Praise for *Is Bill Cosby Right?*

"Dyson, who can coin a phrase with the best of them . . . roundly defends the black youngsters whose circumstances sparked the Cosby campaign."   —William Raspberry, *Washington Post*

"Dyson deconstructs the logic of Cosby's comments and defends poor Blacks."   —*Ebony*

"Dyson is seen by many as the heir apparent to such black intellectual luminaries as Princeton's Cornel West and Harvard's Henry Louis Gates Jr. . . . In his Cosby book, Dyson uses history and social science to raise nuanced images of poor black people. . . . And these virtues are abundant in Dyson's own fluent and gorgeous multilingualism. There is syncopation, repetition, call and response, variations of idiom; there is hilarity, grief, the sly rattle and snap of the rhetorical snare; he samples like a rapper, with scholarly footnotes."   —*Princeton Alumni Weekly*

"Well-researched . . . Dyson then dissects these remarks, offering ironic observations that contrast what Cosby is saying about poor people with Cosby's own unseemly behavior over the years. Dyson's . . . keen observations, wit and intellectual skills have allowed him to report the material . . . in fresh ways and make this a highly readable book."   —*St. Louis Post-Dispatch*

"Dyson is evenhanded . . . [and] passionate about this subject, and his advocacy for the poor is admirable. . . . Substantive and well-expressed."   —Cleveland *Plain Dealer*

"Dyson makes a number of genuinely provocative points, particularly while outlining the seemingly insurmountable structural challenges facing those mired in poverty. . . . *Is Bill Cosby Right?* should get a thorough and rigorous airing, because Dyson is onto something: the maturation (some would say collapse) of the black body politic. . . . As I read, I found myself wishing that this book could be debated in a public manner by a panel of thoughtful African-Americans from all walks of life."
> —Anthony Walton, *The News & Observer*
> (Raleigh, North Carolina)

"Withering attack on Cosby for his criticisms of the black poor and why Cosby is letting other factors off the hook that keep the underclass where they are . . . A good reminder to look at the whole picture, including self-help and personal responsibility."
> —Greg Moore, *Denver Post*

"Informative history and social analysis . . . [of] the long history of black middle-class disdain toward the poor, much of which is rooted in a desire not to give white people a reason to look askance at them. . . . I don't think the black middle class has lost its mind, but sometimes we all need to take a deep breath and consider what is in our hearts before we engage our mouths."   —*Seattle Times*

"Dyson does more than just take off the gloves . . . he's got brass knuckles underneath 'em, two sets worth, and he's ready to rumble. . . . Dyson angrily rises up in defense of what he sees as an attack on the black poor by the 'Afristocracy' of intellectuals, civil rights leaders and other members of the African-American establishment."   —The San Diego *Union-Tribune*

"Dyson deconstructs Cosby's career of 40 years as one of the most famous black men in America, and finds him sorely lacking in terms of his relevance or commitment to civil rights issues. . . . [Dyson] is a compelling writer with a keen analytical mind."
> —Eugene Kane, Milwaukee *Journal Sentinel*

"[Dyson] examines Cosby's complaints in a new book and concludes that the rage of elders such as Cosby does little to bring about prison reform, better jobs or adequate funding for public schools. Dyson challenges all of us to work together to find answers to enduring social problems."   —Tucson *Citizen*

"A provocative book that will provide fodder for debate and discussion."   —*Rocky Mountain News*

"Dyson's insightful book challenges Blacks and Whites to confront the social problems in the Black community."   —*Jet*

"The primary value that [Dyson's] book serves is to hold the mirror of historical, sociological, political and moral reflection so that one can engage in the debate in a more judicious and less emotional manner."   —Byron Williams, *Oakland Tribune*

"Dyson is at least aware that class conflict in the black community goes back to the very beginning. The most striking thing about the discussion that has followed the Cosby comments is the extent to which even well-educated Americans have been surprised to learn that class antagonism exists in the black community at all. This entrenched ignorance about black life was a long time in the making, and is only now being dislodged."
                    —Brent Staples, *New York Times*

Is Bill Cosby Right?

*Or Has the
Black Middle Class
Lost Its Mind?*

Michael Eric Dyson

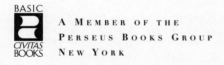

BASIC
CIVITAS
BOOKS

A MEMBER OF THE
PERSEUS BOOKS GROUP
NEW YORK

Books published by Basic *Civitas* Books are available at special
discounts for bulk purchases in the United States by corporations,
institutions, and other organizations. For more information, please
contact the Special Markets Department at the Perseus Books Group,
11 Cambridge Center, Cambridge, MA 02142, or call (617) 252-5298
or (800) 255-1514, or email special.markets@perseusbooksgroup.com

Designed by Lovedog Studio

Library of Congress Cataloging-in-Publication Data

Dyson, Michael Eric.
  Is Bill Cosby right? : or has the Black middle class lost its mind? / by Michael
Eric Dyson.
    p. cm.
  ISBN-13: 978-0-465-01719-5
  ISBN-10: 0-465-01719-3
1. African Americans—Social conditions—1975- 2. African American families.
3. Middle class—United States. 4. Conflict of generations—United States. 5.
Intergenerational relations—United States. 6. Social values—United States. 7.
United States—Race relations. 8. United States—Social conditions—1980- I.
Title.

  E185.86.D945 2005
  306.87'089'96073—dc22

                                                        2005004100
Paperback: ISBN-13: 978-0-465-01720-1; ISBN-10: 0-465-01720-7

06 07 08 / 10 9 8 7 6 5 4 3 2 1

To
The Rev. Dr. Frederick George Sampson, III
The Rev. Orlando Arnold
Ms. Delores Sampson
Ms. Tommye Arnold
Dear friends who allowed a young, poor father
to live with them in Detroit

To
The Rev. Dr. William Douglas Booth and
Mrs. Ruth Booth
Beloved Second Father in the Ministry
and Motherly Conscience
Who fed me and taught me the true meaning
of ministry and manhood
and
The Rev. Dr. Riggins R. Earl, Jr., and
the late Mrs. Lovelene Earl
Marvelous Mentor and Soul Encourager
Who fed me and first inspired a young pastor
to pursue a Ph.D.

And to
Mwata Omotiyo Dyson, M.D.
Beloved son of the heart, who, despite being
told no three times
Pursued his dream and went from anonymous
to Anesthesiologist
Your Mother and I are so proud

Contents

Preface

The Afristocracy
Versus the
Ghettocracy

On May 17, 2004, Bill Cosby stepped to the podium in Washington, D.C.'s Constitution Hall. The famed entertainer was to receive an award for his philanthropic endeavors during a gala event commemorating the fiftieth anniversary of the *Brown v. Board of Education* decision, sponsored by the NAACP, the NAACP Legal Fund, and Howard University. When Cosby opened his mouth, instead of lauding the efforts of civil rights pioneers, he bitterly scorned poor blacks for "*not* holding up their end in this deal." The *Washington Post*, which broke the story, reports that Cosby lamented that activists "marched and were hit in the face with rocks . . . to get an education, and now we've got these knuckleheads walking around," referring to the "lower economic people" of the race. Cosby accused them of "not parenting," and said that they "cry when their son is standing there in an orange suit"—meaning those in jail and prison—while failing to prevent their children's criminal behavior. "Where were you when he was two? Where were you when he was twelve? Where were you when he was eighteen, and how come you didn't know that he had a pistol? And where is his father?"

Cosby also attacked black youth who "put their clothes on backward: Isn't that a sign of something gone wrong?" He assailed the young black girl who "got all type of needles [piercing] and things going through her body. What part of Africa did this come from? We are not Africans. Those people are not Africans; they don't know a damned thing about Africa." The venerable father figure also lambasted black parents who give their children "names like Shaniqua, Taliqua and *Muhammad* and all that crap," adding that "all of 'em are in jail." Cosby repeatedly accosted the black poor—with a few black millionaire ball players thrown in for good measure—for their failure to master literacy. He said—referring to black children as inanimate objects—that "[i]t's standing on da corner. It can't speak English. It doesn't want to speak English. I can't even talk the way these people talk. 'Why you ain't, where you is go. . . .' I don't know who these people are."

The entertainer also assailed poor black mothers and fathers for their horrible parenting skills, saying they buy their kids "$500 sneakers" but refuse to "spend $250 on Hooked on Phonics." Cosby claimed that most black inmates are not "political criminals" but folk who go "around stealing Coca Cola" and who get "shot in the back of the head over a piece of pound cake! And then we all run out and we're outraged,

'Ah, the cops shouldn'ta shot him.' What the hell was he doing with the pound cake in his hand?" Cosby pounded the black poor for their abysmal educational track record, citing their "50 percent drop out [rate]" from high school and charging that black folk are "raising our own ingrown immigrants." On and on Cosby went, berating black parents and youth for their numerous faults, his ramblings united by one theme: the miserable condition of the black poor brought on by their own self-destructive behavior. More recently, Cosby appeared at Jesse Jackson's Rainbow/PUSH Coalition Citizenship Fund's annual conference and widened his attack on the black poor, saying that the charge of airing dirty laundry leveled against him paled in comparison to the bleak reality of blasphemous black children. "Let me tell you something, your dirty laundry gets out of school at 2:30 every day, it's cursing and calling each other nigga as they're walking up and down the street. They think they're hip. They can't read; they can't write. They're laughing and giggling, and they're going nowhere."[1]

Cosby's remarks are not the isolated ranting of a solo rhetorical gun slinger, but simply the most recent, and the most visible, shot taken at poor blacks in a more-than-century-old class war in black America. His views are widely held among a number of black constituencies—it is not unusual to hear some black poor and working-class members themselves joining Cosby's ranks in barbershops and beauty salons across America. But Cosby's beliefs are most notably espoused by the *Afristocracy:* upper-middle-class blacks and the black elite who rain down fire and brimstone upon poor blacks for their deviance and pathology, and for their lack of couth and culture. The Afristrocracy—composed of lawyers, physicians, intellectuals, civil rights leaders, entertainers, athletes, bankers and the like—rail in private (which includes, ironically enough, spaces in the "black public," including churches, schools, conventions and social gatherings, that are usually beyond the reach, or the interest, of the masses of whites, especially the white media) about the pernicious habits of the black poor but rarely make the sort of news Cosby did by letting their bilious beliefs slip into wide public view.

The black poor—the *Ghettocracy*—consists of the desperately unemployed and underemployed, those trapped in underground economies, and those working poor folk who slave in menial jobs at the edge of the economy. The Ghettocracy is composed of single mothers on welfare, single working mothers and fathers, poor fathers, married poor and working folk, the incarcerated, and a battalion of impoverished children. Ironically enough, the Ghettocracy extends into the ranks of athletes and entertainers—especially basketball and football players, but, above all, hip-hop stars—whose values and habits are alleged to be negatively influenced by their poor origins. Thus, the conflict between the Afristocracy and the Ghettocracy takes on generational overtones, since the values and behaviors that are detested by Afristocrats are largely—though by no means exclusively—located among the young.

Is Bill Cosby Right? Or Has the Black Middle Class Lost Its Mind? examines, and responds to, the claims made by Cosby—and, by extension, the lunging phalanx of Afristocrats—in his now infamous speech, and in speeches he has since given across the country in what I have dubbed his "Blame-the-Poor Tour." I will dissect Cosby's flawed logic, reveal the thin descriptive web he weaves to characterize the poor, and address the complex dimensions of the problems he bitterly broaches. It is clear that my subtitle is provocative, perhaps inflammatory, though not nearly as inflammatory and offensive as Cosby's remarks and the wide support they have garnered among black people, especially the black middle classes. Indeed, there are many black middle classes: the one barely a paycheck or two from poverty; the one a notch above, with jobs in the service economy; the one more solidly in the middle, with low-level professional jobs; and the one in the upper stratum, with high-level professional employment and the esteem such labor yields.

Moreover, class in black America has never been viewed in strictly literal economic terms; the black definition of class embraces style and behavior as well. Hence, it is not uncommon to hear "that's so ghetto" used to describe behavior associated with poor folk, whether one picks up garbage or sets a pick-and-roll on the basketball court for a living. And the charge of "acting seditty"—or, putting on airs—can be leveled at the poor and rich alike. I simply aim to provoke black folk into serious self-examination, the sort we claim the poor should undertake, but one that we in other classes may seek to avoid. If Cosby's implicit claim is that the black poor have lost their way, then I don't mind suggesting, with only half my tongue in cheek, that the black middle class, of which I am a member, has, in its views of the poor and its support of Cosby's sentiments, lost its mind. I hope to lay bare the vicious assault of the Afristocracy on the Ghettocracy and offer a principled defense of poor black folk, one rooted in clear-eyed acknowledgment of deficiencies and responsibility but anchored by an abiding compassion for the most vulnerable members of *our* community.

Introduction

An Afristocrat
in Winter

"Do you view Bill Cosby as a race traitor?" journalist Paula Zahn bluntly asked me on her nighttime television show.

Zahn was referring to the broadside the entertainer had launched against irresponsible black parents who are poor and their delinquent children. Cosby's rebuke came in a May 2004 speech on the fiftieth anniversary of the landmark Supreme Court decision *Brown v. Board of Education*. Not content with a one-off tirade, Cosby since then has bitterly and visibly crusaded against the declining morality and bad behavior of poor blacks. Six months into his battle, Zahn snagged the comic legend turned cultural warrior for his first in-depth interview. Cosby clarified his comments and reinforced his position. No, he wasn't wrong to air the black community's dirty laundry. Yes, he would ratchet up the noise and pace of his racial offensive. And he surely didn't give a damn about what white folk thought about his campaign or what nefarious uses they might make of his public diatribe. One could see it on Cosby's face: This is war, the stakes are high and being polite or politically correct simply won't do.

Since I was one of the few blacks to publicly disagree with Cosby, I ended up in numerous media outlets arguing in snippets, sound bites, or ripostes to contrary points of view. In the *New York Times* a few days after his remarks, I offered that Cosby's comments "betray classist, elitist viewpoints rooted in generational warfare," that he was "ill-informed on the critical and complex issues that shape people's lives," and that his words only "reinforce suspicions about black humanity."[1]

Still, I don't consider Cosby a traitor, and I said so to Zahn. In fact, I defended his right to speak his mind in full public view. After all, I'd been similarly stung by claims of racial disloyalty when I wrote my controversial book on Martin Luther King, Jr. I also said that while Cosby is right to emphasize personal behavior (a lesson, by the way, that many wealthy people should bone up on), we must never lose sight of the big social forces that make it difficult for poor parents to do their best jobs and for poor children to prosper. Before going on Zahn's show, I'd already decided to write a book in response to Cosby's relentless assault. But my appearances in the media, and the frustrating fragmentation of voice that one risks in such venues, pushed me to gain a bigger say in the issues Cosby has desperately if clumsily grabbed hold of. This book is my attempt to unpack those issues with the clarity and complexity they demand.

Of course, the ink and applause Cosby has won rest largely on a faulty assumption: that he is the first black figure to stare down the "pathology" that plagues poor blacks. But to believe that ignores how figures from black intellectual W.E.B. Du Bois to civil rights leader Jesse Jackson, in varying contexts, with differing results, have spoken controversially about the black poor. Equally intriguing is the leap of faith one must make in granting Cosby revered status as a racial spokesman and critic. He has famously demurred in his duties as a racial representative. He has flatly refused over the years to deal with blackness and color in his comedy. Cosby was defensive, even defiant, in his views, as prickly a racial avoider as one might imagine for a man who traded so brilliantly on dimensions of black culture in his comedy. While Cosby took full advantage of the civil rights struggle, he resolutely denied it a seat at his artistic table. Thus it's hard to swallow Cosby's flailing away at youth for neglecting their history, and overlooking the gains paid for by the blood of their ancestors, when he reneged on its service when it beckoned at his door. It is ironic that Cosby has finally answered the call to racial leadership forty years after it might have made a constructive difference. But it is downright tragic that he should use his perch to lob rhetorical bombs at the poor.

For those who overlook the uneven history of black engagement with the race's social dislocations and moral struggles—and who conveniently ignore Cosby's Johnny-come-lately standing as a racial critic—Cosby is an ethical pioneer, a racial hero. In this view, Cosby is brave to admit that "lower economic people" are "not parenting" and are failing the civil rights movement by "*not* holding up their end in this deal." Single mothers are no longer "embarrassed because they're pregnant without a husband." A single father is no longer "considered an embarrassment if he tries to run away from being the father" of his child. And what do we make of their criminal children? Cosby's "courage" does not fail. "In our own neighborhood, we have men in prison. . . . I'm talking about these people who cry when their son is standing there in an orange suit. Where were you when he was two? Where were you when he was twelve? Where were you when he was eighteen, and how come you don't know he had a pistol?" Before he is finished, Cosby beats up on the black poor for their horrible education, their style of dress, the names they give their children, their backward speech and their consumptive habits. As a cruel coda, Cosby even suggests to the black poor that "God is tired of you."

It is not remarkable that such sentiments exist. Similar comments can be heard in countless black spaces: barbershops and beauty shops; pulpits and pavement platforms; street corners and suite hallways; and civil rights conventions and political conferences. These cultural settings give such ideas an interpretive context that they often lack when they bleed beyond ghetto walls and comfortable black meeting places and homes into the wider world. Cosby bypassed, or, more accurately, short-circuited, the policing mechanism the black elite—the Afristocracy—habitually use to keep such thoughts from public view.[2] (This is done not so much to spare the poor but to save the black elite from further embarrassment. And no matter how you judge Cosby's comments, you can't help but believe that a great deal of his consternation with the poor stems from his desire to remove the shame he feels in their presence and about their activity in the world.)

Usually the sort of bile that Cosby spilled is more expertly contained, or at least poured on its targets in ways that escape white notice. Cosby's remarks betray seething class warfare in black America that has finally boiled over to the general public. It is that general public, especially white social critics and other prophets of black ethical erosion, that has been eager for Cosby's dispatches from the tortured front of black class war. Cosby's comments let many of these whites off the hook. If what Cosby says is true, then critics who have said the same, but who courted charges of racism, are vindicated. There's nothing like a formerly poor black multimillionaire bashing poor blacks to lend credence to the ancient assaults they've endured from the dominant culture.

Cosby's overemphasis on personal responsibility, not structural features, wrongly locates the source of poor black suffering—and by implication its remedy—in the lives of the poor. When you think the problems are personal, you think the solutions are the same. If only the poor were willing to work harder, act better, get educated, stay out of jail and parent more effectively, their problems would go away. It's hard to argue against any of these things in the abstract; in principle such suggestions sound just fine. But one could do all of these things and still be in bad shape at home, work or school. For instance, Cosby completely ignores shifts in the economy that give value to some work while other work, in the words of William Julius Wilson, "disappears."[3] In our high-tech, high-skilled economy where low-skilled work is being scaled back, phased out, exported, or severely under-compensated, all the right behavior in the world won't create better jobs with more pay. And without such support, all the goals that Cosby expresses for the black poor are not likely to become reality. If the rigidly segregated educational system continues to miserably fail poor blacks by failing to prepare their children for the world of work, then admonitions to "stay in school" may ring hollow.

In this light, the imprisonment of black people takes on political consequence. Cosby may be right that most black folk in jail are not "political prisoners," but it doesn't mean that their imprisonment has not been politicized. Given the vicious way blacks have been targeted for incarceration, Cosby's comments about poor blacks who end up in jail are dangerously naïve and empirically wrong. Cosby's critique of criminal behavior among poor blacks neglects the massive body of work that catalogs the unjust imprisonment of young blacks. This is not to suggest an apologia for black thugs; instead, it suggests that a disproportionate number of black (men) are incarcerated for nonviolent drug offenses. Moreover, Cosby seems to offer justification for the police killing a young black for a trivial offense (the theft of a Coca-Cola or pound cake), neglecting the heinous injustices of the police against blacks across the land. Further, Cosby neglects to mention that crime occurs in all classes and races, though it is not equally judged and prosecuted.

Cosby also slights the economic, social, political and other structural barriers that poor black parents are up against: welfare reform, dwindling resources, export of jobs and ongoing racial stigma. And then there are the problems of the working poor: folk who rise up early every day and often work more than forty hours a week, and yet barely, if ever, make it above the poverty level. We must acknowledge the plight of both poor black (single) mothers and poor black fathers, and the lack of social support they confront. Hence, it is incredibly difficult to spend as much time with children as poor black parents might like, especially since they will be demonized if they fail to provide for their children's basic needs. But doing so deflects critical attention and time from child-rearing duties—duties that are difficult enough for two-parent, two-income, intact middle-class families.[4] The characteristics Cosby cites are typical of all families that confront poverty the world over. They are not indigenous to the black poor; they are symptomatic of the predicament of poor people in general. And Cosby's mean-spirited characterizations of the black poor as licentious, sexually promiscuous, materialistic and wantonly irresponsible can be made of all classes in the nation. (Paris Hilton, after all, is a huge star for just these reasons.) Moreover, Cosby's own problems—particularly the affair he had that led to the very public charge that he may have fathered a child—suggest that not only poor people do desperate things. In fact, as we reflect on his family troubles over the years, we get a glimpse of the unavoidable pain and contradictions that plague all families, rich and poor.

Cosby's views on education have in some respects changed for the worse. His earlier take on the prospects of schooling for the poor was more humane and balanced. In his 1976 dissertation, Cosby argued against "institutional racism" and maintained that school systems failed the poorest and most vulnerable black students. It is necessary as well to acknowledge the resegregation of American education (when in truth it was hardly desegregated to begin with). The failure of *Brown v. Board* to instigate sufficient change in the nation's schools suggests that the greatest burden—and responsibility—should be on crumbling educational infrastructures. In suburban neighborhoods, there are $60-million schools with state-of-the-art technology, while inner city schools fight desperately for funding for their students. And anti-intellectualism, despite Cosby's claims, is hardly a black phenomenon; it is endemic to the culture. Cosby also spies the critical deficiency of the black poor in their linguistic habits, displaying his ignorance about "black English" and "Ebonics." But the intent of Ebonics, according to its advocates, is to help poor black youth speak "standard" English while retaining an appreciation for their dialects and "native tongues." All of this suggests that structural barriers, much more than personal desire, shape the educational experiences of poor blacks. In fact, *Fat Albert and the Cosby Kids*, Cosby's lauded '70s television cartoon series, won greater acceptance for a new cast of black identities and vernacular language styles. Cosby has made money and gained further influence from using forms of Black English he now violently detests.

Cosby's comments betray the ugly generational divide in black America. His disregard for the hip-hop generation is not unique, but it is still disheartening. Cosby's poisonous view of young folk who speak a language he can barely parse simmers with hostility and resentment. And yet, some of the engaged critique he seeks to make of black folk—of their materialism, their consumptive desires, their personal choices, their moral aspirations, their social conscience—is broadcast with much more imagination and insight in certain quarters of hip-hop culture. (Think of Kanye West's track, "All Falls Down," which displays a self-critical approach to the link between consumption and the effort to ward off racial degradation.)[5] Cosby detests youth for their hip-hop dress, body piercing and the pseudo-African-sounding names they have. Yet, body piercing and baggy clothes express identity among black youth, and not just beginning with hip-hop culture. Moreover, young black entrepreneurs like Sean "P. Diddy" Combs and Russell Simmons have made millions from their clothing lines. There are generational tensions over self-definition; arguments over clothes and body markings reflect class, age and intracultural conflicts as well. I think that, contrary to Cosby's argument, it *does* have something to do with the African roots of black identity, and perhaps with Cosby's ignorance of and discomfort with those roots. And Cosby's ornery, ill-informed diatribe against black naming is a snapshot of his assault on poor black identity. Names like Shaniqua and Taliqua are meaningful cultural expressions of self-determination and allow relatively powerless blacks to fashion their identities outside the glare of white society. And it didn't just start in this generation. Cosby's inability to discern the difference between Taliqua and Muhammad, an ancient Muslim name, is as remarkable as it is depressing—and bigoted in its rebuff to venerable forms of black identity and culture.

Cosby's comments don't exist in a cultural or political vacuum. His views have traction in conservative (and some liberal) circles because they bolster the belief that *less* money, political action and societal intervention—and more hard work and personal responsibility—are the key to black success. While Cosby can surely afford to ignore what white folk think, the majority of black folk can't reasonably dismiss whites in influential places. Cosby has said that he's not worried about how the white right wing might use his speech, but it certainly fits nicely with their twisted views of the black poor. The poor folk Cosby has hit the hardest are most vulnerable to the decisions of the powerful groups of which he has demanded the least: public policy makers, the business and social elite, and political activists. Poor black folk cannot gain asylum from the potentially negative effects of Cosby's words on public policy makers and politicians who decide to put into play measures that support Cosby's narrow beliefs.

Cosby also contends that black folk can't blame white folk for our plight. His discounting of structural forces and his exclusive focus on personal responsibility, and black self-help, ignore the persistence of the institutional racism Cosby lamented in his dissertation. To be sure, even when black folk argued for social justice, we never neglected the simultaneous pursuit of personal responsibility and self-help, since that's often the only help we had. In the end, Cosby's views may make white and black liberal fence-sitters unfairly critical of the black poor. Cosby may even convince them that personal behavior will help the poor more than social programs, thus letting white and black elites off the hook. There is a strong counterpoint to Cosby's evasive, and dismissive, racial politics in his own home. I think it is important to recall the famous letter Cosby's wife, Camille, penned in 1998 in *USA Today*—written in the aftermath of the tragic murder of their son by a Russian immigrant, excoriating America for teaching her son's murderer the bigotry that fueled his lethal act. Unlike Cosby's comments, Camille's essay drew the ire and rebuke of pundits and the political establishment. Camille Cosby was told that America provided the opportunity for her husband to become a rich artist. By contrast, Bill Cosby's remarks were embraced by the same establishment, as Cosby was praised for his self-help strategy of pulling himself up from poverty to plenty. Thus, these critics want it both ways. I think when it comes to the issues at hand, contrasting Camille's letter and Cosby's remarks proves that she is the Cosby with genuine insight into race relations.

It is clear that Cosby has touched a raw nerve of class and generation in black America. What he said—and our response to it—goes far beyond a single speech before a group of blacks who were celebrating the achievements of the past. This story is so powerful and controversial, and continues to resonate in our society, because it goes to the heart of the struggle for the identity of a culture. It also embodies the different visions put forth by older and younger members of the race. In a sense, Cosby is Moses, Elijah and King Lear rolled into one. Like Moses, he has laid down the law, but he is realizing, as we all must at some point, that he may not get the chance to see the Promised Land in his own day. The sweet reward of hard work slips through the hands as easily as water in a rushing stream. But finally, as it says in the book of Hebrews, "these all died in faith not having received the promises."[6] We must all face the reality at some point that the fulfillment of our hopes and dreams is ever in the distance, flung to a horizon that recedes as we march forward, and can only be brought closer in the collective push ahead, and often not through one's own energy but through the efforts of some Joshua—the younger helper of Moses, the one God appointed to lead the people after Moses' great journey came to a close. It's hard to hand over the reins and embrace the transition, but it must be done. This doesn't mean that old prophets and sages are of no use; it means they must learn to coexist with an upcoming phalanx of rebels with new spirits and vision. Even if they wear dreads and baggy pants or speak in ways foreign to the elders.

Like Elijah, Cosby has thrown in the towel and embraced his frustration; like Elijah, he has said, "It is enough!"[7] Elijah felt that he was the only one left to do God's work and that everyone else had sold out to godless hedonism and corrupt morality. But God told Elijah to rest up, since he was exhausted—Cosby, too, has said, "I'm a tired man"—and, after replenishing himself, to recognize God not in the thunder but in the still small voice, in the serenity of inner circumstances that nourish hope. And then God pointed out to

Elijah that there were literally thousands more who had a righteous cause and who were not in Elijah's camp. Cosby must accept that others have the truth, too, and that they are working in their own way to make things better—for the race, the culture, the community and our struggle.

And finally, like King Lear, Cosby is at war with his children, feeling their fatal betrayal of his fatherly leadership, saying, as did Lear, that "I am more sinned against than sinning." That, to be sure, is the claim of every generation, of every visionary who feels that the people he has loved and brought along have somehow fatally departed from the path of wisdom and morality when they go their own way. There are undoubtedly lethal circumstances afoot in black America, and we do indeed need the voices of the elders to ring out and the wisdom of the fathers and mothers to resonate loudly. But transition and transformation bring inevitable struggles between generations, or at least between their leading lights, and sometimes the wrestling is bloody and unraveling. We must resist the temptation to take refuge in hurt feelings and raging resentment as we grapple with how our children live, or choose to leave us, or even how we handle our recognition of their betrayals and disaffections. Loyalty to particular figures may not be as important, in the end, as loyalty to the cause of enlarging the hopes of the individual and racial family.

The conversation that Cosby has started endures because the people who must engage him, and the issues he has raised, are likewise enduring. Thus, what Cosby said reflects on the griefs and hopes and losses and pains of an entire generation of noble men and women who nonetheless, like the rest of us, are human and at times frail and misled. We must learn from each other, listen to each other, correct each other and struggle with each other if the destiny of our people is to be secure. And we must fight for the best that is within our reach, even if that means disagreeing with icons and resisting the myopia of mighty men. What Cosby started is left to us to finish.

Chapter One

Speaking of Race — Or Not

Ladies and gentlemen, these people set, they opened the doors, they gave us the right . . . and all of these people who lined up and done whatever, they've got to be wondering what the hell happened . . . Brown V. the Board of Education, these people who marched and were hit in the face with rocks and punched in the face to get an education and we got these knuckleheads walking around, don't want to learn English. (clapping) I know that you all know it. But I just want to get you as angry as you ought to be . . . But these people, the ones up here in the balcony fought so hard.

For most of his career Bill Cosby has avoided race with religious zeal. His role as racial prophet to lower-class blacks, therefore, screams of irony and suggests Cosby's profound confusion and the tragic misuse of his fame to assault the poor. By tracing his career against the backdrop of race, we gain a clearer understanding of how Cosby's present position departs dangerously from his storied path—and how that departure signals the sacrifice of his principles and points to his being way out of his depth. I think Cosby's faults are both poor comprehension and thin description of the problems he sees.

Cosby came of age during a shift in cultural sensibilities that shaped comedy's landscape. Stand-up comedians like Lenny Bruce, Mort Sahl and Dick Gregory cast off the social conformity of the 1950s and sank their comic fangs into the repressed psyches and repressive politics of Cold War America. Gregory built on the work of black comics who were among the first to perform before mainstream crowds, including Timmie Rogers, Nipsey Russell, George Kirby and Slappy White.[1] But his penetrating racial observations catapulted Gregory to greater acclaim and a bigger white audience than any black comic before him. By the time Cosby burst onto the national scene (joined later by Godfrey Cambridge, Flip Wilson and Richard Pryor), Gregory's influence was at once mythic and smothering. Any young black comic hoping to share even a fraction of Gregory's spotlight would have to shine with the gifts Gregory bequeathed: acerbic attacks on the color line, witty self-mockery and telling the truth about black life in white America.

At first, Cosby was content in Gregory's shadow. He did his best to harness the master's rhetorical fire. He conjured just enough anger to be authentically black in the comic mold Gregory had forged. The *New York Times* took notice of young Cosby and lauded him for "hurling verbal spears at the relations between whites and Negroes."[2] Soon Cosby gave up hope of matching Gregory's wily racial shtick. "I was telling racial jokes then," Cosby recalled in 1964. "You know, the biting, witty kind about the Negro's role in America. But pretty soon critics began to regard me as a sort of hip Nipsey Russell and a Philadelphia Dick Gregory. Well, I decided then and there that I had to be original if I wanted to fulfill my aspirations of becoming a big man in show business."[3] Cosby's originality lay in reclaiming the comedic and literary past to fashion a distinctive comic style. He told stories about his childhood, football and public transportation, sprawling, jazz-like tales that unfolded over as much as half an hour, just like the stories he had heard his mother read to him from the writings of Mark Twain, the brothers Grimm, Swift and the Bible.[4]

But Cosby's revamped comic vision was even more radical: He would discard the use of color in his comedy since it was little more than a "crutch."[5] Cosby was challenged by a fellow comic's argument that if he changed color tomorrow he'd have no material, sending him in search of jokes that bypassed pigment. He took comfort in neither the spoiled clichés of color nor the comic relief they offered. Cosby was even convinced of the divisive consequences of racial humor. "Color humor, like off-color humor, makes audiences uncomfortable," Cosby said in 1965. "When I began telling racial jokes, the Negroes looked at the whites, the whites at the Negroes, and no one laughed—and then I had to tell the jokes all over again. So I tried reaching all the public, so folks would say, 'Hey, man, here's a Negro who doesn't use racial material.'"[6] Cosby's resort to color-blind rhetoric wasn't simply a means to bridge the racial gap in his audiences; it also suggested his philosophy of race beyond the comedy club. "I don't think you can bring the races together by joking about the differences between them. I'd rather talk about the similarities, about what's universal in their experiences."[7]

Cosby's determined effort to keep race from coloring his life and career gained more visibility when he won a role in 1965 alongside Robert Culp on NBC's *I Spy*. As one half of an interracial duo who trotted the globe entangled in espionage, Cosby shattered television's race barrier as the first Negro to star in a network series, leading *Variety* magazine to tag him "TV's Jackie Robinson."[8] Cosby's meteoric rise made news, but just as much ink was devoted to his racial politics as to his acting, which, as a twenty-seven-year-old novice, he had surely not refined. The press noted Cosby's adroit stereotype-shattering—his character on *I Spy* had been a Rhodes Scholar, was fluent in seven languages and didn't sing, dance or widen his eyes in paroxysms of fear like so many black actors before him were forced to do. But they couldn't resist noting that Cosby's race on the series was no big deal at all, a point that made him the darling of many white critics.

Newsweek observed that on *I Spy*, "his lines provide the color, not his skin," while *National Review* chimed in that "watching along, one does not notice him *as a Negro* but as a rough, tough, generous, loyal, fine, funny fellow."[9] One review of his *I Spy* role noted that race "will be of no importance, just as in Cosby's comedy act. He is a stand-up satirist who happens to be colored."[10] Another critic agreed. "Cosby is anything but self-conscious as an entertainer about the fact that he is a Negro. Indeed, he vaulted onto TV by way of his enormous success as about the only Negro nightclub comedian who avoided rather than leaned on racial themes."[11] Another writer trumpeted Cosby's raceless persona by saying, "he is concerned more with dropouts than discrimination, bothered more by air pollution than prejudice."[12] For still another critic, Cosby had a distinct advantage over Sammy Davis, Jr., Sidney Poitier and Nat King Cole: "Cosby's great achievement is that he . . . is not primarily a Negro, he is primarily a guy."[13] A journalist saw parallels between Cosby's professional identity and racial reticence. "As Cosby's humor is devoid of race, so too is his public image. He doesn't speak out on racial matters."[14] Finally, one reporter sketched Cosby's broad appeal on the canvas of racial struggle. "He was a Negro standing against a background of black rage and revolution who told stories without regard to race or color. Time was when another generation of Negro comics like the late Bert Williams was afraid to joke about race before white *or* black audiences. . . . Bill Cosby came along cool and color-blind, choosing to ignore the hang-ups of blacks and whites, and making jokes about everyday life as though all men were created equal."[15]

During *I Spy*'s three-year run and after, Cosby enhanced his image as a colorless comic, as one who told "colorful jokes which in my opinion have no relation to a person's color at all."[16] Cosby was delighted that he was called "to play a spy instead of a problem."[17] Cosby's costar Bob Culp also exulted in their color-blind bond on the show. "We're two guys who don't know the difference between a colored and a white man. That's doing more than 100 marches. We're showing what it could be like if there had been no hate."[18] Downplaying Cosby's race can be seen as a noble effort to stem racism's hurtful ubiquity and to stamp out all cultural presumptions keyed to color. Still, one can't help but notice the irony of Cosby's situation: His ability to be color-blind was tied directly to the fierce struggles for racial justice being waged by blacks in the streets and courts of the nation.[19] Cosby admitted as much when he noted their roles while defining his own. "Negroes like Martin Luther King and Dick Gregory; Negro groups like the Deacons and the Muslims— all are dedicated to the cause of civil rights, but they do their jobs in their own way. My way is to show white people that Negroes are human beings with the same aspirations and abilities that whites have."[20]

The burden of race that Cosby bore clashed with some of the beliefs the movement encouraged—that blacks be treated as individuals and that color cease to matter as much as character in establishing personal relations. But until society fundamentally changed, these ideals could be cruelly twisted to intimidate blacks who—unlike those who naïvely believed they had already become reality—knew their realization was still far off. These blacks knew that color, whether we liked it or not, still intruded where it shouldn't. Cosby's choice to go color-blind in this context obligated him to ignore race—at worst, to pretend that it didn't exist and at best, to act as if it were incidental to national life. In either case, Cosby's lofty goal of proving that blacks are human struck a nerve in white communities eager to be rid of guilt because racism still existed. In the bargain of Cosby's racial politics, both sides were shortchanged. Black folk failed to find as clear a voice for our humanity as we might have had if Cosby had been willing in his comedy to flesh out the nuances of black identity. Cosby would have had to acknowledge the differences, not just the similarities, of white and black life—differences in infant mortality rates, living standards, education, life expectancy, economic status and the like, all of which could be empirically confirmed and not left to subjective perception. And whites were freed from the responsibility to mend the social relations they had fractured, or in any case had benefited from, in the first place.

Both sides were also called on to pretend a bit, in fact, quite a bit. There is little doubt that Cosby's efforts to prove our humanity flowed from the impossible position he occupied—of being forced to represent his race when all he wanted was to be a human being allowed to go his own way without the encumbrances of color or caste. Yet, it must be remembered that it was the same impossible position that *all* black folk in one way or another, depending on our gifts and fate, wrestle with as a condition of our existence. If Cosby had shown he understood that in some noticeable fashion, it may have been as helpful to us as his insistence that race would not ruin his art. Even as he fled its tyranny, race marked Cosby's route of resistance. As those who have sought a similar path can testify, the decision to ditch race is not simply a matter of will. Cultures and classes and societies with all their folkways and mores and politics matter as well. Color *has* shaped Cosby's life and career, and not only in brutal, negative fashion. Unfortunately, Cosby has for the most part banished the galvanizing virtues of blackness to the realm of inference. It is not that he has refused to acknowledge them, or to take pleasure in the cultural modes they provide; he has simply disavowed the need to explain or justify them. He has taken them for granted, which is heartening in some contexts and less than courageous in others. Though he has repeatedly said that he wants to help whites to understand our humanity, Cosby has been shy, and sometimes downright resentful, about the duties of racial exposition such a role entails. That is, until quite recently, when his mean-spirited explanations of the black poor began to metastasize across the globe.

Cosby's critics grew along with his fame and fortune. He knew from the start that his racial politics left him "open to skeptics who would like to brand him as a deserter of the cause."[21] Some of those critics noted that while Cosby dodged stereotypes on *I Spy*, he still played Culp's valet and tennis trainer as part of their undercover act. Cosby's character Alexander Scott wasn't allowed to smoke or drink. Others suggested that Scott's sexless existence proved that Cosby would never be equal to Culp until he also got the girl.[22] Then, when he occasionally got the girl, other critics like the *London Times* openly questioned, as their headline blared, "Why Cosby Never Gets a White Girl."[23] But there were more substantive critiques, and one critic, Faith Berry, stands out for the sharpness of her views. Berry argued that, unlike Dick Gregory, Cosby "didn't have a reputation for putting his career on the line to tell it like it is."[24] Despite the pride some

blacks took in Cosby's pioneering role on *I Spy*, Berry
lamented his role as a spy "fist-fighting and gunning down
darker people in the service of American espionage around
the globe." Berry argued that none of the Emmy awards
Cosby received for *I Spy* "counted so much as the image he
projected: that of a kind of half-man who, had he lived during
the days of Nat Turner, might have sold Turner down the
river and been applauded for it by too many people." Perhaps
Berry's most telling critique of Cosby is that his role, and
those of other black actors on television shows in his wake,
"created a new black stereotype of overwhelming dishonesty:
the black man with no real personal life or vision of his own,
the black man who is in the plot as a useful tool, the cooperative, all-too-often flunky accomplice made to look heroic in a
scenario reminiscent of the old Lone Ranger-Tonto put-on."[25]

Berry was mixed in her review of *The Bill Cosby Show*,
Cosby's half-hour television comedy series that debuted as the
number one new show in 1969 but was canceled after two
seasons, lasting a year less than *I Spy*. Cosby played likable,
fun-loving high school gym teacher Chet Kincaid, again
without explicit reference to his color. Berry admits that
"what does come through much of the time, thanks to Cosby
and a raft of black performers, is that black people are
human—even if, as the show would have us believe, they
don't have a problem in the world."[26] Berry understands the
importance of Cosby's approach since "the blacks-as-humans
factor has rarely been stressed in the theatrical business,
including television." She praises the show for featuring a
black mathematics student as the brightest pupil in an algebra

class, which is "nothing extraordinary, except that it's surely the first time on television." In the end, however, *The Bill Cosby Show* fails to deliver to black viewers what they hoped for: "black actors [that] project the black image honestly; and, in this day and time, the *new black image* and not a *new stereotype*." For Berry, Cosby had a new image, "but to call it honest, to refer to it as a show with a black man in situations that actually portray the black experience, would be to state an untruth."[27]

Berry's critique, and those of other writers, underscore the difficulty Cosby faced in carving out a career that flew beyond race—the talk of it, the disputes about it, the contradictions and paradoxes of it that dogged his path. And neither would Berry be the last critic to charge Cosby with playing a stereotype, the very thing he has warred against in a career that also includes over twenty comedy albums, nearly as many movies, more than a half-dozen books, nearly ten music albums, and just as many television series, including a groundbreaking cartoon series, *Fat Albert and the Cosby Kids*. After he tried his hand at a comedy-variety series in 1972, *The New Bill Cosby Show*, which lasted only one season (another series, *Cos*, didn't last two months in 1976), Cosby turned to film, including a well-received comedy trilogy in the mid-'70s directed by and costarring Sidney Poitier.

In *California Suite*, a four-segment ensemble comedy based on Neil Simon's play that also featured Walter Matthau, Jane Fonda, Maggie Smith and Michael Caine, Cosby appeared in an all-black segment costarring Richard Pryor. Cosby and Pryor's slapstick performances as two black physicians who face one mishap after another while on vacation were skewered by noted critic Pauline Kael. Kael admitted that the Cosby and Pryor roles were originally played by white actors when the comedy was staged on Broadway. "When the roles are played by black actors," Kael wrote, "the skit seems to be saying that the men may be doctors but they're still uncontrollable, dumb blacks."[28] Kael argued that the film's art direction and choice of "recessive whitened décor turns them into tar babies." Kael contended that the slapstick setting transformed Cosby and Pryor into vicious stereotypes. "When they stumble around a flooded room, crash into each other, step on broken glass, or even worse, when Cosby bites Pryor's nose, it all has horrifying racist overtones." Kael concluded that the film showed "blacks who act like clowning savages."[29]

Cosby was so incensed at Kael that he took out a full-page ad in *Variety* and fired back. "Are we to be denied a right to romp through hotels, bite noses, and, in general, beat up one another in the way Abbott & Costello, Laurel & Hardy, Martin & Lewis, Buster Keaton, and Charlie Chaplin did— and more recently as those actors in the movie *Animal House?* I heard no cries of racism in those reviews. If my work is not funny—it's not funny. But this industry does not need projected racism from critics."[30] Cosby's querulous exchange with Kael and, before that, Berry's critique, were deeply ironic: Despite his efforts to explore black humanity while purging his art of overt racial reference, and especially racial stereotypes, Cosby was ensnared in controversy over his alleged stereotypical portrayals of blacks on the small and silver screens.[31]

While the letter to Kael was one of his most visible retorts, Cosby, and a few of his friends, constantly responded to critics of his image and his color-blind, race-avoiding politics. In 1965, Cosby suggested to skeptics that his approach benefited race relations. "If my material is without race consciousness, maybe I can promote equality better. After all, if something applies equally to black and white, the underlying assumption is the sameness of both."[32] He was pricklier in 1969 when he defended his philosophy.

> Well, I think there are some people who are disappointed when I don't tell my audiences that white people are mis-treating black people. White critics will write about Cosby not doing any racial material, because they think that now is the time for me to stand up and tell my audi-ences what color I am and what's going on in America. But I don't see people knocking the black elevator man in their building just because he isn't doing anything for civil rights by running that elevator. . . . The fact that I'm not trying to win converts on stage bugs some people, but I don't think an entertainer can win converts. So I don't spend my hours worrying how to slip a social message into my act.[33]

Sammy Davis, Jr., an equally controversial figure in black circles for his race-transcending, race-denying politics, defended his friend Cosby, saying that he "carries as much weight on his shoulders as any Negro I know," and that while Cosby wasn't "a front-runner in the cause—that's not his

nature," he was nevertheless "totally committed."[34] Cosby was
even more transparent in resenting the racial representation
thrust on his shoulders. "I don't have time to sit around and
worry whether all the black people of the world make it
because of me. I have my own gig to worry about. If a white
man falls off a chair, it's just a guy. If a Negro does it, it's the
whole damn Negro race. I don't want to be a crusader or a
leader."[35]

Even after Cosby rewrote the rules of the TV sitcom with
the unprecedented success of *The Cosby Show* in 1984, he
wasn't spared the critic's lash.[36] Tired of the endless cycle of
"car chases and breasts and characters yelling at each other
and saying Yowie!" Cosby turned his attention to crafting a
half-hour series that would showcase the strengths of the
American family.[37] As early as 1966, Cosby said that "[s]ome-
day I want to do a family situation comedy on television and
it will be a hit because people want to see what goes on in a
Negro home today."[38] A few years later, Cosby was more
forthright than ever about the prospects of a series with a
black, non-stereotypical cast. When asked if such a show
could be successful on TV in 1969, Cosby was blunt.

> Probably not. The kind of show you mean would have to
> be about the life of a black family, with all its struggles.
> But if you're really going to do a series about a black fam-
> ily, you're going to have to bring out the heavy; and who
> is the heavy but the white bigot? This would be very
> painful for most whites to see, a show that talks about the
> white man and puts him down. It would strike indifferent

whites as dangerous; it would be called controversial and they probably wouldn't tune in. But when there's a right and a wrong, where's the controversy? The white bigot is *wrong*. The indifferent person sitting on the fence is *wrong*. Instead of having occasional shows that present the black viewpoint on educational channels, the networks should be in there pitching now.[39]

By the time Cosby got his wish more than fifteen years later, his views had drastically changed. He no longer believed that a show about the family should explore the struggles of the average *black* family. Neither did he feel in any way compelled to address racism or the plight of black folk in a world still populated by white bigots. The Huxtable family that Cosby created was solidly upper middle class— Cosby played an obstetrician, his TV wife a lawyer—and hardly ever uttered a sentence about racial or class struggle. In fact, no sign of poor black folk was spotted until near the end of the series' run when a visiting relative of modest means was embraced by her wealthier kinfolk. Cosby's statement about the black family sitcom in 1969 proved to be an aberration in his solidly color-blind philosophy. By 1984, with the arrival of the Huxtables in American homes and at the top of the Nielsen ratings, Cosby's dream television family just happened to be black. One critic gushed, "Yes, the family is black, but that fact is totally ignored. No racial jokes are made, no problems of prejudice discussed. The Huxtables are comfortable middle-class Americans . . . and their stories could take place almost anywhere. Nobody actually says this family represents the whole human family, but the delicious ordinariness of its pleasures and tribulations has given millions a fresh, laughter-splashed perspective on their own domestic lives."[40]

In *The Cosby Show* the comedian found the most influential vehicle yet to promulgate his color-blind politics and to swipe at critics who believed that he comforted whites and copped out of addressing the problems of black America. Cosby, and his show's consultant, noted Harvard psychiatrist Alvin Poussaint, bristled at the charge that the Huxtables weren't black enough, or that they were minstrel makeovers of fifties sitcom characters. Poussaint contended that "it is racist to suggest that the series is merely *Father Knows Best* in blackface."[41] Relying on the inferential racial politics Cosby has mastered, Poussaint argued that the "Black style of the characters is evident in their speech, intonations and nuances."[42] As for Cosby, he, too, blanched at the suggestion that his television family hadn't dealt with controversial issues like racism, poverty and interracial dating, and that they ignored the masses of blacks who were far less wealthy than the Huxtables.

Why do they want to deny me the pleasure of being just an American and just enjoying life? Why must I make all the Black social statements? My family here is not going to sit around for half an hour and do Black versus White versus Brown versus Asian jokes so people can say "This is a Black show." What they [the critics] are doing is saying, "Well, if you're not going to talk about these [Black] issues, then why are you there?" And then comes the arrogance on my part. "I'm here because I'm a human being and I want to have fun. I want to show the happiness within our people. I want to show that we have the same kind of wants and needs as other American families." I'm going to take this show and make it last as long as I can to show Black people that they have something to be proud of.[43]

* * *

Cosby's racial politics—made up of his belief that color is a crutch that has no place in his art; his desire to bring the races together by focusing on their similarities, not their differences; his yearning to be seen as a human being and an American without reference to race; and his resistance to racial representation and crusading—spin out from, and wash back against, broader currents of debate in black culture. Failing to identify these currents dooms us to believe that Cosby's racial politics are exceptional or original, when they are neither. Along the way it will become clear how Cosby's recent views ratify certain beliefs while rejecting others in black culture. In light of Cosby's beliefs over the last forty years—about race, universalism and human identity—it is hard not to conclude that his public denunciation of the black poor sullies his principles.

Cosby's words about lower-class blacks have not spiraled into a vacuum. His comments have been received in a specific cultural and political context. Cosby's remarks also have reinforced and discarded views about how poor black folk behave and how they ought to be treated. I will address these views, and the contexts that frame them, later in the book, especially in Chapter 5. For now, Cosby's views should be placed within black cultural debates that have to do with the *stages, status, styles* and *strategies* of black identity. As with any outline of thought and reaction, these categories are meant to provide a convenient handle on broad trends within black culture. They are neither exhaustive nor pure, since they bleed between lines of strict definition. Yet, they can help to identify and organize ideas of cultural identity that unmistakably imprint Cosby's beliefs.

The stages of black identity refer to how blacks dynamically negotiate offensive, misleading or troubling information about black life. The first stage is stereotype, where white prejudiced beliefs and bigoted intuitions are dressed as objective observation and common sense—from D. W. Griffith's film *Birth of a Nation*, portraying black males as rapist thugs, to Smith and Murray's book *The Bell Curve,* offering "scientific" proof of black intellectual inferiority. Racial stereotypes may contain strands of truth wrapped around knots of willful ignorance and deadly distortion. At its heart, a stereotype is a lazy assessment of the other, a sloppy projection of bias onto a vulnerable target: Blacks are dumb, lazy, criminal, sex-crazed and so on. In early film and television, blacks were only seen as coons, maids, cooks, butlers and the like. Blacks spend a great deal of time fighting these labels and proving they're not true.[44] Cosby has attempted to resist stereotypes from the start of his career.[45]

The second stage is archetype, or the projection by blacks of the defining characteristics of black identity. Since most stereotypes are negative—and even when they involve ostensibly flattering traits like sexual prowess or the ability to dance and sing, they are tinged with paternalism and condescension—black archetypes are usually positive and spotlight the virtues of black identity. Thus, blacks reject Stepin Fetchit's shuffling, bowing, dim-witted, demeaning portrayals of black masculinity in film and offer in its place the dignity and poise of Sidney Poitier's legendary film roles, or Bill Cosby's vast body of work on television. (But millionaire Fetchit, born Lincoln Theodore Perry, said before his death at age eighty-three in 1985 that all "the things that [Bill] Cosby and [Sidney] Poitier have done wouldn't be possible if I hadn't broken that law.")[46] Blacks argue that Harriet Beecher Stowe's novel *Uncle Tom's Cabin* is not as accurate a reflection of black life and identity, and not nearly as heroic, as the one presented in Toni Morrison's *Beloved*. Archetypes embody the efforts of black folk to wrest the authority of self-definition from whites who fail to see the beauty and power of black life, and to redefine our identities in more edifying terms.

The third stage is antitype, or the expression by blacks of the irreverent meanings of blackness that transgress against received beliefs or accepted norms. The creation of antitypes—from blaxploitation films to hip-hop music, from the comic routines of Richard Pryor to the silhouette art of Kara Walker, from Audre Lorde's lesbian scholarship and activism to "homothug" gay drug dealer Omar portrayed on television's

The Wire by Michael K. Williams—permits blacks to challenge visions of blackness that exclude the unsavory and the
politically incorrect. Antitypes embody efforts to explore
the experiences and identities of blacks who are usually
kept—because of class status, lack of power, gender and sexual orientation—from being visible in archetypal black representations. Black archetypes provide the backdrop for
influential blacks to elevate or sink antitypical visions of
blackness—for instance, Cosby's embrace of antitype through
his support of nontraditional gender roles on *The Cosby Show*
and his resistance to antitype through his criticisms of the
new black comics and hip-hop culture. The appeal to archetypes also permits powerful blacks to heap scorn and stigma
on blacks who fall within antitypes' borders, whether they are
poor or gay or single mothers. Cosby's blasting of poor blacks
for their failure to hold "up their end in this deal" is a perfect
example.

It should be noted that the work of some blacks crosses
between the stages of black identity. Toni Morrison's novels,
and her literary and cultural criticism, may be viewed as both
archetypal and antitypical, since they support *and* subvert
beliefs about black identity. And Kara Walker's visual art
experiments with the images of blacks produced by racist
whites, appropriating and signifying on stereotypes of black
identity while veering into antitypical territory. At times, as
with the comedy of Keenan Ivory Wayans on his 1990s
sketch variety series, *In Living Color*, or the gangsta raps of
Snoop Dogg, the line between stereotype and antitype is
barely discernible, a point not always lost on creators of

black art who seek to play with negative portrayals of black life in order to explore, and, sometimes, unmask them.[47] In the main, Cosby has been hugely unsympathetic to such efforts.

The stages of black identity are closely related to the styles of black identity, which have to do with seeing black culture and identity in either complex or simple terms. By extension, the styles of black identity concern whether we will be absolute or comparative, fundamental or flexible, in our views of blackness. Is black identity a once-and-for-all proposition that is settled in advance of social and psychological factors, or is it continually transformed by these and other forces? For instance, in the stages of black identity, stereotypes are seen by many blacks as negative, archetypes are seen as positive, and antitypes are viewed with great suspicion, depending on the kinds of political and racial struggles one seeks to wage. Often, black identity is reduced to the mantra of "positive" versus "negative": An image or identity either uplifts or degrades black folk. Cosby is squarely in this tradition of interpretation. He decries "what many of today's black comics are doing with the legacy he left them. Where Cosby's routines were mostly good-natured and colorblind, he thinks comics are now foulmouthed, misogynistic and too eager to reinforce negative stereotypes of black people."[48] While positive-versus-negative conversations are often productive when directed at obvious examples—few blacks would disagree with the contention that Rush Limbaugh's 2003 attack on the talent of black quarterback Donovan McNabb was laden with vicious stereotype—they are just as likely to stall in more difficult cases, especially when competing visions of black identity are evoked within the culture.

For example, is rap music positive or negative? In the archetypal vision of blackness, that question is almost always answered in the negative because it is believed that rap embraces stereotypes of black people as violent, over-sexed and criminally inclined, an argument Cosby has made on numerous occasions.[49] The question of negative-versus-positive is seen as valuable because it yields the greatest insight about the processes and contexts of black identity. The antitypical vision of blackness might answer that despite rap's admitted vices, it possesses, at its best, redeeming virtues: It counters official visions of history with narratives drawn from despised young folk; it joins the word and the drum, elemental aspects of black expressive culture; and it permits poor black folk another exit from the ghetto, even as its formerly poor artists continue to tout its virtues with mixed results. The answer to the question of rap's influence points to competing visions of black identity, represented on one side by positive-versus-negative and on the other by complex-versus-simple.

In the positive-versus-negative framework, questions of black identity usually attract black-and-white answers because there is often a black-and-white view of the issues at hand. In complex-versus-simple views of black identity, there is a much more complicated and multilayered view of black culture at work. Simple views of black life—whether stereo-typical, archetypal or antitypical, and to be sure, there is a big difference between them—chase nuance and contradiction to the sidelines. An identity or issue is either positive or negative, either right or wrong. The positive-versus-negative outlook obscures the way challenging concepts of identity can be dismissed as negative because they don't accord with dominant black views. For many blacks, gays and lesbians are viewed negatively because their lifestyles challenge rigid, fundamental black theological beliefs. A book that uplifts the radical legacy of Martin Luther King, Jr., is viewed by many blacks as negative because it also honestly treats his alleged promiscuity and plagiarism.[50] A focus on the positive simply can't guarantee a full and engaging view of black life. A preference for hip-hop artists who are positive (no cursing, no self-denigrating epithets, no violent references to the ghetto) often overlooks the question of whether they have intellectual depth and the ability to flow. By contrast, rappers viewed as negative—if for no other reason than they employ the word "nigga" in their repertoire, a charge, by the way, that can be made against many rappers otherwise considered to be positive—may possess these abilities in abundance. And the same rapper who revels in a woman's finely proportioned behind may also speak against racism and on behalf of the poor, even as he encourages them not to look at hip-hop as their salvation.[51]

There is a larger question at stake for the advocates of complex black identity: Does this notion of blackness honor the variability and multiplicity of black identity, and does it account for the contradictions and conflicts, and the good and bad, that characterize black life? Black folk have often avoided such complexity because destructive white stereotypes of black identity have been so widely disseminated. We are loath to expose ugly dimensions of black life to a white public that is often hungry for confirmation of black pathology while failing to see the same problems in its own backyard. Black culture has, therefore, become fixed in defining black identity; only the positive, redeeming and virtuous will do. That's understandable, but still shortsighted and, on occasion, needlessly defensive. Although most groups don't have to pay the heavy identity tax that blacks do for negative information circulating in the culture, it is still a gesture of racial maturity to embrace our complexity, a move that pains those stuck on positive-versus-negative, as Cosby often has been. The only exception he has been willing to make is to "air the dirty laundry" of poor black folk, while the habits and behaviors of other black communities are spared public hashing.

The styles of black identity offer help in addressing the status of black identity, or the thorny issue of black authenticity, of what is real in black culture. The nagging worry of authenticity is whether black folk have strayed too far from the old landmarks of cultural identity. The status of black identity has become urgent with the rise of hip-hop culture and its mantra of "keep it real," which often means honoring the ghetto roots of black identity. But a prior question of black authenticity, raised by jazz musician Gene McDaniels thirty-five years ago, still resonates, namely, "make it real compared to what?"[52] Black folk engage the question of authenticity to distinguish between identities that are intrinsic and organic to the culture and those that are imported, or even imposed. This is what Cosby has in mind when he chides black youth for wearing their "hat on backwards, pants down around the crack . . . and all kinds of needles and things" in their bodies, asking, "What part of Africa did this come from? We are not Africans." He's defining what is authentic to black American culture by implying that these traits don't reflect African roots, and by arguing that black Americans are *not* Africans, offering a double dose of authenticity claims.

Authenticity anxiety is only heightened as figures and forces outside the culture play a bigger role in helping those inside it find their voices. There is heated debate, for instance, about whether hip-hop culture reflects genuine aspects of black culture or whether it is manufactured by advocates of consumer culture out to exploit black identity for the marketplace. Of course, a complex vision of black identity holds that both of these things are true. It is those who resent the marketplace's intrusions and its corruptions of black identity—and that certainly includes archetypal advocates like Cosby as well as many fans of the art form, those most likely lumped under the antitypical rubric—who question whether "real" black youth culture really draws from emotional and intellectual roots within the culture. Some go even further and question whether the identities proclaimed in hip-hop as cutting-edge and countercultural are largely the creations of shrewd marketers out to make a buck by merchandising black pathologies. While those who fall inside the antitypical camp might hold this to be true—and those who have a complex view of black culture might agree—this position is most forcefully argued by defenders of a simple view of black culture. Marketing and merchandising are not new, even if they bear closer scrutiny because they have rarely been as strong and seductive a force as they are now. Neither should we forget that some of the ideas and images presently circulating in hip-hop, from the black rebel and outlaw to the cultural griot, have been around for quite a while in the culture.

The question of authenticity shouldn't be dismissed, just rendered in more complex fashion as we probe the roots of black identity. It makes sense, for example, to ask whether low-slung, beltless pants and stringless shoes, both styles of urban gear that mimic prison clothing, are authentically black. It should be obvious that such styles can claim no direct lineage in black life; but it is equally obvious that the commercial and creative use made by blacks of elements outside the culture is indeed an authentic black cultural trait. It should also be obvious that claims to authenticity do not resolve the ethical issues of identity. Whether something is authentic or not doesn't settle whether authenticity is a good or bad thing, a productive or destructive force.

The Cosby Show was integral to heated cultural debates about whether the images projected on the show were real, that is, representative of actual black life and the conditions we confront, or creations of commercial television that distort the facts. As Henry Louis Gates, Jr., argued in his essay, "TV's Black World Turns—But Stays Unreal," the black "fixation with the presence of black characters on TV has blinded us to an important fact that 'Cosby,' which began in 1984, and its offshoots over the years demonstrate convincingly: There is very little connection between the social status of black Americans and the fabricated images of black people that Americans consume each day."[53] Speaking to another dimension of "real," the relation between aesthetic creations and political status, Gates contends that "the representations of blacks on TV is a very poor index to our social advancement or political progress." Gates also suggests that the blending of Cosby's television image and his real-life persona, like that of other successful blacks, increases the likelihood that their individual prosperity will be seen as representative of all blacks, especially as the boundaries between fiction and fact are overcome through marketing and advertising. "Today, blacks are doing much better on TV than they are in real life," Gates writes, "an irony underscored by the use of black public figures (Mr. Cosby, Michael Jackson, Michael Jordan, Bobby McFerrin) as spokesmen for major businesses." Gates says that when "Mr. Cosby, deadpan, faces the camera squarely and says, 'E. F. Hutton. Because it's my money,' the line blurs between Cliff Huxtable's successful career and Mr. Cosby."[54]

The question of black authenticity gathers all the intersections of black life in miniature; it portrays the relation between identity and class, culture, gender, ideology, sexual orientation, region, religion, age and the like. Some blacks think that "real" blacks don't vote Republican, marry outside the race, adopt gay lifestyles, support abortion, bungee jump, climb mountains, attend the opera, or love country music. These views reveal the tribalism that can trump complex views of black life. Proud of their roots, some blacks worship them. But roots should nourish, not strangle, black identity. To be sure, some versions of black identity that were offered as an alternative to simple archetypes, for instance, antitypi-cal celebrations of the thug, gangsta or the "real nigga," often come off as the only authentic vision of blackness going, a temptation for the exponents of all notions of blackness. I'm afraid that's the trap into which Cosby has too often fallen in his criticisms of young people and the poor. Ultimately, "real" or "fake" has as much to do with the politics we practice, the goals we project for black life and the means we advocate to achieve freedom and self-expression as it does with the exis-tence of an objective blackness. "Real" is the by-product of a dynamic struggle, one that is still very much alive.

The strategies of black identity promote a provisional response to the stages, styles and status of black identity. The strategies of blackness point to how black folk manage their identities on a cosmic level. These strategies have primarily to do with how we view our black identities—and how they play out—in relation to the dominant culture. If status is internal to black culture, then strategies are the outward face of black identity, how we offer the world a picture of our blackness. The first strategy is accidental blackness; we are human beings who by accident of birth *happen* to be black. The message this strategy of blackness sends to the white world is: "Our blackness is only the most obvious—but surely not the most important—element of our identities. We are human beings with the same likes, wants, needs, desires and aspirations as you." Cosby has consistently held true to this position, and as the journalistic sources cited above prove, he has been received that way in white society. As *Newsweek* suggested, "Bill Cosby is not a Negro comic; he is a comic who happens to be a Negro."[55] And as Cosby insisted, "The story about me is not the story of a black man, but of a man. What happens to me, happens to just a man."[56] Clarence Thomas, Condoleezza Rice and Tiger Woods ("The bottom line is that I am an American . . . and proud of it! That is who I am and what I am. Now with your cooperation, I hope I can just be a golfer and a human being") join Cosby in this category.[57]

The second strategy is incidental blackness; we are proud to be black, but it is only one strand of our identity. The message this strategy of blackness presents to the white world is: "Our blackness is important, but we do not spend our days thinking about it, nor do we believe that race is nearly as important a factor in the nation as it used to be." The strategy of incidental blackness relies upon cautiously acknowledging the historic force of race while proclaiming its erosion in contemporary affairs. Colin Powell and Barack Obama, among others, fit here. Finally, there is intentional blackness; we are human beings who are proud of our blackness and see it as a critical, though surely not the exclusive, aspect of our identity. The message this strategy of blackness sends to the white world is: "We love ourselves and our culture, and other cultures as well. We embrace the political aspect of our blackness. We don't want to forget our blackness because it is central to our identities, but we also understand that in a culture still plagued by racism, we can't afford to forget our identities because we know the dominant culture hasn't either." Martin Luther King, Jr., Jesse Jackson, Ella Baker, Malcolm X and a host of others belong here.

The strategies of blackness permit black folk to negotiate the white world while remaining sane and balanced. Black folk may pass in and out of various strategies over a lifetime. And the focus on race in these strategies surely doesn't block the consideration of other equally compelling features of identity rooted in gender or sexual orientation or religion or class. Those with a simple view of blackness fixed on archetypal representations of identity may find comfort in strategies of accidental blackness that treat racism as if it didn't exist. Even if blacks disagree with such a strategy, they understand the racial fatigue that can make such a prospect enticing. In turn, those with a complex view of blackness who may embrace antitypical black identities might favor an intentional strategy in making arguments for racial justice in the workplace or in higher education. These strategies of blackness are used in varying ways and degrees in different contexts at different times, so that a person who is intentional in one setting—say, on the front lines of a protest before the Supreme Court to preserve affirmative action—may be incidental at the company picnic. Circumstances, and, of course, political and ideological factors, and one's take on the stages, struggles and status of black identity, determine what strategy one employs to survive. Cosby has favored the strategy of accidental blackness for most of his career; his departure from it to evoke intentional blackness, and thus to bolster his authority to criticize the poor, shouldn't be overlooked.

* * *

If Bill Cosby's views derive from profound debates about black identity, these debates can shed greater light on his racial philosophy and, more recently, his comments about the black poor. To be sure, Cosby's decision to kick the habit of race in his art in the early sixties—a decision "urged on him" by white manager Roy Silver—had many advantages.[58] First, Cosby's strategy of accidental black identity countered the clumsy way white television writers used racial humor to get laughs. Next, Cosby's strategy met racial stereotype at its roots and cut it off; thus he wouldn't have to face the problem of how to explain an offensive sketch, since it would be stopped before it began. For instance, Cosby refused to become the "token" Negro on *I Spy* who drew unnecessary attention to his race. Cosby and his manager culled the scripts for potential offenses.[59] In one script, an Asian child was supposed to rub Cosby's face and be surprised that his color didn't come off. Cosby was annoyed and promised that should it happen again, "I'll rub back."[60] Third, viewing race as a crutch caused Cosby to work harder to be funny without playing his race for easy laughs. In Cosby's view, color was the lazy comedian's ruse, used in lieu of digging deeper into the human psyche and the world outside of race to find humor.

Cosby's views were simple and absolute: Race-conscious comedy is less authentic, and certainly less compelling, than color-blind humor. Cosby failed to see that while the easy reliance on color *could* be a crutch, it didn't have to be. There are many ways to probe the complex interiors of color—to hold it up in the light of comedic day and peer inside its prismatic effect. Moreover, Cosby overlooked how much work such an enterprise might demand. Lazy comedians are lazy comedians, in whatever guise or genre they operate. Diligent artists can bring new insight by relentlessly stretching their art. Dick Gregory did it before Cosby, and Richard Pryor and Chris Rock have done it since. Despite Cosby's brilliant work, race hasn't disappeared; it seems he might have as usefully led us *through* the battlefields of race instead of *around* them. Or, failing that, he might have more loudly applauded comedians besides Gregory and Pryor who did. While Cosby's comedy elegantly conjures the nonexistence of race, there is moral beauty as well in confronting the beast and slaying it with a laugh, a strategy used by black folk through the ages.[61]

A convincing argument can be made for playing with stereotypes to deconstruct them; it is just as reasonable to critically engage black archetypes and experiment with anti-types. Cosby's way of proceeding, as if stereotypes didn't exist, or as if most antitypes were useless and self-defeating, is *one* way, a sometimes helpful way, of dismantling them. But there can be value in hammering away at stereotypes—or signifying on them, or relishing the demystification of their esoteric lunacies, and thus resisting their rule laugh by laugh. The same can be said for black comedy's role in treating arche-types and antitypes. Keenan Ivory Wayans's sketch variety series, *In Living Color*, often assaulted plastic archetypes of blackness and exploded—and, yes, often extended—racial stereotypes in the risky endeavor of probing rather than idol-izing black culture. *In Living Color*, through its irreverent antitypes and its signifying excesses, showcased a different, complex side of the black humanity Cosby longs to affirm. If nothing else, Wayans proved that art doesn't exist merely to reinforce "positive" views of black life, but to invite blacks and others to confront our identities, to reflect on them, to be bothered by them and to probe, often in uncomfortable ways, the racial pieties we hold dear. In one brilliant stroke, *In Living Color* addressed the stages, status and styles of black identity. Comedy shouldn't just soothe; it should also disturb. Color needn't be a crutch; it can also be a catalyst—to self-reflection and greater understanding.

Cosby's effort to bring the races together through his comedy was both courageous and flawed. The yen for truths that unite blacks and whites reflected the integrationist ethos of the civil rights movement Cosby wished neither to join nor lead. Cosby's comedy enlivened the ideals of universality and color blindness at which branches of the movement aimed. But there was often a huge gap between what the movement meant by "universal" and "color-blind" and what the broader society understood them to be. Cosby's frequent failure to understand that difference has made his vision of color blindness and universalism much less salient, and, quite frankly, much less useful, to black folk. The whites who came to Cosby because he failed to unnerve them, to shake them, or to challenge them at all, felt just fine. As Cosby boasted to Rex Reed, "People accept me because I'm not controversial. Most of them don't even think of me as a Negro."[62]

The civil rights movement perceived universalism in the guiding ideals of democracy and justice that should benefit all peoples. The movement also argued that the "self-evident" claims of humanity for *each* community must be respected;

one needn't destroy one's particular identity to fit in. As W.E.B. Du Bois argued in 1903, black folk didn't want to lose our identity as the price of our survival. For Du Bois, the American Negro "would not bleach his Negro soul in a flood of white Americanism, for he knows that Negro blood has a message for the world. He simply wishes to make it possible for a man to be both a Negro and an American, without being cursed and spit upon by his fellows, without having the doors of Opportunity closed roughly in his face."[63] Unlike Du Bois, Cosby didn't see that black identities needn't give up their particular ethnic or racial slants to be universal; that's a false dichotomy engineered by the white merchants of a variety of universalism that seeks to project the normative as the universal. The two surely aren't the same.

It is supremely ironic that, under the banner of universalism and "self-evident" rights, black folk fought to gain benefits of citizenship that turned out to be neither self-evident nor universal. It should give pause to folk like Cosby that the universal as it was conceived in areas of white society was a masquerade of racial privilege that only *appeared* to be welcoming and inclusive. By contrast, black folk were often viewed by their white opponents, the upholders of the universal, as shattering the political compact by asking for "special" rights—except that those "special" rights turned out to be the rights that were guaranteed to all white male citizens. Black folk made their arguments about being included in the center of political privilege while being shunted to the social periphery; they were often regarded as vulgarly particular in their claims. Paradoxically, as blacks begged to be included in the universal from an allegedly particularistic standpoint, they were denied access by the advocates of an allegedly universal perspective.

The justification for keeping blacks from their universally recognized rights of citizenship was an alleged cultural and moral inferiority. Black folk fell literally and metaphorically beyond the pale of white identity, which, during the time Cosby rose to fame in the early sixties, was viewed as the divining rod for normalcy. Most whites and a large number of blacks—and who can blame them, since it was beat into their brows from the time they got here—viewed white identity as normative, and hence universal, since whites were able to impose their interpretation of its meaning on the nation. Whiteness, a particular slant on the universal, was enshrined as its very definition. In reality, in its white supremacist mode, it was a gross defection from the very spirit of the universal, though in other aspects it needn't have been, since all universals must find local footing. This cultural situation understandably confused citizens of all colors, including gifted folk like Cosby who could expect no exemption from the seeming omnipresence of white culture.

Each time Cosby cringed at *the very thought* of color or race in comedy, he bought the logic of normative white identity hook, punch line and sinker. Cosby didn't cringe at race or color per se; he cringed at *blackness*. He didn't see the color of whiteness; it was the "universal" he embraced. When Cosby talked of doing comedy that both blacks and whites could enjoy, its ideals and standards were often derived from a white base. (As proof, Cosby and his early white managers ruthlessly scrutinized his routines with the intent that Cosby should be color-blind, or, in their words, "work white.")[64] Even when Cosby turned to his family for material for one of his legendary routines, say, about his brother Russell, he undermined the universal character of the story by ignoring its racial dimensions and an important lesson of the civil rights movement: The "particular" that is not conceived as exclusively or exhaustively representative is the path to the universal.

Universalism may be composed of either vicious or virtuous specificities. The use of race didn't have to mean that Cosby had to forsake his dream to become universal; he simply needed to avoid the illusion that any particular identity, white or black, could possibly capture *the* truth. His decision to go color-blind just as color could legitimately be explored through humor was a missed opportunity for us and Cosby, who, given his desire for uplifting art, might have taught us all a great deal about race through his stand-up routines, television shows, comedy albums and films. To do so, he didn't have to leave comedy and become an activist like Dick Gregory, who, by 1967, viewed himself "as a social commentator who uses humor to interpret the needs and wants of Negroes to the white community, rather than as a comedian who happens to deal in topical social material."[65] Cosby might have benefited, however, from a complex view of black identity instead of the simple view of blackness that seemed to hold him back.

Cosby's racial confusion and embrace of simple blackness didn't end there, but flashed as well in his reluctance to speak out on race. The comic's stern refusal to be a leader is under-standable. "I'm *tired* of those people who say, 'You should be doing more to help your people.' I'm a comedian, *that's all*."[66] It is extremely difficult to balance the obligations to excel as a black entertainer, or more generally as a black professional, with the demands that one speak for one's race. If it is true now, it was even truer when Cosby first blazed to celebrity. The sheer unavoidability of racial representation, however, looms for the gifted and blessed, for those whose talents make them, willy-nilly, role models and de facto spokespeople for a race still under siege, with one-quarter of its members mired in poverty. That there is little choice in the matter often gnaws at those whose natural inclination is to recede into the woodwork of their given profession. Cosby has insisted that he is better suited for quiet, behind-the-scenes race work, a claim that is odd to some given the public life well-known comedians lead.

We should draw a distinction, however, between a comic's professional persona and his public position as a private citizen. A comic's privacies—of emotion, of experience, of evolution—fuel artistic expression. But his public actions as a private citi-zen, as one not elected or appointed to office, appeal to a different dimension of his identity. The comic-citizen is a species of all articulations of role switching and the frequent genre blurring that occur when celebrity enters the equation. To be of use to his group, the well-known comic of color has to occasionally breach the pact he makes with himself—that he will act out on stage his encounter with personal and social issues that can be turned to creative advantage, but otherwise, for the sake of his sanity and dignity, he will try to keep everything to himself. (Of course, comics like Richard Pryor shredded this agreement in ways that were both spectacular and utterly horrifying.) The comic-citizen affirms members of his race who identify with him even as his celebrity amplifies their influence through his identification with them. Fair or not, the comic of color, just like most black professionals, is *presumed* to have a contribution to make—a presumption fed by the desperation to be validated by the fortunate of the race—and it is the *public* character of that contribution that is critical to his constituents.

If the comic of color can't help being representative, it is because she embodies in her art the turmoil and suffering that anonymous blacks regularly endure without the platform or public sympathy the celebrity comic may enjoy. The black comic need not surrender a complex or antitypical or independent vision of black identity to uphold her critical function; part of the appeal of black comics is their irreverent perspectives that encourage pitiless cultural inventory and relentless self-critique.[67] The black comic's artful engagement with the stages and styles of black identity only bolster her position of authority and representation, especially if she has chosen the strategy of intentional blackness and opted to publicly identify *as* a black figure *with* her black people. If, however, the comic has declined those representational duties and has instead chosen the strategy of accidental blackness, then her words may be interpreted as hostile, unloving and harsh. This is Cosby's dilemma: Having been accidentally black for forty years, he has suddenly and vio-

lently switched strategies of self-presentation to an intentional blackness that can be supported by neither his politics
nor his past. Cosby's choice to go public as a crusader against
poor blacks—those who may have looked up to him over the
years with memories of *Uptown Saturday Night*, where he
appeared more intentionally "black" than in most other roles,
or who may have fondly reminisced about *Fat Albert and the
Cosby Kids*'s marvelously vernacular intonations, contrary to
Cosby's present mission to stamp out Ebonics—is remarkably
troubling, for reasons I explore throughout this book. For
now, two problems are most pressing.

First, by attacking the poor, Cosby has made tragic use of
his public capital. Despite black folk criticizing and begging
him for forty years, Cosby has refused to explore race in his
comedy, rejected the role of crusader or leader on issues of
race and resisted bearing the burdens of racial representation
in public with grace. Not only has Cosby refused to speak *for*
black folk, but he has refused, with rare exception, to speak
against a host of ills during his day, including white supremacy,
unfair housing practices, segregated public accommodations,
Jim Crow laws, unequal health insurance, racial disparities in
wealth, disproportionately high infant mortality rates, unjust
criminal justice sentencing practices, unequal higher education access, environmental racism, crumbling ghetto infrastructures, lead poisoning and asbestos consumption among
poor children, and, on the evening he made his infamous
remarks about the ghetto poor at a ceremony commemorating
Brown v. Board, the persistent and harmful resegregation of
black children in schools across the country.

Cosby has chosen instead to direct one of the most powerful and influential voices in the culture, and one of the brightest media spotlights in the land, *against* some of the nation's most vulnerable citizens, who are in need of support and love, not humiliation and belittlement. It is tempting to dismiss Cosby as a crotchety, self-loathing hypocrite—after all, he has suffered, sometimes publicly, from some of the very ills he deplores (including admission of an affair and charges of a child out of wedlock, though the latter claim has not been proved). But that would be too easy and in some ways unfair, since Cosby's claims are either true or false regardless of his moral status. However, Cosby's standing does have relevance in discussing whether or not he has been able to as strictly adhere to his lessons as he counsels. As we shall see later, he hasn't.

Cosby's media assault has been defended by those who say he's built up sufficient capital to diss poor blacks through his majestic philanthropy over the years. (The word literally means "love of humanity," but writers have also warned of the concentration of power in the hands of the few in a "philanthocracy" that is peculiarly American, and distinctly plutocratic.)[68] But that's like saying that it's all right to rape a young lady because you've given a million dollars to a women's college. One is never granted permission to do wrong as the reward for doing right. One can't accumulate enough goodwill to undermine the common good of the neediest members of our culture.

Second, Cosby has lurched far beyond the circumference of his talent in making sweeping social pronouncements on race. It is not merely a matter of whether one agrees or not with Cosby; it is the fact that Cosby has not been practiced or articulate in matters of public negotiation with the subtleties, nuances and complexities of racial rhetoric. He has been ingenious, if misled, in creating comedy that has insisted on the nonexistence of race as the condition of our agreement on universally recognized values. In his nonracial comedy, Cosby has been sharp, luminous, humorous and sometimes sophisticated. Even when he was feigning anger or enacting bluster, he was usually analytically generous—that is, in his search for the roots of the behavior he lampooned, he was willing to cede the humanity of the people he surveyed. Cosby was often lucid and elegantly improvisational, even multivocal, playing to his strengths in routines honed over a brilliant stand-up career where, like a jazz artist, he constructed narratives of sometimes haunting ethical beauty that offered insight into the human condition.

In striking contrast, as a social critic of late, Cosby, in his observations about the black poor, is flat, univocal, literal, his monologue marred by dreadful analysis and wailing monotones, his speech bruised by disgust and nearly uncontrollable contempt. In the past, he has been mostly unwilling to speak up in traditional, representational fashion when it might count for the poor black people he now attacks. One of his defenders even admitted that "Cosby would not be at his best as a professional civil rights leader, a Black Panther, or the head of a poverty program."[69] Or, he might add, as a social critic. Although Cosby has chided the black poor for failing those brave blacks who "marched and were hit in the face with rocks," he fails to mention that when he had the chance to join the pioneers he now pits against the poor, he reneged. "I don't want to go someplace where they're throwing rocks unless I have some rocks to throw back," Cosby said.[70] And when he went on the *Phil Donahue Show* in 1985, he resented being asked about the black culture whose poor members he now unhesitatingly discusses. "I am not an authority on blackness," Cosby angrily insisted. "I didn't come on this program to discuss blackness. I came on this show to discuss human beings and let's get into that. . . . I don't want to spend the time when a black person shows up on a show talking about blackness and what you all have to do in order to make America better. . . . Right now, why don't you see if I can be a h-u-m-a-n b-e-i-n-g."[71]

Cosby's recent crusade underscores how much he has contradicted his color-blind, leader-reluctant principles, and suggests the manner in which he has scarily ranged far from his arena of competence. On the *Donahue Show*, when audience members wanted to learn Cosby's views on racial matters and to know what they could do to improve race relations, he rebuffed them with surprising gruffness. Apparently Cosby was neither ready nor willing to impart his wisdom. Only now he can't keep quiet; the unguarded words tumble from his mouth in unforgiving fury. And they hurt poor black people much more than anything Cosby has done to help them in the past. His relentless attack is symptomatic of the huge generational and class divide in black America. Our response is a measure of our willingness to meet him on the intellectual and cultural battlefield and provide good reasons why he is wrong. The reputation of millions of young people and poor folk hangs in the balance.

Chapter Two

Classrooms and
Cell Blocks

[I]n our cities and public schools we have fifty percent drop out . . . Those of us sitting out here who have gone on to some college or whatever we've done, we still fear our parents (clapping and laughter). And these people are not parenting. They're buying things for the kid. $500 sneakers. For what? And won't buy or spend $250 on Hooked on Phonics. (clapping) . . . All this child knows is "gimme, gimme, gimme." And these people wanna buy the friendship of a child. . . . and the child couldn't care less . . . Just forget telling your child to go to Peace Corps. It's right around da corner. (laughter) It's standing on da corner. It can't speak English. It doesn't want to speak English. I can't even talk the way these people talk. "Why you ain't, where you is go, ra." I don't know who these people are. And I blamed the kid until I heard the mother talk (laughter). And then I heard the father talk. This is all in the house. You used to talk a certain way on da corner and you

got in the house and you switched to English. Everybody knows it's important to speak English except these knuckle- heads. You can't land a plane with "why you ain't. . ." You can't be a doctor with that kind of crap coming out of your mouth. There is no Bible that has that language. Where did these people get the idea that they're moving ahead on this? Well, they know they're not, they're just hanging out in the same place, five, six generations, sitting in the projects. Well you're just supposed to stay there long enough to get a job and move out . . . Now look, I'm telling you. It's not what they're doing to us. It's what we're not doing. 50 percent drop out. Look, we're raising our own ingrown immigrants. These peo- ple are fighting hard to be ignorant. There's no English being spoken, and they're walking and they're angry. Oh God, they're angry . . . It's time for you to not accept this language that these people are speaking, which will take them nowhere. What the hell good is Brown Vs. the Board of Education if nobody wants it? And if they're getting in the way? . . . These are children. They don't know anything. They don't have any- thing. They're homeless people. All they know how to do is beg. And you give it to 'em, trying to win their friendship. And what are they good for? . . . When you walk around the neighborhood and you see this stuff, that stuff's not funny. These people are not funny anymore. And that's not my brother. And that's not my sister. They're faking and they're dragging me way down. Because the state, the city and all these people have to pick up the tab on them, because they don't want to accept that they have to study to get an educa- tion. And so, ladies and gentlemen, please, Dorothy Height, where ever she's sitting, she didn't do all that stuff so that she could hear somebody say, "I can't stand algebra, I can't stand. . .and what you, why you wanna," with holes in them . . . It's horrible. Basketball players, multimillionaires, can't write a paragraph. Football players, multimillionaires, can't read. Yes. Multimillionaires. Well, Brown V. the Board of Education. But where are we today? It's there; they paved the way. What did we do with it? The white man, he's laughing, got to be laughing. 50 percent drop out, rest of 'em in prison.

In our own neighborhood, we have men in prison . . . I'm talking about these people who cry when their son is standing there in an orange suit. Where were you when he was two? (clapping) Where were you when he was twelve? Where were you when he was eighteen, and how come you don't know he had a pistol? (clapping) And where is his father, and why don't you know where he is? And why don't the father show up to talk to this boy? . . . Looking at the incarcerated, these are not political criminals. These are people going around stealing Coca Cola. People getting shot in the back of the head over a piece of pound cake! And then we all run out and we're outraged, "Ah, the cops shouldn'ta shot him." What the hell was he doing with the pound cake in his hand? (laughter and clapping). I wanted a piece of pound cake just as bad as anybody else (laughter) . . . And they have pistols and they shoot and they do stupid things. And after they kill somebody, they don't have a plan. Just murder somebody. Boom. Over what? A pizza. And then run to the poor cousin's house. They sit there and the cousin says "what are you doing here?" "I just killed somebody, man." "What?" "I just killed somebody, I've

got to stay here." "No, you don't." "Well, give me some money,
I'm going. . ." "Where are you going?" "North Carolina."
Everybody wanted to go to North Carolina. And the police
know where you're going, because your cousin has a record. . .
And then they stand there in an orange suit and you drop to
your knees, and say, (crying sound), "Please, he didn't do any-
thing, he didn't do anything." Yes, he did do it. And you need
to have an orange suit on too (laughter, clapping) . . . You got
to tell me that if there was parenting, help me, that if there
was parenting, he wouldn'ta picked up the Coca Cola bottle
and walked out with it to get shot in the back of da head. He
wouldn't have. Not if he loved his parents. And not if they
were parenting! Not if the father would come home. Not if the
boy that dropped the sperm cell inside of da girl and the girl
said, "No, you have to come back here and be the father of this
child." They don't have to.

Bill Cosby, by his own admission, was a bad student, and
"compiled a lackluster academic record from the moment he
set foot in school."[1] His sixth-grade teacher noted on his
report card that "William would rather clown than study."[2]
He dropped out of high school after he flunked the tenth
grade *three* times. He enlisted in the navy, where he got his
GED, and then enrolled at Temple University, where he
dropped out to pursue a show business career. His unfinished
bachelor's degree from Temple was eventually bestowed on
him because of "life experience."[3] Cosby enrolled as a part-
time doctoral student at the University of Massachusetts at

Amherst, which awarded him the Ed.D. degree in 1977 for a dissertation on *Fat Albert and the Cosby Kids*. But not even that degree was unsullied by controversy: A professor who served on Cosby's dissertation committee, Reginald Damerell, said that Cosby hardly took a class—and that he got course credit for appearing on *Sesame Street* and *The Electric Company*, "and wrote a dissertation that analyzed the impact of his show."[4] Damerell concluded that degrees like Cosby's "do not attest to genuine academic achievement. They are empty credentials."[5] (While I think Damerell's conclusion is harsh and unfair, it does underscore the ironic route Cosby has traveled to become nearly as acclaimed for his educational pedigree as for his comedic genius.) Given his difficult educational background, it's a good thing Cosby didn't have Bill Cosby around to discourage him from achieving his goals by citing statistics about black high school dropouts that don't square with the facts. It's a shame that Cosby skewered the victims of educational neoapartheid, the very folk that *Brown v. Board* sought to help, instead of pointing to the social inequities and disparities in resources that continue to make American schools "separate and unequal." And for Cosby to overlook how the criminal justice system mercilessly feeds on social inequality is just as tragic.

It may be partially accurate to describe the contemporary social and educational landscape for blacks in Dickensian terms: It is the best and worst of times, but only if we admit that one's perception of the times rests on rigid class divisions in black communities. For an expanded black middle class, which enjoys unprecedented success at work and in school, the times are much better than before *Brown*, though exorbitant optimism must be chastened by the racist barriers that remain. In 1954, the year of the *Brown* decision, the neonatal mortality rate for blacks per one thousand live births registered at 27 percent, compared to 17.8 percent for whites. The maternal mortality rates per one thousand live births were 14.4 percent for blacks and only 3.7 percent for whites. The average black household income was $2,890, 55 percent of the white average of $5,228. In 1952, black illiteracy for those age fourteen and above was 10.2 percent, five times the 1.8 percent level of white illiteracy. At the time, more than a quarter of black males had no more than four years of schooling, compared to less than 9 percent for white males.[6]

Today, the picture is dramatically different for the most well-to-do blacks. For instance, black households in the upper income bracket, those making $75,000 to $99,000, increased fourfold between 1967 and 2003, composing 7 percent of the black population.[7] And while the picture got far better for the bulk of the black middle class, they had a far less sure grasp of economic security. In 1960, for instance, there were only 385,586 blacks who were professionals, semiprofessionals, business owners, managers or officials, a number that swelled to 1,317,080 by 1980. By 1995, there were nearly seven million black folk employed in middle-class occupations, boosted by blacks joining the ranks of social workers, receptionists, insurance salespeople and government bureaucrats.[8] But signs of trouble persist. Despite the fact that the black median household income rose by 47 percent from 1967 to $29,026 in 2003, it still lagged by $16,000 the white

median household income of $46,900.[9] Plus, the median
household income for blacks fell by 3 percent in 2002 and
fell by more than 6 percent between 2000 and 2003.[10] And
the unemployment rate among blacks, at 10.1 percent, is
twice the national rate of 5.6 percent. Between 1992 and
2002, the number of blacks with manufacturing jobs declined
by 18 percent, forcing blacks into the service sector—
including professions like data processing, advertising and
housekeeping—which employs 43 percent of the black
workforce, a larger percentage than for whites in the economy.[11] The problem with these jobs is that they have shown
weak growth and provide fewer benefits. As a result, blacks,
at 52 percent, lag far behind whites, at 71 percent, in
employer-sponsored health care, and less than 40 percent of
blacks have private pension plans, while more than 46 percent of whites are covered.[12] All in all, nearly two in five
nonelderly black folk had no health insurance between 2002
and 2003. And since more than half of all black families live
in major metropolitan areas, the steadily increasing cost of
public transportation is a huge problem. More than 12 percent of the black population relies on public transportation to
get to work—and many others must also get to school and
other vital destinations—while only 3.1 percent of whites
must do the same.[13] Finally, the poverty rate of black households is more than 24 percent, compared to 6.1 percent for
white households.[14]

The educational prospects of black folk have suffered as
well, but one may have never picked this up by listening to
Cosby's comments. There is a direct link between the social

and economic status of the most vulnerable and the quality of education they receive. As Stanford education professor Linda Darling-Hammond has eloquently argued, disparities in wealth and resources result in a significantly unequal education for the poorest members of society, especially minority students.

> [E]ducational outcomes for students of color are much more a function of their unequal access to key educational resources, including skilled teachers and quality curriculum, than they are a function of race. In fact, the United States educational system is one of the most unequal in the industrialized world, and students routinely receive dramatically different learning opportunities based on their social status. In contrast to European and Asian nations that fund schools centrally and equally, the wealthiest 10% of school districts in the United States spend nearly ten times more than the poorest 10%, and spending ratios of three to one are common within states. These disparities reinforce the wide inequalities in income among families, with the most resources being spent on children from the wealthiest communities, and the fewest on the children of the poor, especially in high-minority communities.[15]

The profound gulf between the wealthiest and poorest members of our society affects a huge portion of the black population and stretches between suburban schools and urban schools, where minorities account for between 95 and

99 percent of the student body.[16] As Jonathan Kozol showed in *Savage Inequalities*, there are telling differences between how much money suburban and urban schools spend on each student: In 1989, Chicago public schools spent a little more than $5,000 per student, while Niles Township High School, in a nearby suburb, spent $9,371 per student; central city Camden, New Jersey, schools expended $3,500 per student, while each student in suburban Princeton enjoyed an expenditure of $7,725; and in 1990 New York City schools invested $7,300 in each student, while schools in suburban Manhasset and Great Neck spent over $15,000 per student, even though they didn't have nearly as many special needs.[17]

As a result of the wide disparity in wealth in school districts—since schools often get revenue from the local property tax, the wealthier the district and the higher its property values the more resources it has—and huge differences in expenditures on each student, there are corresponding differences between suburban and urban schools, especially in the quality of teachers (higher paid and more experienced in the suburbs), the courses presented (smaller class size and more offerings in the suburbs), curriculum materials (out of date in urban schools) and equipment and facilities (up to date in the suburbs). In most suburban schools, computer technology is cutting edge; in many urban schools, it is barebones. Textbooks are often in wretched condition in urban schools, offering outdated material—for example, in a Chicago elementary school, fifteen-year-old textbooks were used, which led to the impression that Richard Nixon was still in office—

and in many cases can't be taken home by students because there are barely enough to go around. The infrastructures of urban schools are often in grave disrepair, featuring toilets that don't work, rooms without air conditioning and poor heating, and cracked or missing ceiling tiles in recreation rooms.

In the end, the huge wealth disparity not only enables white students to enjoy superior primary and secondary education but gives them an enormous advantage in the college sweepstakes.

> In higher education, wealth confers stunning prerogatives and advantages. Affluent families can sidestep poor-quality education by sending their children to high-quality private schools. This gives them a major leg up for admission to our most prestigious universities. Judicial rulings that command an equalizing of expenditures on public schools have been consistently ignored. . . . These resource differences give students in the white districts a very big head start in the competition for places at quality colleges and universities. On top of this, it is students from affluent families who are able to afford $1,000 test-coaching seminars that typically improve a student's performance on the Scholastic Assessment Test by 100 points or more. Students from affluent families are more likely to have computers in the home and have broadband access to the Internet. These tools can give students very great advantages in preparing for the standardized tests that count so much in college applications.[18]

The wide resource gulf between suburban and urban schools is exacerbated by the profound resegregation of American schools.[19] Although *Brown* was to have destroyed the vicious segregation of American schools, patterns of disturbing neoapartheid have endured, bringing in their wake substantive inequalities. More than 70 percent of black students in the country attend schools that are composed largely of minority students. Even though the segregation of black students falls more than 25 points below its level in 1969, the existence of financially strapped, resource-starved, technologically underserved predominantly minority schools is a rebuke to the judicial mandate to integrate students, and, it was thought, resources, in schools attended by all races. But the mythology of either resource sharing or true integration lapses in the face of current trends. White students usually attend schools where less than 20 percent of the student body is drawn from races other than their own, while black and brown students attend schools composed of 53 to 55 percent of their own race. In some cases, the percentage is much higher, as more than a third of them attend schools with a 90 to 100 percent minority population.[20] As black and brown students get concentrated in knots of ethnicity, and often poverty, in central city schools, their educational resources are, likewise, increasingly depleted, resulting in gross inequities between white students and their black and brown peers. If Cosby was aware of this disturbing trend, he gave little indication as he railed against the poor parents and their children who are victims of resegregation.

It wasn't always the case that Cosby blamed poor parents and students for their plight while ignoring the structural features of educational inequality. In his doctoral thesis, entitled, in the unwieldy fashion common to most dissertations, *An Integration of the Visual Media Via* Fat Albert and the Cosby Kids *into the Elementary School Curriculum as a Teaching Aid and Vehicle to Achieve Increased Learning*, Cosby got right to the heart of the matter as he argued that two fundamental issues had to be addressed if educators were to ensure equal education for all students: the development of a curriculum that would help students reach their full potential, but before that, "the need to eliminate institutional racism."[21] Cosby lucidly characterized his view of institutional racism when he elaborated on how schools instill harmful beliefs in black children.

Schools are supposed to be the vehicle by which children are equipped with the skills and attitudes necessary to enter society. But a black child, because of the inherent racism in American schools will be ill prepared to meet the challenges of an adult future. The "American Dream" of upward mobility is just another myth. . . . Far from being prepared to move along an established career lattice, black children are trained to occupy those same positions held by their parents in a society economically dominated and maintained by a white status quo. Through a series of subtly inflicted failures black children are taught early not to aspire to or compete with their white counterparts for those "esteemed" jobs. . . . It has become increasingly difficult to reconcile the urban child to his education. . . . Inner-city children not only dislike school but tend to be dissatisfied with themselves. They react negatively to the entire educational process for the simple reason that school does not provide them with successful and rewarding experiences. Further, school curricula lacks congruence with the realities of their world.[22]

It is evident from his dissertation that Cosby saw schools as hotbeds of ideology and politics that are transmitted through the curriculum, and more subtly through the attitudes of teachers as they interact with black students. Cosby also insisted on the link between systemic inequities and the diminished self-esteem of the student; he refused to unfairly blame black children for lacking the desire to succeed when the classroom passed along diseased ideas about black identity. Cosby argued that the "American Dream" is a myth—a myth, however, that he eagerly embraced a decade later, especially when he defended his *Cosby Show* family against critics who claimed that the Huxtables were insufficiently black. "To say they are not black enough is a denial of the American dream and the American way of life. My point is that this is an American family—an *American* family—and if you want to live like they do, and you're willing to work, the opportunity is there."[23] In his dissertation, however, Cosby acknowledged that such a dream was denied to black children taught to mark time by filling the jobs their parents filled before them, a way to preserve white privilege.

Cosby also spoke passionately in his dissertation about the reasons black students fail: because of the urban school's indifference to changing learning conditions; because they have had the right to fail removed; because they are bored, due to the unimaginative methods of teachers interested in controlling the student; and because little of what goes on in class makes sense. Cosby argued that the failure black children experienced would only reinforce "the debilitating sense of worthlessness whites convey in a variety of ways," feeding the self-hatred of the black student.[24] Cosby pleaded with urban schools to give urban children a sense of competence to ward off attitudes and behaviors that would destroy their character and intelligence. Thus, the urban schools had to develop a curriculum to fight institutional racism. Cosby concluded that blacks were not "the only victims" of racism, although they "bear the deepest scars of time-worn racial and intellectual inferiority myth preaching"; in his mind, "whites suffer in a more subtle way."[25] Cosby argued that the myth of black inferiority and white superiority was equally disastrous for black and white children. He said that whites

are raised with a counter myth of white supremacy (power and domination) and intellectual superiority (by which to assert their power and domination). . . . Neither myth is healthy. Each breeds a negative ego position. On the one hand, there is a feeling of abject failure and pronounced inferiority, while on the other, there exists a super ego fed by continuous and demonstrated successes leading to an aggrandized sense of superiority. In combination they are combustible ingredients of a divided society.[26]

When Cosby raged against poor black parents and children in his recent comments, he forgot the lessons he had eloquently expressed nearly thirty years before. When he demanded, "What the hell good is *Brown v. the Board of Education* if nobody wants it?" he forgot what he had understood earlier: that desire is the child of environment, that vision is the gift of context, and, as he said, black "children are taught early not to aspire to or compete with their white counterparts" for jobs, or, we might add, for education either.

Of course, on some matters, Cosby in his recent statements was plain misinformed. He said more than once that 50 percent of black students drop out of high school. That is simply not true. Cosby was nowhere near the facts on this one, since the dropout rate for blacks is 17 percent.[27] And while the white dropout rate is 9 percent, the dropout rate for black high school students has actually declined 44 percent since 1968, while the white dropout rate has slightly increased over the same period.[28] In 1960, only 20.1 percent of black adults had completed high school; today it is nearly 79 percent, compared to 89 percent for whites.[29] Despite the brutal obstacles blacks have faced, and which Cosby outlined in his dissertation, they have fought to become educated in far greater numbers than the generation he applauds, a fact that Cosby fails to recognize when he says that the black poor "don't want to accept that they have to study to get an education." Thus, contemporary blacks have not failed the civil rights generation; neither have they failed to extend the legacy of literacy we have created since our time here as slaves.[30]

Cosby also asserted that black youth—referring to them with the objectifying, abstracting, thing-like "it," not a new practice with Cosby, to be sure, but no less disconcerting in any case—"can't speak English," that "[i]t doesn't want to speak English," that Cosby can't speak like them (his speech, one supposes, notwithstanding), and that everyone knows "it's important to speak English except these knuckleheads." It is utterly remarkable that Cosby, after the mountain of scholarship on Ebonics (coined by Robert Williams in the '70s, Ebony + Phonics = Ebonics) and Black English, could with one wave of his Ebonics-indebted rhetorical wand dismiss what he has so brilliantly deployed, and commercially exploited, over the years.[31] Black English captures the beautiful cadences, sensuous tones, kinetic rhythms, forensic articulations, and idiosyncrasies of expression that form the black vernacular voice. Bad grammar does not Black English make; it is a rhetorical practice laden with complex and technical rules—for instance, the use in Black English of zero copulas, or forms of the verb "to be." To say "I am going" is one thing, suggesting a present activity; but to say "I *be* going" in Black English is something else, suggesting a habitual practice, a repeated action.

Black English grows out of the fierce linguisticality of black existence, the insistence by blacks of carving a speech of their own from the remnants of African languages and piecing and stitching those remnants together in the New World with extant patterns of English for the purpose of communication and survival. Of course, much of that communication had to be masked through ranges and intensities of signifying, in terms of not only the content of black speech but its very form as well. Thus, complex linguistic rules emerged from the existential and political exigencies that shaped black destiny: speaking about white folk in their face without doing so in a way that resulted in punishment or perhaps death, leading to verbal hiccups, grammatical hesitations and linguistic lapses; articulating the moral certainties of black worldviews without compromising the ability to transmit them in the linguistic forms that best suited their expression, while adapting them to the religious passions of the white world; capturing in sound the seismic shifts in being and meaning of New World blacks that came in staccato phrases or elongated syllables; unleashing through the palette a percussive sense of time peculiar to the negotiation of an ever-evolving identity with grace and humor (when I was in grad school, my German professor said about a certain phrase, "the tense can only be translated in the Black English terms, 'It bes like that'"); and situating the absurdity of modern blackness through the constantly modulating forms of diction that lent a protective veneer of spontaneous rationality to rapidly evolving patterns of speech.

And by their creative linguistic transformations, black slaves inflected, and infected, the speech of their masters. As one observer proclaimed, "It must be confessed, to the shame of the white population of the South, that they perpetuate many of these pronunciations in common with their Negro dependents."[32] For Cosby to dismiss *that*, the very kernel of black life in Black English, verges on self-denial; for him to ridicule its most vulnerable practitioners borders on racial disdain. As James Baldwin argued in his powerful essay "If Black English Isn't a Language, Then Tell Me, What Is?" black English

> is the creation of the black diaspora. . . . *A language comes into existence by means of brutal necessity, and the rules of the language are dictated by what the language must convey.* . . . There was a moment, in time, and in this place, when my brother, or my mother or my father, or my sister, had to convey to me, for example, the danger in which I was standing from the white man standing just behind me, and to convey this with a speed and in a language, that the white man could not possibly understand, and that, indeed, he cannot understand, until today. He cannot afford to understand it. This understanding would reveal to him too much about himself and smash that mirror before which he has been frozen for so long. . . . Now if this passion, this skill, this (to quote Toni Morrison) "sheer intelligence," this incredible music, the mighty achievement of having brought a people utterly unknown to, or despised by "history" . . . if this absolutely unprecedented journey does not indicate that black English is a language, I am curious to know what definition of language is to be trusted.[33]

Cosby has over the years, despite his rabid resistance to Black English, deployed its rhythms, tics and habits of speech.

As linguist John McWhorter recently commented, "Bill Cosby speaks more ebonics than he knows . . . and people don't want to hear it. It's not their favorite flavor."[34] The theme song to *The Bill Cosby Show* included a string of non-sensical articulations, such as "flizzum flazzum," that owed their spirit of playful verbal invention, if not their content, to Ebonics. The speech Cosby gave damning poor black parents and their children is loaded with Ebonics, from its inflections, intonations, diction and stylistic flourishes to its grammatical eliminations (of syllables) and, simultaneously, its vernacular substitutions. That's also why it was especially troubling at the 2003 Emmys when comedienne Wanda Sykes, in all of her vernacular splendor and her animated shtick, asked an obviously peeved Cosby the secret of his and other early black comics' success, and he stared at her with menacing intensity and fatal scowl and said, icily, "We spoke English."[35]

Even earlier when *Fat Albert and the Cosby Kids*—not in the cleaned-up, linguistically correct language of the 2004 film but in the original cartoon series—appeared on the scene, they brought verbal resonances to Saturday morning television that were rooted in black community. A cartoon series set in the projects, with the intonations of black children ruling their roost through stories with moral meaning, it was *visual vernacular*; the aesthetic communicated a dialect of style. And when Mushmouth created a distinct pattern of speech, he created a linguistic rule of his own—by inserting the "B" sound into his speech, he asserted the rule of the ubiquitous "B" in syllabic construction. "Hey man" became "hey-ba man-ba," and his own name became "Mush-ba

Mouth-ba." Cosby has reaped huge financial dividends, and cultural capital, off of that cartoon and its film; it seems disingenuous for him now to deprive real-life children of the very legitimacy of perspective and verbal creativity he allotted to cartoon and cinematic characters.

Cosby seemed not to notice his own Black English in 1997 when he penned an op-ed for the *Wall Street Journal*, "Elements of Igno-Ebonics Style."[36] Cosby was responding to the Oakland School Board's controversial, and widely misinterpreted, decision to use Ebonics in the classroom to help black children bridge the gulf between their native dialects and speech habits and "standard" English. Cosby lampooned Ebonics speakers in feigned dialects and then scolded the Oakland School Board: "Granted, if you don't teach Ebonics, the children will find it anyway. But legitimizing the street in the classroom is backwards. We should be working hard to legitimize the classroom—and English—in the street. On the other hand, we could jes letem do wha ever they wanna. Either way, Ima go over heanh an learn some maffa matics an then ge-sum 'n tee na' then I'll be witchya."[37] But Cosby, and many more besides, missed the point. The Oakland School Board made the decision to boost black children's literacy in "standard" English by meeting the students where they were rhetorically; like all good teachers, they began with the given and then used it to arrive at the goal. Between the given and the goal lay expanses of black linguistic practice that the Oakland teachers sought to use in their efforts to respect the speech of their students while bringing them up to snuff on "standard English."

The Oakland teachers realized, as do most black folk, that we must code-switch, or, as Cosby phrased it, speak one variety of English on the streets and another in the home, on the job and the like. The recognition of Black English's legitimacy is not an argument against learning "standard" English; it is to recognize that discussions of language, especially involving poor and minority peoples, are discussions about the issues Cosby addressed in his dissertation: power, domination, black inferiority, white superiority and white supremacy. Who can, or should, determine what language is legitimate and useful, and when it can or cannot be spoken? Of course Cosby is right to stress the need for black youth, and their parents, to understand the contexts where some languages are more useful than others. But the sense of propriety is driven as much by power and the cultural normalizing of the taken-for-granted (and hence taken for standard and taken for true and right) linguistic styles of the white mainstream as by an innate sense of what is good or bad language. The more languages folk have at their disposal, the more easily they are able to negotiate with the hidden premises of power that underlie discussions about linguistic appropriateness. To ignore the cultural and racial contexts that deny access to such multilinguisticality, and to overlook the rigid racial and educational hierarchy that reinforces privilege and stigma, are intellectually dishonest.

Perhaps there is a deep element of shame that Cosby has not yet overcome in the use of black style and Black English. In a 1969 interview, Cosby movingly spoke of how he confronted the black embarrassment associated with black style.

In his junior high school, at Christmastime, Cosby and his schoolmates had been allowed to bring in sound recordings to share with the class and celebrate the holiday season. Cosby didn't own any records, but a couple of black girls brought in Mahalia Jackson's version of *Silent Night*, while white kids brought in recordings like the Mormon Tabernacle Choir's version of the *Hallelujah Chorus* and Bing Crosby's *White Christmas*. When the white kids listened to Mahalia Jackson, they snickered, "because of their own ignorance and, at the same time, we were embarrassed because it wasn't white. Mahalia just didn't sound like the Mormon Tabernacle Choir, and Clara Ward didn't sound like Bing Crosby." Cosby said at the time that "this no longer happens, because of the black-is-beautiful re-education, because of the fact that our culture, our music is something to be proud of."[38] Cosby admitted that it hadn't been easy to "throw out all the brainwashing," but black folk were making the effort. As an example, he told another, perhaps even more poignant, story from his life.

Black people from the South have a common accent; it's almost a foreign language. I can't speak it, but I understand it, because my 85-year-old grandfather speaks it. I remember hearing him use the word "jimmin" and I had to go up to my grandmother to find out what he was saying. She told me he was saying "gentlemen." That was black; it's the way my grandfather talks, the way my Aunt Min talks, because she was down South picking cotton while I was in Philadelphia picking up white middle-class values and feeling embarrassed about hearing people talk like that and wanting to send them to school to straighten them out. I now accept this as black, the same way I accept an Italian whose father from the old country has a heavy accent. I accept it as black the same way chitlins and crab fingers and corn bread and collard greens and hush puppies and hog jaws and black-eyed peas and grits are black. This is what we were given to eat; this was our diet in the South, and we've done some groovy things with it. Now even white people are talking about Uncle So-and-So's sparerib place.[39]

If Cosby could only see Black English in this light, with this compassion and this discerning of the social and racial networks that sustain cultural expression, he might appreciate its power and beauty.

When Cosby claimed that black parents bought their kids $500 sneakers instead of spending $250 on Hooked on Phonics, I immediately had two thoughts. First, I recalled that in 1994 Hooked on Phonics had agreed to settle charges brought by the FTC that it lacked sufficient evidence to support its widely advertised claim that its products could rapidly teach children with learning disabilities to read, regardless of the problems they had. Educational experts countered the Hooked on Phonics advertising juggernaut by suggesting it only worked as an "after-school adjunct to comprehensive reading instruction that teaches children more than sounding out letters and words."[40] Hooked on Phonics has been the subject of very little academic research and, as a result, is not looked upon by many knowledgeable education specialists as an important means to help children to read. At best, it plays a supplementary role that helps with some of the skills necessary for children to read. Perhaps the black parents that Cosby blasted were more aware of the overstated claims of Hooked on Phonics than he appears to have been. If one has limited resources, spending $250 on a product that has not been proved to deliver what it promises is sound educational and consumer practice.

But I also thought of Elizabeth Chin's marvelous ethnographic study of the consumer behavior of poor black children, *Purchasing Power: Black Kids and American Consumer Culture.*[41] Although Cosby targeted poor black parents, a great deal of the consumption for youth in poor communities is done by youth themselves. The point of Chin's book is to dispel the sort of myths perpetuated by Cosby and many others, black and white, whose perceptions of black youth are strangled by stereotype. She thus chides those who make judgments about black youth based more on "guesswork" than "fieldwork."[42] Chin contends that black youth are not the "combat consumers" they are portrayed as being: either captives of a powerful fetish for brand names or predatory consumers willing to steal for Air Jordans or kill for a bike. Chin argues that "consumption is at its base a social process, and one that children use in powerful ways to make connections between themselves and the people around them."[43] Chin also notices that, unlike their middle-class and upper-class peers, the children she studied were made profoundly conscious of what it costs to clothe, feed and take care of them; hence, they usually spent part of the money they had on necessary, not pleasurable, items. Chin explains her work in a powerful anecdote about the prejudice she confronted and, by extension, the black youth she studied, in examining the consumer behavior of black youth. She says she had developed, as do most researchers, a one-line response to questions at cocktail parties about the nature of her research in New Haven.

> "I'm studying the role of consumption in the lives of poor and working-class black children." Here I would more often than not get a knowing look. "Ah," the response would be, "you must have seen a lot of Air Jordans.". . . "Actually, no," I'd answer. "I only saw two pairs of Air Jordans on the kids I worked with." [T]his statement was nearly always met with incredulity. More than once people responded with something to the effect of "There must have been something wrong with your sample." . . . [T]hese comments also disturb me because so many people seemed to prefer hanging on to ideas about poor black kids that had been gleaned from the pseudo experience provided by the kinds of news stories I have so extensively critiqued in the preceding pages. Like the terms *inner city* and *ghetto*, the "Air Jordans" response to thinking about poor and working-class black children and consumption obscures more about those children than it reveals.[44]

Cosby's gross generalizations about poor black parents and their consumptive behavior—based on his commonsense observations and likely not on a systematic examination of the buying habits of poor black parents or their children—reinforce the biases that Chin sought to challenge in her study. Cosby belongs to a group of critics who have, according to Chin, made black consumer behavior appear pathological.[45] And I couldn't help thinking when I read Cosby's "Igno-Ebonics" op-ed (which begins, "I remember one day 15 years ago, a friend of mine told me a racist joke. Question: Do you know what Toys 'R' Us is called in Harlem? Answer: We Be Toys,") of the touching story Chin tells of a shopping trip to Toys "R" Us with a black youth who had never heard of the store before, much less visited it, but who agonized greatly over the choice between two inexpensive toys that would enhance different social relationships.

Cosby's remark hints at the priorities of poor black parents and youth: are they educationally oriented or materially focused? It is interesting that Cosby expects poor parents, and youth, to be more fiscally responsible than those with far greater resources prove to be. Immediately, the defense of their consumer habits, however, rests on the assertion that wealthier parents and children have more latitude, while poor parents must be ever so careful about how they spend their money. There is a cruelty to such an observation, however; not only is the poor parent, or child, at a great disadvantage economically, but they are expected to be more judicious and responsible than their well-to-do counterparts, with far fewer resources. Moreover, the materialism that obviously can strike poor folk as well is, nevertheless, far less likely to do them or society as much harm as it does those with far greater wealth in our country. The perception that the meager resources of the poor are somehow atrociously misspent on expensive consumer items is far out of proportion to the facts of the case. And to begrudge poor parents the desire to provide their children some of the trinkets of capital in a profoundly rapacious consumer culture that endlessly promotes acquiring things as a mark of status and citizenship (didn't George Bush, in the aftermath of 9/11, direct Americans to prove they were uncowed by terrorists by returning to the stores?) is plain dishonest.

Perhaps Cosby has forgotten what it was like to be young, black and poor, or to be hungry for even more capital in the wake of a real first taste of money and the comforts it can bring. *Ebony* magazine reports that when Cosby was asked in 1965 why he entered the acting field, he had a one-word reply: "Money!"[46] He told the *Saturday Evening Post* that "I've got no great artistic ambitions. What show business mainly means to me is cash."[47] Neither should we forget that Cosby was once, and for a long while, one of the most recognized and successful pitchmen in American history, promoting products to the American public—from Jell-O to Ford automobiles, from Coca-Cola to E. F. Hutton—for our eager consumption. (It is not hard to imagine that Cosby, had he come along at the right time, might have pushed $250 sneakers [they don't cost $500, but we got his point], engaging in what cultural theorists term "the social construction of desire.") It even led to a brief, pungent, satirical editorial by Edward Sorel, "The Noble Cos," in *The Nation* in 1986 that assumes Cosby's voice: "So this buddy says, 'I didn't mind your commercials for Jello, Del Monte, Ford cars . . . Ideal Toys, or

Cola-Cola, although Coke does do business in South Africa. . . . But, Bill, why do commercials for those crooks at E. F. Hutton?' My buddy didn't understand my commercials improve race relations. Y'see, by showing that a black man can be just as money-hungry as a white man . . . I'm proving that all men are brothers."[48]

Cosby's insistence, in his infamous May 2004 speech and on National Public Radio's *Talk of the Nation* in July 2004, that black youth are anti-intellectual because they chide high achievement as "acting white," repeats what is the academic equivalent of an urban legend.[49] Claiming that black youth are anti-intellectual is pretending somehow that *America* is not consumed with anti-intellectualism. Cosby's claim has the dubious virtue of being both true and uninformative. It is not that black anti-intellectualism doesn't exist, shouldn't be admitted, or doesn't reveal itself in ways that need to be vigorously opposed. But it is highly misleading to tag black communities as any more anti-intellectual than the mainstream. Richard Hofstadter wrote a book in 1963 entitled *Anti-Intellectualism in American Life*.[50] He blamed McCarthyism's withering assault in the 1950s on "the critical mind" and the choice of Dwight D. Eisenhower—who, as Hofstadter says, was "conventional in mind [and] relatively inarticulate"—over Adlai Stevenson—whom Hofstadter termed "a politician of uncommon mind and style, whose appeal to intellectuals overshadowed anything in recent history"—as the defining moments of modern anti-intellectualism.[51] (One wonders if Hofstadter might today see parallels in the choice of George W. Bush over Al Gore, or even John

Kerry, though Bush isn't Eisenhower and Gore and Kerry aren't Stevenson.)

But, according to Hofstadter, the plague of anti-intellectualism is even more ancient than the 1950s. Hofstadter says that "[o]ur anti-intellectualism is, in fact, older than our national identity."[52] And a recent National Endowment for the Arts report says that book reading has dramatically declined in the United States over the last ten years.[53] Neither is the anxiety especially American: There is hand-wringing over anti-intellectualism around the globe. There is the study that decries the effect of modernization on Russian youth, saying that anti-intellectualism might result if Russian intellectual life is ignored while Western education is celebrated.[54] And then there is the study, first done in the '60s and replicated in the '80s, of anti-intellectualism among Korean teachers because they favored athletic and nonstudious pupils over academically brilliant, studious and nonathletic pupils.[55] That certainly shreds the myth of the Asian model minority. And then there is the study of "Victorian Anti-Intellectualism."[56] The twist here is that it was the middle and upper classes who scorned intellectual engagement. Cosby should take note: They weren't worried about Puffy; they were putting down Puffendorf!

The notion that black youth who are smart and who study hard are accused by their black peers of "acting white" is rooted in a single 1986 study of a Washington, D.C., high school conducted by Signithia Fordham, a black anthropologist at Rutgers University, and John Ogbu, the late Nigerian professor of anthropology at the University of California at

Berkeley.[57] According to Fordham and Ogbu, many black students at the school didn't study and deliberately got bad grades because their classmates thought they were "selling out" and "acting white." Fordham and Ogbu's study has gained iconic status in the anecdotage not only of Cosby but of figures like Henry Louis Gates, Jr., in the pages of the *New York Times* and Barack Obama in his thrilling keynote speech at the 2004 Democratic Convention.[58]

The trouble with such citations is that they help to circulate and give legitimacy to a theory that is in large part untrue. First, in 1997, Duke professor Philip J. Cook and Georgetown professor Jens Ludwig set out to determine, through field research, if the alleged grief visited upon those black students who study actually existed.[59] While Fordham and Ogbu studied one school, Cook and Ludwig studied 25,000 public and private school students, following them from eighth grade through high school. Cook and Ludwig concluded that black students were just as eager to excel in school as whites and that black students dropped out of school only slightly more than white students, largely due to low family incomes or absent fathers.[60] Cook and Ludwig discovered that blacks and whites with similar family characteristics cut class, missed school and completed homework at nearly the same rate.[61]

Cook and Ludwig uncovered an intriguing fact: that the black students who were members of academic honor societies were *more* likely than other black students to view themselves as "popular." Further, they found that students who belonged to honor societies in predominantly black schools were more popular than their peers who had not received such an honor. Cook and Ludwig concluded that there was little evidence to support the notion of an oppositional peer culture to black academic achievement. In fact, other studies suggest that the parents of black students are more likely than white or Asian parents to have assisted their children with their homework or met with their children's teachers, and just as likely to encourage them to put forth their best effort in school. Black parents are more likely than white parents to place their children in educational camps, attend PTA meetings, check their children's homework and reward their children for academic success.[62] Moreover, while only 6 percent of white students in grades 6 through 12 reported discussing national news events with a parent on a daily basis, 26 percent of black students in comparable grades reported that they did so.[63] And there is evidence that high school black peer groups were more likely than comparable white peer groups to believe that it is important to study hard and get good grades, leading to the conclusion that white, not black, academic peer culture opposes academic achievement.[64]

More recently, University of North Carolina professors Karolyn Tyson, a sociologist, and William Darity, Jr., an economist, coordinated an eighteen-month ethnographic study of eleven schools in North Carolina and concluded that black and white students are fundamentally the same when it comes to the desire to succeed, knowing that doing well in school can positively impact later life, and feeling good about themselves when they do well.[65] They also concluded that when anti-intellectual activity occurs in white culture, "it is seen as inevitable, but when the same dynamic is observed among black students, it is pathologized as racial neurosis."[66] The authors also argue that the single case where they found any evidence of the anxiety of "acting white" occurred at a school where there was an overrepresentation of whites in gifted-and-talented classes and a drastic underrepresentation of black students. But the anxiety occurred most frequently not among the students, but among the teachers and administrators, who accused the black students of being "averse to success" and placing a low value on education, underscoring how racial hierarchy and the social mythology of low black academic desire collude to deprive black students of an equal education.[67]

Finally, Cosby's remarks about black youth and the criminal justice system are incredibly naïve, mean-spirited or woefully uninformed. While it is true that most black men who are incarcerated are not "political prisoners," that doesn't mean that their imprisonment doesn't have political contexts and consequences. For instance, Ronald Reagan's "War on Drugs"—which, as both Lani Guinier and Tupac Shakur contended, is a war on black and brown people—inaugurated changes in public policy and policing measures (leading eventually to racial profiling) that greatly increased the odds that blacks would do serious time for nonviolent, and often first-time, offenses. This political decision had grave, and foreseeable, consequences that disproportionately affected young blacks: They were more likely to become incarcerated. The increase of black incarceration was driven by political considerations, not a boost in, for instance, drug consumption. In fact, self-report surveys of students and adults suggest that black folk do not report greater rates of illegal drug consumption than do whites. In fact, it's often lower. For instance, in 2003, 26.5 percent of white students in the twelfth grade reported using illegal drugs within the past thirty days; for the same cohort among blacks, it was just 17.9 percent.[68] However, by a huge margin, black folk are much more likely to be arrested and to serve real prison time for drug-related offenses. This situation is unavoidably, unmistakably political, contrary to what Cosby contends.

It is also ironic that Cosby seems to justify the shooting by police of a black man who steals a piece of pound cake. Most black folk surely don't approve of stealing and certainly want criminals removed from the community, especially violent ones who menace neighborhoods. Yet, too many of us understand the nexus between poor schooling, severely limited life options and the subsequent self-destructive choices made by desperate young men. Moreover, despite a strong desire to see criminals arrested, black folk are justifiably wary of police who often seem incapable of distinguishing legitimate criminals from law-abiding citizens who call the police for protection—not for harassment or brutality. Years ago, Cosby understood the complex social arrangements that provided the backdrop for explaining certain forms of criminal behavior. He also understood how disparities in money offered differing brands of justice.

Cats with dough don't commit armed robbery or most of the crimes poor people commit. Yet rich guys' crimes—

like embezzling a bank or moving a million dollars' worth of heroin a year—hurt a hell of a lot more people than some guy who sticks up a candy store and gets away with $12. So I think something's a little wrong there. When the rich man comes to court, he's got the best lawyers money can buy. But the poor man, the black man, gets a lawyer who's not necessarily interested in the case and may even consider it a pain in the ass. And then there's the whole thing about under-the-table payoffs to judges, which I won't attempt to document but which exist. What I'm saying is that there are two kinds of justice in this country: one for the rich and one for the poor—and blacks are poor. When the black people keep getting shafted by cops and courts, how can they have respect for people who are supposed to represent the law?

Cosby's blistering, brilliant analysis captures the harsh, excessive and unjust penalties imposed on poor blacks. It also situates in its historical and racial context the criminal justice system, and clarifies the link between class and justice. Of course, Cosby's powerful critique of the two-tiered justice system, one for the wealthy, the other for the poor, offers another jarring contrast between his past thought and his present practice. For instance, while condemning the black pound cake stealer, Cosby stood by Martha Stewart's side, and showed up in court to support her, even though she fit Cosby's description of a person with huge resources who buys justice and whose crime, perhaps, has a more harmful effect than the man robbing a candy store or stealing a piece of pound cake.

The disparity in the distribution of justice is painfully apparent in the case of black males. From 1974 to 2001, the percentage of black males who had been in state or federal prison increased from 8.7 percent to 16.6 percent, while the percentage for white males went from 1.4 percent to 2.6 percent during the same period. The percentage of black women who had been in state or federal prison rose from 0.6 percent to 1.7 percent, even as the rate for white women increased from 0.1 percent to 0.3 percent.[69] Blacks are six times as likely as whites to have gone to prison at some time in their lives. If the trends hold up, one out of three black males born in 2001 will be imprisoned at some point in his lifetime. In 1974, that number was one out of eleven. Only 5.9 percent of white males born in 2001 have a chance of imprisonment in their lifetimes. For black females, the number is 5.6 percent and for white females, a paltry 0.9 percent.[70]

And when one considers the relation between education and incarceration, things look even bleaker for black men. According to the Justice Policy Institute (JPI) report "Cellblocks or Classrooms? The Funding of Higher Education and Corrections and Its Impact on African American Men," we have a lethal public policy of prizing prisons over education.[71] There is a swelling prison industry that is sweeping ever larger numbers of blacks into local penitentiaries. The more black bodies fill the jails, the more cells are built and the more revenue is generated, particularly in the rural white communities where many prisons are located. The prison-industrial complex literally provides white economic opportunity across the class strata, from the lower- or working-class maintenance worker, the moderately middle-class guard and the solidly middle-class prison executive to the wealthy merchants of incarceration capital who manufacture and produce prison life. In 1995 alone, 150 new prisons were constructed and filled, while 171 more were expanded.[72]

Big money is at stake when it comes to making a crucial choice: to support blacks in the state university or the state penitentiary. As the report makes clear, we have chosen the latter. During the 1980s and 1990s, state spending on corrections grew at six times the rate of state spending on higher education. By the end of the last century, there were nearly a third more black men in prison and jail than in colleges and universities. The number of black men in jail or prison has increased fivefold in the last twenty years. In 1980, at the dawn of the prison construction boom, black men were three times more likely to be enrolled in college than incarcerated. In 1980, there were 143,000 black men in jail or prison and 463,700 enrolled in higher educational institutions. In 2000, there were 791,600 black men in jail or prison, while only 603,032 were enrolled in colleges or universities. It's not a matter of whether "Junior" stole the pound cake; it's a matter of whether he can get into a school that will train him to cook rather than incarcerate him because he stole when he was hungry.

None of this is meant to dismiss black crime or serve as an apologia for destructive behavior, but it is necessary to underline the social and personal forces that drive criminal activity, even as we fight against an unjust criminal justice system that targets black men with vicious regularity. I speak as one who has been a victim of crime. As it is with most victims, I can remember the most recent event, though more than twenty-five years ago, with chilling accuracy.

"Give me yo' money, nigga," a voice icily demanded of me as I walked with a female companion on a hot summer night in Detroit in 1977.

I had barely glimpsed in my peripheral vision the approach of his grim, steely figure—young, black and male like me—before he pressed his demand on us, ominously backed by a coal black .357 Magnum. The threat evoked by his sudden appearance choked my vocal cords, and squashed any fantasies I may have had of heroic action under desperate circumstances. I hardly managed a reply, which, by tone and terseness, was calculated to inform him that we had no money (why else would we be walking near midnight in the ghetto neighborhood where the '67 riots began?) and to cushion the rebuke he would undoubtedly feel with my admission.

"Man, all I got in my pocket is a dollar and thirty-five cents," I uneasily pleaded, praying that my precision about my indigence would force him to acknowledge that we were poor targets for an armed robbery.

"I don't believe you," he angrily protested. "Now give me *all* yo' money."

My companion and I grew tenser, fearing that we were about to meet the fate of so many others who failed to have the goods when robbers came calling in Detroit, then known as the murder capital of the nation. By now, the hand that held our assailant's gun was visibly trembling, as much, I sensed, out of fear as out of frustration that we had no money. His quaking posture betrayed a vulnerability I desperately sought to exploit, hoping I might forge a bond of racial empathy with him beyond whatever forces drove him to assault us.

"Man, you don't look like the type of brother that would be doin' something like this," I hastily offered.

"I wouldn't be doin' this, man," he exclaimed, seemingly as surprised by his own willingness to explain his actions as by my desperation in provoking his response. "But I got a wife and three kids and we ain't got nothin' to eat."

Then came the cruel twist to his rationale for robbery, the partial cause of so-called black-on-black crime contained in his near-repentant revelation.

"And besides, last week, a brother did the same thing to me that I'm doin' to you."

Perhaps the irony lying awake in his own words burdened his conscience. Maybe it nudged him to reevaluate the laws of street survival that turn the victims of crime into its perpetrators. Or perhaps he took pity on our frightened but sympathetic faces. Whatever the case, he allowed us to flee from his potentially harmful grasp. We thanked God and our lucky stars, but only after we were at a safe enough distance to escape should he change his mind.

Too many others, particularly black men, are not as fortunate as I was that night. I know that's what angers Bill Cosby, in part: the sense that the carnage has become routine, perhaps acceptable. With chilling redundancy, black males are dying at the hands of other black males. The mutual harming of black males has furnished the themes of too many films to count, and too many rap narratives as well. The situation for black males, especially juvenile and young adult males, has darkened the outermost regions of hopelessness. Terms usually reserved for large-scale social catastrophes—terms like "genocide" and "endangered species"—are now applied to black men with troubling frequency.[73]

More foreboding is the common belief that relief appears nowhere in sight. There are over fifteen million black males in America, and despite the success and happiness that some enjoy, many others are snared in unhealthy and unproductive lifestyles. Matched in extremity by the outsize cultural attainments of figures like LeBron James or, for many, Bill Cosby, millions of ordinary, anonymous black males are robbed of social standing and personal dignity by poverty and racial injustice. Often, these men are left to fend for themselves and their families with little more than mother wit and diligent labor that is poorly rewarded. Still others seek more satisfying and immediate material rewards in criminal lifestyles.

The social injuries to black male well-being are indexed in the mind-numbing statistical litany whose mere recitation testifies to the crisis at hand. Black males are more likely than any other group to be spontaneously aborted. Of all babies, black males have the lowest birth weights. Black males have the greatest chance of dying before they reach twenty. Although they are only 6 percent of the U.S. population, blacks make up half the male prisoners in local, state and federal jails. An overwhelming majority of the twenty thousand

Americans killed in crime-related incidents each year are black males. Over 35 percent of all black males in American cities are drug and alcohol abusers. Twenty-five percent of the victims of AIDS are black men. Fifty percent of black men between sixteen and sixty-two are not active in the labor force. Thirty-two percent of black men have incomes below the poverty level.[74]

The situation is equally perilous for black youth, especially those trapped by the justice system. More than six in ten juvenile offenders in residential placement are minority youth. Minority youth accounted for seven in ten juveniles held in custody for a violent offense. Recently, I visited a detention center and jail for young people. Of course, most of the youth locked up—for petty thievery and, yes, for double murder—were black boys and girls. My wife and I spoke to them, and we were touched, even moved to tears, by their stories. They were young folk eager to make amends for what they had done wrong. But many of them were also hungry for love and affection. As I read Cosby's words, I thought about these young people often trapped by forces larger than their minds can explain. They wrote to us when we returned home, and every nice thing they said about us would be said about anybody who spent just a little time with them. Here are some of the things they wrote to me after my visit, in their own spelling, their own voices, which speak to the deep need our youth have to be loved, held and redeemed. They are responding to questions posed to them by the wonderful woman who runs the literacy program.

WHAT DID YOU LIKE BEST ABOUT THE AUTHOR VISIT?

Boys

* I like when he was talking about me learning how to read because I need help.
* He told everybody the truth and he was real and what he said touched me.
* He was real but at the same time he was educated.
* The way he talked about music and the way he used it to show us how we live.
* How he said that youth now days lisen to what rapers talk about an then we go do it.
* They cared about the people.

Girls

* He was funny and funny.
* I like the way he acknowledged the group and he spoke very bluntly
* The way he talked to us because he said the true.

THE VISIT WOULD HAVE BEEN BETTER IF. . .

Boys

* had more time to talk with us

* he would have used words we could understand
* he did not talk as fast

Girls
* Nothing could have been better, he was excellent
* Had more time to talk with us

IS THERE ANYTHING YOU WOULD LIKE TO SAY DIRECTLY TO THE AUTHOR?

Boys
* Yes I would like to say to you that I love what you do.
* Thanks for the book, also when talk to younger people that are not in collage you should use words that are more commonly used and understanded.
* Thanks for coming to talk to us about real stuff we need to know about.

Girls
* Thank you for putting a smile on my face. You should come back again. Thank you for helping not only people of color but all people.
* Thank you for coming and you helped me out with what you were talking about. I always thought it was my falt and you explaned that it

wasn't. Thank you for everything! I'm the one you said looked like your daughter. Thank you!!

WERE YOU INSPIRED BY MEETING THE AUTHOR?

Boys

*   I always wanted to meet an author that write books because I wanted to know how did they ever think about doing that.
*   I was inspired to learn more words and more educated words
*   He was speaking the truth about black people.
*   To read a lot more cause when he and his wife talked to us they sound smart and knew what they were saying. I used to think reading was only for entertainment but now I read for inteligents.
*   not inspired but honored, because knowledge is power and they have inlighted me on sertain aspects about my self.

Girls

*   I just want to read his book called *Why I Love Black Women*
*   Yes I want to respect myself first.
*   Yes, to respect myself as a woman.
*   He inspired me to say how I feel and express my feelings.

*   Yes, strength within and women coming together to support one another.

DID THE AUTHOR CHANGE THE WAY YOU THINK/FEEL ABOUT YOUR LIFE?

Boys

*   To me the author change the way I think. When he gave his speech I thought in my mind I need to start doing right and stay out of trouble and stop coming to jail.

*   Yes he did because now I know there are some people who care about us.

*   Made me feel better about myself inside.

Girls

*   Yes, he proved you didn't have to sell your body to have some one to love you.

*   Yes, because I like to see authors alot

*   He made me think a little more

*   Yes, I wasn't thinking about my feelings or my body until he came and spoke with us.

*   I feel better about myself

If we could reach more, many, many, more, of our young people, and touch them, hold them and love them, then we might be able to change their lives and how they view themselves. But until we radically alter our educational system, and solve the problems of poverty and social deprivation, our children will continue to spiral down stairwells of suffering and oppression. While Bill Cosby's frustration is understandable, his mean-spirited attacks on the vulnerable and the poor will do nothing to lift them from the catastrophes they endure. Until we fight on the educational, political and social fronts—and change the way resources are drained from black schools, homes and neighborhoods, and redistribute them within our own black spaces—all of the raving and ranting in the world will only embolden the vicious enemies of black children to do even less, while it will dishearten those who want to see a better world for some of the most beautiful but buffeted children on the globe.

Chapter Three

What's in a Name (Brand)?

Are you not paying attention, people with the hat on back-wards, pants down around the crack. Isn't that a sign of sometin', or you waitin' for Jesus to pull his pants up? (laugh-ter and clapping). Isn't it a sign of sometin' when she's got her dress all the way up into the crack . . . and got all kinds of needles and things going through her body. What part of Africa did this come from? (laughter). We are not Africans. Those people are not Africans, they don't know a damned thing about Africa. Wit' names like Shaniqua, Taliqua, and Muhammad and all that crap, and all of 'em are in jail.

Bill Cosby is not the first person to lash out at poor black youth for how their bodies are clothed and modified, and for what seems to be the infernal nonsense of their names. His disgust echoes ancient white and black protests of strutting and signifying black flesh. It is impossible to gauge Cosby's disdain, and the culture's too, without following the black body on the plantations and streets where its styles were seen as monstrous and irresistible. We might then see how depressing it is for Cosby to be so ignorant of black youth and the issues they are up against, and what's more, we should mourn his determination, and that of many more, to stay that way.

Human beings use clothing to create and control their identities.[1] That's especially true for poor youth, who often feel powerless to influence the world around them. For young people, styles of fashion often encourage extravagant self-expression. When they select clothes, young folk do more than drape their bodies in the latest styles; they are also helping to shape identities they have either inherited or invented. Their clothes may suggest playful excess or curious understatement, depending on their moods or needs, and young folk often see their bodies as works of art in need of relentless restyling.

Black urban youth can hardly help viewing their bodies as targets—of cultural opposition and creative opportunity. Since they are so widely talked about and often feared, their flesh is a mobile laboratory of personal expression where style is both the hypothesis and the experiment. There is little doubt that fashion in black urban circles rises to performance art, a necessary trait in a culture where performance has always been at a premium. Black urban fashion constantly reminds young folk of just how culturally durable they are, since they are among the most imitated and appropriated people on the globe, though often without footnotes, copyrights or royalties. But they are vulnerable too, and despite their achievements they are often devalued by elders like Cosby who have already made up their minds about black youth's bodies. Their flesh may be celebrated in stylish cultural theories of resistance, but the plain fact is that hating the dress of black youth, or, really, the lower classes in general, is older than the baggy pants and short dresses that ride up Cosby's nerves.

Ever since we have been free, black folk's style of dress in urban centers has been a concern to white society and bourgeois Negroes.[2] At first, whites laughed at ex-slaves as they strolled along the streets of southern cities in the late nineteenth century. Black folk were considered repulsive and ludicrous in their imitation of the fine clothing worn in white society. Hateful whites, and even less vicious commentators, played up the contrast between fine clothing and awful, ugly black flesh. Darker hued black women were singled out for their alleged grotesqueness: big lips, noses and eyes protruding beneath bonnets and lace caps as their blue-dark skin shined remorselessly out from get-ups deemed unsuitable for the Negro body.[3] The very stylishness of blacks also angered many whites. They were not used to seeing well-dressed blacks during slavery and became severely agitated by the sight of elegantly dressed men and women attending social gatherings in northern cities like New York in the 1820s. Whites called the New York police when they were outraged at seeing *in public* well-adorned blacks strolling in style to their rare place of recreation, a club called the African Grove, which was immediately shut down. Later, when an African theater that fea-

tured the debut of legendary actor Ira Aldridge was established on the same spot, white rioting and police harassment
closed its doors as well.[4]

But white laughter soon turned to scorn as whites caught
on to blacks who were using the streets as a performance
arena. Forced by economic hardship and racial segregation
into the public spaces of black neighborhoods, especially the
corners and main walkways, black folk were literally performing their newfound freedom from slavery by moving and dis-
playing their bodies. Making a virtue of necessity, since they
had to compete with whites for public space, blacks in the
late nineteenth century took to the streets and remade them
into a theater of self-expression, parading and strolling back
and forth in the clothing that was the most visible sign of
their emancipation. There was certainly a compensatory
function to their raiment: Blacks who were otherwise poor
and deprived would nevertheless invest in clothing and perform their liberty by freely experimenting with fashion.

This trend continued into the early twentieth century. By
then, whites resented and feared the ways that black bodies
invaded sectors of southern urban culture. The black streets
had by then become a largely masculine domain where black
males experimented as extravagantly with their social identities as they did with their colorful dress. Despite the brutal
confinement of black life under Jim Crow law, black folk in
the early 1900s refashioned the streets with some of their
most uplifting and imaginative performances: A constant
parade of black bodies claimed formerly terrorized social space

with stylish abandon. Blacks still had to be careful, however, because looking too good offended whites. They didn't want to believe that the same colored folk who had scraped the bottom of the barrel could now rise higher than whites had either hoped or expected. Good dressing among blacks signaled resistance to the lowly status they had been forced to accept. A great outfit carried ominous symbolic weight far beyond the segregated borders of black life.

The social customs of subordination on southern streets revolved around clothing: Black men had to have their hats in their hands to show deference, or tip their hats to whites to show respect.[5] Whites aimed to control and monitor black life—which was the meaning, after all, of laws that restricted black mobility in the white world—and bore down on even the most intimate details of black life before they, well, got out of control. The black sense of the ornate carried political meanings that whites surely didn't miss; they were insulted by good black dress because it meant that blacks had, however subtly, shredded social barriers. Their way of dress gestured to the beginning of the long, slow death of social apartheid. If black folk could wear the clothes that white folk wore, and look good in their defiance of white culture, it wouldn't be long before they would want to slip into the prestige and authority whites enjoyed as well. As Shane White and Graham White write, just as "slaves, in the antebellum world, had been expected to look the part, shunning any sign of assertiveness and even demonstrating their contentment, so, under the racial system that had crystallized by the turn of the century, African Americans were required to dress, walk, comport themselves, and direct their gaze in a manner that registered uncomplaining subservience."[6]

In the north, where the Great Migration in the early 1900s swept Negroes by the thousands into industrial cities from Chicago to Detroit, city sidewalks were jammed with signifying black bodies that were to a degree free of the intrusive eye of white society. Although they contained women and girls, the streets remained a masculine haven, filtering the mores and values, the styles and sensibilities, the worries and fears, and the joys and hopes of black males, accounting for the streets' vibrancy and their occasional, unavoidable terror, given the cramped circumstances of black living. Lower-class men overtook the streets to perform their distinctive modes of masculine identity: in the clothes they wore, the walks they perfected—including "shooting the agate," or strutting coolly with one's hands at one's sides with the index fingers protruding—and the thrilling way they captivated the corners with their commerce, recreation and carousing.[7]

Looking good on *their* streets was of high value to the black middle class and black elite as well.[8] In Afristocratic circles, sartorial splendor was differently judged; the aesthetic of black elegance and dignity countered stereotypes of black savagery and contrasted favorably with the gaudy extremes associated with lower-class blacks. The class divide found a sure index in competing styles of dress. Middle-class blacks "and members of the elite were keen to distance themselves from the dress and demeanor of ordinary African Americans and, at the same time, to curb what they viewed as the sartorial and kinesic excesses of those they saw as their social inferiors."[9] The black elite saw their dress as part of "genteel performance," where black aristocrats "exercised the self-restraint, both in the parlor and on the street, that were the prime attributes of gentility. For them, the genteel perform-ance no more allowed boisterous laughter and conversation on a streetcar than it did shouting during a church service."[10] Black aristocrats disdained "overdressing" and the "exagger-ated styles" that black female aristocrats associated with "Boulevard women."[11]

The extravagant dress of lower-class blacks, perfected in the stroll down any number of northern streets, is part of what may be termed *jubilant performance*, marked by social verve, resistance to convention, and the willingness to exper-iment. There was a freer, more improvisational character to dress as well: Blacks embraced unique fashion combinations that reflected the hodgepodge manner in which black urban identities were carved together. To be sure, jubilant perfor-mance was also associated with antitypes of secular black cul-ture, including "pimps, prostitutes, gamblers, hustlers, numbers runners, bootleggers, and drug dealers," evoking crit-icism from white and black quarters.[12]

The black aristocracy was unnerved by the black poor— how they dressed, how they spoke, how they behaved— because they constantly felt the stares of white disapproval. Although blacks successfully battled whites to garner space in the urban north and transact their cultural affairs, they still fell under white scrutiny. The black elite's fear that the ways of poor black folk would make their own tenuous positions in society even more vulnerable prompted black aristocrats to carry out a program of moral rebuke disguised as social uplift. They lectured, preached, cajoled, beseeched and condemned the black poor for the good of the race, or, rather, for the good of members of the race who were fatally obsessed with white approval. To a degree, the black elite acted out of necessity, but perhaps to a larger degree, their actions proved how they had unconsciously drank in the poisonous view of the black poor that whites forced on them. The Afristocracy, therefore, became accomplices to white panic and surveillance.

To be sure, strong traditions of black conservative morality make it hard to write the black elite off as mere tokens of white consciousness or pawns of white control. But there was a measure of ethical substitution involved, as the ideals of white society were part of a reverse invasion of black life: Having endured the occupation of blacks in significant, though largely destitute, social spaces, white authority struck back with a black hand. Every time the black aristocratic finger pointed at poor black folk's pathology, four more fingers of white moral unease folded into its palm. There is little doubt that Afristocrats were mercilessly prodded into their reactionary pose by white society, and that they were themselves the subject of extraordinary scrutiny. But it must be acknowledged that in the black elite's strained relations with poorer blacks, white supremacy got two for the price of one. The overly watched black aristocracy over-watched the black poor, themselves already fixed by a damning white gaze in the optics of racial paranoia. No matter how each clothed itself, whether in elegant concession to white culture or in extravagant resistance, black aristocrats and the black poor were stitched together in the fabric of white rejection.

Up north, the black poor and struggling weren't interested in performing deference to whites in public with demeaning rituals like those practiced by their southern kin. There would be little hat holding, eye averting or brim tipping to accommodate white authority. Instead, blacks on northern streets riotously explored jubilant performance through fashion, song and recreation, wringing as much joy as possible from a harsh existence of constant toil and meager wages. The black elite were frightened and enraged by the refusals of the black poor to color their lives with white values and black bourgeois demands. The black aristocracy used newspapers and pulpits to whip the black poor into order, to shame them, if they could, into acting right, which often meant acting white.[13] Not only did black aristocrats fear that jubilant performance would be seen as too aggressive, but they felt that poor and struggling blacks confirmed every stereotype of uncouth behavior. The conflicts among blacks of different classes were nearly as bruising as those between the races, blasting the delusion that, before segregation's demise, black folk of every station were knit together in harmony.

There was great harmony, and melody, too, in the triumphant musical notes that black folk blew into the midst of their struggles. Besides relief from doldrums and despair, black musicians supplied an example of what could happen when black expression was unfettered by self-doubt or cultural sneering. To be sure, there were many cultured despisers of popular black art, especially jazz, on both sides of the racial divide, but black musicians outlasted and outplayed their opposition with their colossal gifts. They performed a vision of excellence in which their people took enormous pride. Their talent often extended to elegant and stylish dress as well, and in the 1920s, as now, black musicians were "arbiters of fashion, as well as its avant garde."[14] Their styles ranged from the formal, well-coiffed elegance of Earl Hines, decked out in tuxedo and Chesterfield overcoat, to the sharp-as-blades sartorial extravagance of Cab Calloway's colorful zoot suits. Black musicians often blended aristocratic bearing with jubilant performance in elevating the illicit meanings of the streets (one thinks of the zoot suit's political meanings of resistance to white fashion and values and how its literally outlawed extravagance came into play in prestigious artistic circles and beyond).[15] In the art and clothing of these musicians, black urban culture marked the cultural landscape in unforgettable fashion.

Today, the relation between the streets and art holds steady. Developments in black life, technology and race relations over the last few decades have only increased the influence of black urban culture in the nation. Black artists still shape the world's perception of black street culture, except now, instead of jazz, they draw from the bravado and flourish of rap music. Rarely has a secular black culture as proudly, and defiantly, embraced the extravagant excesses and exaggerated poses of poor black identity as they do hip-hop. Even more than their predecessors, hip-hop artists play a critical role in circulating the meanings and messages of urban black culture. Hip-hop stars and impresarios like Sean "P. Diddy" Combs

(Sean John), Jay-Z (Rocawear) and Russell Simmons (Phat Farm) have branded their products—compact discs, films and especially fashion lines—across a number of media, proving that black urban styles have global reach in the international marketplace. Like all youth subcultures, black urban youth shape their identities through style and appearance.[16] Black youth both embrace and resist the mainstream in finding their place in the aesthetic ecology, the living environment of style and image that thrives on organic forms of self-presentation. The working class, in particular, became a locus of youth rebellion against social convention; their clothing expressed outrage, alienation and distrust of the sartorial and moral standards of adult society. Moreover, by selecting clothes whose style was associated with lower and working classes, youth were able to express antiestablishment attitudes through "garments that are unclean, unkempt and disordered."[17]

Black youth explore their cultural roots through clothing because they have "a much greater awareness of fashion and being in style" than their white peers.[18] Black male youth also define their masculinity through their clothes more readily than do white male adolescents.[19] This may have something to do with the social stigma black youth still suffer. Like their forebears in city streets, black youth embody jubilant performance. They experiment with styles, and transform their identities, in a culture still skeptical about their aims and skills, except where playing fields and entertainment arenas are concerned. When black urban youth style their bodies, they do so within the limited social choices they face. Fashion is a default mechanism of self-expression—and social control. The more daring their fashions, the less cooperative they are with bourgeois elegance, and the more they under-mine bland conformism, the more likely black youth are to understand their bodies as battlefields of fierce moral contest.

Fashion is one of the truly democratic options of self-expression left to urban black youth; while they may be as tyr-annized as the rest of us by name brands and exorbitant prices, they are neither passive victims of style nor its oblivi-ous dupes. As consumers with limited options but sometimes expensive tastes, black urban youth style their identities by shifting emphasis away from individual, and original, items—a Versace dress, Gucci shoes—to a style that incorporates knock-offs of those items in its eclectic street repertoire. By making a virtue (a style trend of ghetto extravagance) out of necessity (little money and less credit), black youth discov-ered "ghetto chic" and "ghetto couture." Poor black youth transformed the market from their positions as imaginative, if restricted, consumers, igniting a widespread trend of "individ-ual customization. Tailors . . . took the most expensive and conservative designs of coveted labels and added an extra twist of 'street flavor.'"[20]

Of course, neither ghetto chic nor the black youth who created it are exempt from the same sort of disdain and embarrassment that dogged the styles of their urban forebears a century earlier. Hip-hop has been accused, rightly so, of misogynistic lyrics, though other sectors of the culture that purvey patriarchy's poisons are spared such relentless con-demnations as hip-hop has garnered. Hip-hop culture has also been blamed for giddily embracing consumerism, a charge that is true, again, but even truer of whiter and richer segments of the culture. Similar to the Air Jordan myth discussed in Chapter 2, the perception of black youth consumption is often blown way out of proportion to its actual occurrence. And of course hip-hop has been nailed for casting glamour on thuggish behavior and for heartlessly painting violent portraits of urban life. It's all true, but still, the whole truth of hip-hop isn't contained in these charges of moral corruption and, nearly as often, racial betrayal. The sheer vitality of hip-hop as art form and, because of the generational lag, as agitator of adults, must not be overlooked. Many black elders claim that hip-hop is all macho posturing and stylish bluster in the service of social pathology.

But it is not *merely* posing, and the ethically questionable gesture, that form the culture's base of appeal: At its best, hip-hop summons the richest response in the younger generation to questions of identity and suffering. They may not be as elegantly crafted as were the urban horrors depicted by Wright or Baldwin—after all, we are speaking of different genres, and different modes of intelligence, literate versus postliterate, that is, if the word is narrowly defined and selectively applied—but Scarface and Nas, and, before them, Tupac and Notorious B.I.G., have sketched characterizations of black male angst and moral striving as haunting and beautiful as anything we're likely to read from social critics of the black ghetto. We need not romanticize these pavement poets to appreciate their art. Neither can we deny that the furious resentment that hip-hop evokes—which, curiously enough, often overlooks battles within hip-hop about its future and direction and about whether it has sold its soul to the devil while claiming to lead youth to the Promised Land—is still largely a matter of bourgeois disgust for the economically humbled.

Street fashion is once again at the heart of the war against the urban black poor. Black adults, including Afristocrats like Cosby, have been engulfed in moral panic over baggy pants that sag almost beneath the behind. For these folk, baggy pants express a conscious, or, perhaps worse yet, unconscious, desire to return to the scene of their stylistic origin: the prison. It is true that baggy pants, which often hang on the hips low enough to reveal the color of one's undergarments, are adapted from prisons. Inmates had to discard belts from pants so they wouldn't harm themselves or others by turning leather or buckles into weapons. The style was popularized by California gangs in the '90s. (In the NBA, no less a luminary than Michael Jordan was the first to wear baggy shorts, the sure sign to purists that basketball, too, had become a sport of thugs with tattoos and cornrows.) Some black adults think that black youth are heading for moral suicide when they align themselves with a prison subculture that praises and practices death.

There is no denying that black youth are in deep trouble. The aesthetic ecology in which they are nurtured surely contains poisonous weeds and quicksand, glimpsed in sexist tirades on wax and the hunger to make violence erotic. Alarmist narratives also mirror the worries over working and struggling urban bodies throughout the twentieth century. The extravagant stroll down the street has been supplanted by the gang cruise, the low-riding ESE or the corner-hugging homeboy, whether that corner is for consumption (the mall), creativity (the recording studio) or carnage (the drug den). It is easy to understand why in many instances baggy pants might be fearsome. (Of course, in thousands of crime reports from the media and police, the suspect is often described as wearing such gear.) If this style of dress emerged on streets where black and brown male youth played or preyed, it may be that they decided to adorn their bodies in the styles forced on the men they love, family and friend alike, who have gone to jail or prison. This may be understood as *sympathy dress*, fashion that draws from the overidentification of black and brown youth with their terrorized, or terrorizing, kin, who may have been caught up in bloody urban dramas. Just as one shaves his head because he identifies with a loved one who loses her hair when afflicted by disease, youth may adopt the clothing and style of those who are critical to their survival. It's a way of reclaiming the body of a loved one from its demobilized confinement and granting it, vicariously, the freedom to walk on streets from which it has been removed.

But perhaps we shouldn't be too literal, either; if that was the origin of the baggy aesthetic, it need not be its exclusive, or by now even its primary, frame of reference. Most youth who wear baggy pants and oversize shirts are probably not even aware of their origins, and when they find out are not likely to give up the fashion because its beginnings don't determine their uses of the style. Many black youth who wear baggy pants may feel they are already in prison, at least one of perception, built by the white mainstream and by their dismissive, demeaning elders. The baggy pants style may symbolize, consciously or not, their restricted mobility in the culture. Baggy pants, and oversize clothing in general, may also cover black bodies subject to unhealthy surveillance. Maybe black youth who can't hide in their skin are forced to hide in their clothes. The more they are swallowed up in a sea of denim or cotton, the less likely they are to drown in naked scrutiny of vulnerable limbs. And while the clothes also mark them for suspicion of crime, they no doubt recognize that they are already marked by color and class and age. Why Cosby and more elders don't get this is regrettable and sad. Some argue that Cosby's assault on the bodies and names of our youth is a sign of love. If it is, it is a callous and derisive love.

One supposes the same love shows in Cosby's sarcastic slap at the body modifications of black females. The piercing of ears, noses, tongues, eyebrows and navels (and, less noticeably in public, the labia and nipples) sends Cosby into spasms of disgust. Despite what Cosby implies, many young people do modify their bodies with Africa, and other ancient civilizations, in view. Many non-Western cultures practiced the art of changing the body through extravagant self-styling. As is true with fashion, body modifications—both the temporary sort, including facial makeup, hair removal, coloring of teeth and body painting, and the permanent kind, such as stretching the neck with rings and cosmetic surgery—suggest that the body is both a signifying battlefield and an "unfinished project."[21] The modified body, to a degree, challenges Western myths of beauty and self-image. Body modifications that borrow from ancient cultures get under the skin of civi-

lized body ideals: that the body should be ordered and con-
trolled; that the skin should be free of foreign agents, an ideal
that discourages tattooing and body piercing; that the body
should never be deliberately marked by signs of trauma, a
move against acts of scarification; and that the body should
be subject to ideals of public presentation that embody
restraint and modesty.

In contrast to practices in ancient cultures, body modifications have been dramatically altered by consumer culture.[22] In
many ancient societies, body modifications had many functions and were imposed on tribal members. Body modifications were used to mark one's age, social rank or status as a
slave, or one's relation to a tribe; to signify mourning and to
ward off disease and evil; to secure one's life in the afterworld
and to possess magical powers; to intimidate opponents; and
to enhance one's appeal to the opposite sex.[23] Body modifications were also used to marginalize tribal members and to
mark criminals with stigma and shame. Contemporary practitioners of modifications, including tattooing, scarification
and body piercing, seem to invite or underscore their mar-
ginal status. One may be resisting conventional notions of
"normal," "beautiful" and "appealing," or one may be rejecting the mainstream's views of culture and politics. Whatever
their motivation might be, it is clear that those who practice
body modification can now signify on their bodies, through
their bodies, with their bodies, thus liberating themselves
from certain Western norms.[24]

The freedom to experiment with one's body enhances the
artistic elements of body modification. Tattooing in the con-

temporary vein may be seen as the body's graffiti, encouraging participants to paint maps of identity on the body's surface. Scarification in the modern context may be seen as the body's Braille, inspiring participants to raise the flesh's surfaces to read messages others are blind to. And piercing may now be seen as the body's crochet needle, allowing participants to embroider the skin in striking patterns of self-disclosure. Of course, as was true with disco music, body piercing, which thrives in gay and lesbian cultures, represents the "homosexualization" of American expressive culture while underscoring the exhibitionist impulses of consumer culture.[25]

Body piercing allows some black youth to adapt jubilant performance to their skin and to improvise their identities. Their improvisational identities inspire black youth to use body modification to gain surer self-understanding. Even as black youth applaud and embrace the modified body in white cultures, they must remember that their black skin is already a permanent marker of difference. (Of course, Michael Jackson's chilling reversal of pigment suggests the elasticity of the epidermis, but even so, the disappearance of his color has not kept Jackson from finally being treated like the black man he was remembered to be.) To be sure, black skin is sometimes loved as an exotic fetish, but it is more likely viewed as an uninhabitable and disfiguring border. This fact is undisturbed even as body modifiers adopt "Modern Primitivism" to reject the materialistic values of Western culture and to incorporate the ideals of "primitive" cultures.[26] This concept, quite useful in curing Western myopia, carries cataracts of its own. Some whites fail to see how they have a choice whether

to be identified as "primitives," while for black folk, the bat-
teries are always included and the primitivism is always
assumed, or, rather, there is what can be called a *civilized savagery* ascribed to even the most postmodern, body-modifying
black subject around. Black youth can tap into the broader
history of revulsion to the modified body in the West. But
they can also embrace urban black identities that are scarred
by cultural disdain and tattooed with racial disgust.

For an example, one need look no further than Cosby's cynical insistence, all in the tone of his voice, that the body piercing of black youth is both a sign of their African ancestry and
a signal that they have no idea what that ancestry means. His
words resonate in simple blackness and drip in contradiction.
On the one hand, Cosby seems to suggest that black youth are
both dramatically and irreversibly alienated from their African
roots ("What part of Africa did this come from?"); on the
other hand, he suggests that black youth have no idea about
their African roots because they are *not* African. ("These people are not Africans, they don't know a damned thing about
Africa.") Of course, one might reasonably levy that charge at
Cosby as well, given his stereotypical misrepresentations of
black youth and his ignorance of the African origins of their
jubilant performances on skin and streets. Body modifications
do have roots in African and in many other civilizations.
Scarification and body painting were practiced in Sahara in
8000–5000 B.C.E.; Egyptian mummies of Nubian women had a
series of tattoos across their abdomens in 4200 B.C.E.; and in
4000 B.C.E., men in predynastic Egypt wore decorated penis
sheaths while the women were tattooed.[27]

In today's Africa there is overwhelming evidence of body modifications, enhancements, adornments and decorations that suggests at least a provisional link to *African* American culture. As Cosby's comments reveal, there is still a great deal of ambivalence about the role of Africa in black American culture. The romantic view of Africa has rightly been rejected; it feeds on ignorance or denial of the continent's complex identities and conflicting values. But there is startlingly little appreciation for African cultures and ideas, even among black folk. While we worked to free our bodies from white supremacist rule, and our kin of color from colonialism, we often failed to decolonize our imaginations and update our images of the world that birthed our ancestors. The last frontier of bigotry toward our ancestral homeland to be conquered may lie no further than the mirror.

One need not subscribe to *National Geographic* to learn how Africans have adapted the ancient art of body modification to their current situations. They have largely spurned the stigmas and tribal traumas of the past, with notable exceptions, including female circumcision, an act whose brutality Alice Walker helped bring to the world's attention.[28] Perhaps one of the young women Cosby thinks has no knowledge of Africa may know of Turkana women from Kenya who sport multiple piercings along the rim of their ears; or Suri women in Ethiopia who display scarifications, large ear plugs and body painting; or the young Dinka women whose facial scarification can be read as painful elegance; or the Iwam warrior from the upper Sepik river in New Guinea with a pierced nasal septum.[29]

If Cosby's views on fashion and body modifications prove his disinterest in straying too far from the comforts of his insistent bias, a trait he shares in common with millions more, his take on unique black names is especially dispiriting. Behind those colorful and sometimes extravagant, even outlandish, names is a history of black subjugation that has rattled the black psyche with ungodly precision. There is nothing those names could ever mean that could begin to approach the offense that brought them into existence. Shaniqua never enslaved humans as chattel.[30] Taliqua never tore a child from her mother's breast to rape or sell her. And even though Muhammad isn't in the same class, a slip we may ascribe to Cosby's general disdain for non-European names, even he, in black skin at least, never benefited like his owners from the savage pleasures of white supremacy. Whatever acrimony Cosby has for the unique names of the black poor—and he is surely not alone—he should at least learn, as should we all, even if in the briefest fashion, the story of how black names were dragged through mud and used to denominate us as beasts and fools. But we fought back with a homespun ingenuity that pitted our imaginations against the ghastly terrors of chattel slavery and we took back our dignity, or at least our self-determination, one syllable at a time.

When African slaves got to American soil, their spirits were broken and they were robbed of their identities, a fact most memorably glimpsed in the stripping away of their names and their bleak renaming by their owners. The new names the owners bestowed often bled with the contempt they felt for the slaves; many Africans were named after ani-

mals, inheriting monikers like Jumper, Bossey or Postilion.[31]
In other instances, Africans were given biblical or Puritan
names, or named after classical deities, as if to conjure the distance between their wretchedly inferior beings and the ideals
and achievements those names summoned. They were given
names like Hercules and Cato, or Othello and Claudius.[32] If
an owner thought a slave particularly dumb, he was sure to
stick him with Plato or Socrates; if, hypocritically enough, a
black female was deemed promiscuous, she would get the
name Diana, all the more to pour derision on their heads.[33]
Africans were also given names of titles that marked their
exact opposite status: General and King. (In the generations
after slavery, blacks continued this tradition in various ways,
but, of course, without the vicious signifying that accompa-
nied it. My grandfather, born in the late 1800s, for instance,
was named Major Leonard.)

Later, slaves were named after geography, and received
place names like Quebec and Senegal, Bristol and
Cambridge. Or they were named after famous personages like
Byron, Washington, Lafayette, Napoleon, Lincoln and
Madison.[34] As slavery expanded, African Americans began to
win back the freedom to name themselves—sometimes
overtly, sometimes in more subtle ways, but largely by refusing
to tie their identities to the names their owners gave them.[35]
In the instances they were in control, Africans named their
infants seven days after birth, a sign that they took naming
seriously and that a great deal of thought went into naming
each African child.[36] Some slaves secretly held on to their
African names and referred to themselves by their "country

names," suggesting the provisional control that slaves on pre-dominantly black estates were gaining over some important matters.[37]

Many slaves also kept their ancestral roots alive by giving themselves African nicknames used in their own company, creating a familiar feeling in a strange land. By the mid-eighteenth century, more than one-fifth of slaves on big estates in the lowcountry had African names, proving they had ingeniously battled the usurpation of their identities by white owners.[38] By the second and third generations of enslavement, when blacks gave their children African names, it reflected the effort to stimulate the memory of their African ancestry in their children and grandchildren.[39] Even with the rise of European names in slave communities, slave parents insisted on maintaining African naming practices, like naming their children after important days, events and places.[40] Thus, if a child was named Christmas, he had a European name backed by an African tradition of recognizing an important day.

When Africans insisted on fitting their children with names from their distant homeland, slaves in the South often chose events relating to birth, such as the day the child was born: Quash, Squash, or Quashy for Sunday, for example; Cudjo for Monday; and Cuffy for Friday. Sometimes those names were linguistically deformed in crude substitutions, like Coffee for Cuffie, or by translations into English, so that African children bore the names Monday, Wednesday and Friday.[41] African children were also named after months, with names like April, June and August; times of day, with names like Morning; and seasons or festivals of the year, yielding names like Winter and Easter. There were African names derived from tribal names, such as Hibou from Ibo, Becky from Beke and Fantee from Fanti. African children also bore Anglicized African names: Andoni became Anthony, Nsa became Henshaw, and Effiom became Ephraim.[42] Sometimes, white owners degraded African names and lent them pejorative meanings. For instance, the Hausa name Sambo, usually given to the second son of the tribe's family, was twisted in South Carolina to signify a lazy, stupid black male, a negative meaning that survives to this day. Quaco, the day name for men born on Wednesday, was derisively transliterated as Quack.[43]

The African naming tradition in the New World was often extravagant, similar to traditions in the African cultures blacks left behind. Besides secret nicknames, there were secondary names assigned to blacks to distinguish them from others with the same names on large plantations; names for occupations, such as Engineer Ned, Carpenter John and Headman Frank; names for age and appearance, such as Old Daniel, Great Jenny or Little Mag (later, placing "Big" before a name reflected the southern practice of giving the title to the oldest member of the family with a common name, usually a father whose son was named after him); names showing relationships, such as Katina's York, Jenny's Dolly or Henry's Tom; and finally names that through sheer exuberance and creativity were made up and later generally adopted, names like Pie-Ya, Frog, Monkey, Cooter, John de Baptist, Fat-man, Fly-Up-de-Creek and Cat-Fish.[44] Africans engaged in what may be termed resistive nomenclature: Siblings and parents named their children to combat the broken family ties when kin were sold. Brothers and sisters named their children after each other and sons and daughters were named after their fathers and mothers, though father and son pairings were more usual.[45]

After slavery, black folk took on names that signified their newfound freedom. Their overwhelming choice of Anglo-American names over African names reflected their profound acculturation as well as their emancipation.[46] Freed blacks also chose Anglo-American names to purge their ranks of derisive classical names and of names usually given to mules or dogs—the logic seems to have been that if Anglo-American names were good enough for white folk then they were good enough for black folk seeking to occupy a free society. Blacks also moved from the informal and diminutive, Jim and Betty, to the full and formal, James and Elizabeth.[47] And, for the first time for most blacks, they shed the stigmatizing use of single forenames and selected surnames to match their newly emancipated status. Many of those surnames embodied their liberation, including Freeman, Newman, Freeland and Liberty. Blacks drew other surnames from their trades and skills, an ancient custom, while some blacks chose to be identified with their color, hence the popularity of Brown.

But the bulk of ex-slaves chose Anglo-American surnames, underscoring their deep Americanization. The same can be said for those free blacks in the Upper South who took the surnames of their former masters—sometimes out of "gratitude and respect," as one ex-slave put it, but also because, as he admitted, identifying with an established family would help him in his efforts as a tradesman.[48] Many other ex-slaves followed suit. In the first flush of freedom, black surnames were drawn not only from Anglo-American culture and from former owners, but from notable personages associated with independence and freedom, like Washington, Jefferson, Jackson, Grant and Hamilton, and from biblical names like Isaiah, Moses, Joshua and Ezekiel. Other free blacks adopted certain surnames because of their emotional or cultural appeal, or because they "simply liked the way they sounded, or found them unique."[49]

Unusual or unique names—those names "given to no other child born in that year who is of the same sex and race"—have consistently, if not overwhelmingly, appeared in African American culture.[50] Among black college students in 1938, 15.3 percent of black females and 8.4 percent of black males had unusual names. The proportion of unusual names for these students varied according to the region of the country they lived in: In Ohio, it was 9.9 percent; in the Upper South, it was 10.4 percent; in the Lower South, it was 13.9 percent; and in Oklahoma and Texas, it was 16.3 percent, numbers that paralleled those for whites with unusual names.[51] Some blacks, however, did give their children "highly fantastic" names. In Rockingham County, North Carolina, in 1930, blacks had names like Agenora, Audrivalus, Earvila, Eldeese, Katel, Limmer, Margorilla, Roanza and Venton Orlaydo.[52]

Some unusual black names were "African survivals," while other names, especially those given by Gullahs on the South Carolina and Georgia coastlines, followed African patterns of naming children after circumstances of birth, the mood of the parents, or with the intent of bringing their children good fortune.[53] Gullah children had names like Blossom, Wind, Hail, Storm, Freeze, Morning and Cotton, all reflecting birth circumstances—for instance, Blossom might have been born when flowers were blooming and Cotton was born during cotton-picking time.[54] Black children had names like Pleasant Times and Hard Times, reflecting their parents' mood at the time of their birth. Religious belief and the desire to bless their children led to names like Fortune, Redemption, Refuge and Precious Allgood; sacred and secular phrases resulted in names such as I Will Arise, Try and See, and Daisy Bell Rise Up.[55] Some Gullah children were named after West African nicknames and after totems or clan names such as Frog, Bear, Cat-Fish and Squirrel.

For the most part, however, unusual black names were African only in the sense that they reflected flair and creativity, not because they had direct links to African culture.[56] Those African traits showed through when black folk named their children after brands and consumer products, such as Hershey Bar, Listerine and Creamola. Unusual black names became more prominent in the first half of the twentieth century, but were curtailed in the 1950s, perhaps because of the rise of the modern civil rights movement and the focus in certain quarters on assimilation to white life.[57] The adoption of African names became popular with the dissatisfaction, after the height of the civil rights struggle, with persistent inequality. The trend was aided as well by the rise of black power ideology and black nationalist sentiment in the late sixties and early seventies, with its strong emphasis on black pride, a distinctive black culture and identification with Africa.[58] Prominent black figures, as well as thousands of other blacks, adopted African names: SNCC leader and black freedom fighter Stokely Carmichael became Kwame Toure; writer and activist Leroi Jones became Amiri Baraka; and activist and Kwanzaa founder Ron Karenga took on the first name Maulana. There followed a slew of infant females named Aina, Jamilah, Khadija and Shani, and a host of boys named Hasani, Hakeem, Jabari, Kofi, Quaashie and Sulaiman. The volume *Names from Africa*, put out in 1972 by Johnson Publishing Company, publisher of *Ebony* and *Jet* magazines, became one of its best-selling books.[59] These developments may even account in part for the resurgence of unusual black names since the 1980s.

In the last twenty years, a number of black parents have continued to give their children unique names. In a study of unique African American names in Illinois conducted by Harvard sociologist Stanley Lieberson and then–graduate student Kelly S. Mikelson, for example, 29 percent of black girls and 16 percent of black boys had unique names in 1989.[60] At times, the uniqueness of their names had to do with the unusual spelling variation of a common name; a "standard" name that was no longer popular; or, in the majority of cases, because their names were invented or adapted from existing words, usually nouns, that were not usually used as first names, such as geographical names, surnames, or commercial products.[61] In Illinois, there was a huge jump in the early sixties in unique names for black girls, and while the percentages were lower for black boys, they followed the same pattern. Among white children during the comparable period, there weren't nearly as many unique names given.[62]

While unique black names seem to radically depart from "standard" (African) American names, it seems that these names fulfill the same function provided by first names in at least sixty societies: the indication of the name-holder's sex.[63] In the Illinois study, 224 subjects (122 of them were white, 61 were black and 41 were either "other" or indicated no race) were presented with a list of sixteen unique black names. There was a high degree of consensus about which names were male and which were female, and the majority guesses were usually correct.[64] Since both blacks and whites had an equal ability to guess the gender of the names, it was clear to Lieberson and Mikelson that there "is a widely shared cultural agreement regarding the sounds associated with names for girls and boys."[65] Furthermore, there appear to be linguistic features that influence black parents' selections of invented names. For example, there is the gender cue that *a* endings, such as Lamecca, Timitra, Maleka and Sukoya, are usually female.[66] (Joshua is the only male name among blacks' and whites' top one hundred names that ends with an *a*.) Next, similarity to an Arabic male name—in concert with the fact that a large degree of black, and white, male names end in consonants— usually indicates a unique male name like Husan.[67]

Then there is the gender cue provided by the *Sh* (*Ch* often has the *Sh* sound, as in Charlene) that starts many black female names. (In fact, there are four leading names for black females that begin with *Sh*: Sharon, Shamika, Sheri and

Sheena, and three that begin with C*h*: Chantel, Charlene and Chanel.)[68] Even among black unique names, the *Sh* sound (even when it is made by C*h*) holds true as a likely index of female gender. (This is only likely, since there are black males with the *Sh* sound at the beginning of their names, for instance, actor Shemar Moore.) Also, for boys with unique black names, it is slightly more likely their names will end in *i* or *ie* than for girls. And it is also much more likely that names ending in a hard *d*, such as Olukayod, are male rather than female. All in all, black parents who give their children invented, unique names appear to be guided by the rules that they be gender specific and that certain sounds are appropriate for either gender.[69] There appears to be culture in phonemes.

Of course, prejudice against unique names may not stop when folk learn that there are rules that shape their invention, or that naming in general has a long and complicated history in black America. Many blacks, especially those who are middle class or wealthier, feel just as Cosby does. Journalist Cathy Jackson is upset when black parents give their children distinctive names because, unlike in the case of Africans, or of Muslim groups, these names don't make any sense. "What is the meaning of Zohnitha, Equilla, Lakeisha, Neumoonisha, La Domona, De Andrean or Zanquisha?" Jackson asks.[70] Of course most folk, including blacks who give their children conventional names, may not pass that litmus test of naming: I'm not sure my mother knew the meaning of Michael when she gave me that name. For that matter, I'm not sure she realized that Eric, my middle name, was invented centuries ago by folk who believed the world was flat, though the meaning of that name has since changed.[71] Jackson argues that these names "surely aren't inherited from our African-American ancestors." But, as we learned above, the patterns are the same as those adopted by earlier generations of black folk, Africans and African Americans alike, who were creative in their selections, adaptations and inventions.

Jackson is on to more serious territory when she warns of studies that show behavior problems "occur much more frequently among people who have peculiar names," and that another study found that "criminal misdeeds are four times as frequent among those with unusual names."[72] For a moment it appears as if Cosby's disgust with unique black names may be justified, especially his aside that those with such names "are all in jail." But then, when we recall that some of the worst crimes in history have been committed by folk with perfectly normal names like Charles Manson or Ted Bundy, there's a bit of relief. Moreover, many of the white supremacists who committed untold atrocities against black folk in the South had regular names like Sam and Billy, and segregationist politicians who justified those heinous acts as occupants of the highest office in states like Alabama and Georgia had old-fashioned names like George Wallace and Lester Maddox. To be sure, Pookie might steal your car, which is bad enough, but he isn't likely to participate in acts of racial genocide.

In fact, there might be a more reasonable causal explanation to correlate blacks with unique names and behavioral problems and criminal activity: They usually come from at-risk families and neighborhoods. As Jackson says, "it is mostly poor, very young Black mothers who give their children fanciful names," though she admits she knows upwardly mobile black people have also "saddled their offspring with names that have lots of rhythm but no reason."[73] But then, as we learned above, there are plenty of reasons for how and why black folk choose the names they do, and there are rules that govern even totally made up names. If it is true that mostly working-class and poor black folk give their children unique names, then it is likely that if they gave their children conventional "white" names— say, Richard or Alan or William—it wouldn't make much difference at all in their economic standing.

Even though Jackson claims that she is concerned about the social costs a "burdensome title" imposes on black kids— ridicule at school, names their grandparents can't pronounce, psychological harm—the ultimate explanation for her response to black names may be the same sort of embarrassment before white folk that chagrined earlier generations of the black middle class and elites, and that seems to plague Cosby as well. Trying to explain to one's white colleagues or peers or fellow citizens the raison d'être of some black names brings winces of shame to many black faces. Fortunately, when some black folk find humor or even shock in unique black names—after all, naming one's children Versace, Formica, Moet, Lexus and Toyota, as some black parents have done, may seem a frightening new invention, but, as we discovered earlier, black folk for a long time have turned to famous brands and consumer products for names—they have neither guilt nor embarrassment about the choices poorer and younger black folk make. Instead, they have awareness that a persistently racist society imposes social and racial tariffs on poor blacks, and psychological ones on the more well-to-do blacks among us.[74]

There should be little surprise, then, with the findings of a 2003 study conducted by economists Marianne Bertrand and Sendhil Mullainathan that concluded that employers often discriminate against black job applicants by screening resumes based on applicants' potential race as suggested by their names.[75] The pair crafted resumes with white-sounding and black-sounding names and sent nearly 5,000 of them to 1,300 jobs that were advertised in Chicago and Boston newspapers. Those "applicants" with white-sounding names such as Jay, Brad, Carrie, Kristen, Laurie and Sarah were 50 percent more likely to receive a callback than those with black-sounding names like Ebony, Latonya, Kenya, Latoya, Rasheed and Kareem.

When Bertrand and Mullainathan were designing their study, colleagues predicted that there would indeed be a discrimination effect revealed, but one that pointed to "reverse discrimination," under the assumption, it seems, that affirmative action policies would benefit the resumes of apparently black applicants.[76] But the reverse proved to be true; the racial disparity in callbacks substantiates the existence of persistent discrimination in the workplace. This discrimination affected blacks seeking employment in a wide range of positions as executives and managers, administrative supervisors, sales representatives, sales workers in retail finance and insurance and personal services, clerical workers, administrative support, manufacturing, transportation and communications, wholesale and retail trade, insurance and real estate finance, business and personal services, and health, educational and social services.[77]

Predictably, some economists have tried to reverse the logic of Bertrand and Mullainathan's study and place the onus on the blacks who are the victims of discrimination. In citing a study, "The Causes and Consequences of Distinctively Black Names," by economists Roland G. Fryer, Jr., and Steven D. Levitt, economics professor Robert J. Barro argues that the economists prove that "the more black-sounding a person's name, the more likely the parents have a lower socioeconomic status."[78] Thus, employers "might infer that a job seeker with a black-sounding name is more likely to have grown up in a less educated and poorer family," and if these employers "believe, rightly or wrongly, that such a back-ground lowers the chance of job success, this may help explain why audit studies find that employers react negatively to black-sounding names on resumes."[79] For Barro, the study proves that "a person's name no longer predicts much about later economic outcomes, such as whether he or she winds up living in a rich or poor area," and that "ultimately it matters whether your parents are well-educated or rich but not whether they name you Shanice or Molly."

Barro is not defending the use of black names so much as he is discounting whatever discriminatory effects might result from employers' choosing not to select blacks with unique names because it also suggests that they are poorly educated and less likely to be successful on their jobs. "Thus, the key issue is whether black-white gaps in income and other economic and social indicators are still narrowing rather than whether employers are discriminating against black names."[80] What Barro overlooks is that if blacks continue to be discriminated against based on the likelihood that their names reveal their race, and if they are thus closed out of jobs that could substantially alter their own economic standing as well as that of their children, then that sort of discrimination is precisely the kind of economic and institutional behavior that will result in poor economic outcomes. The prejudices of the employers create a self-fulfilling cycle: As long as employers deny opportunities to black folk on the basis of their names—and since not all black parents who gave their children unique names were poor—they assure the very condition they claim to deplore. These are undoubtedly the sort of institutional barriers that should be eradicated. In Barro's logic, black folk are to blame for the very discrimination they suffer.

It is worth considering that well-known and powerful blacks with unique names have become so accepted that their names no longer sound strange, or even prohibitively black, but resound positively throughout the culture: Oprah, Shaquille, Keyshawn and Condoleezza. Should they, like ordinary blacks, be encouraged to change their names, or to hang their heads in shame when their unique names are mispronounced or misspelled? Are their names signs of inferior intelligence or uncouth behavior? We have learned to love and admire the people, and, as a result, we love and admire their names, or, at the least, we don't hold those names in secret derision or public disgust. Can we really imagine Cosby deriding Oprah or Condoleezza or Shaquille? Should the burden of Cosby's bias, and that of many, many more, rest on the heads of the uniquely named black poor? I think society should learn to name and let name.

The kind of prejudice that poor black folk, especially youth, confront in a persistently racist society, whether about their clothes, body modifications or names, is predictable, but tragic nonetheless. In too many quarters of our society, visions of black identity are still stereotyped, cramped and morally impoverished. But the venomous sentiments directed at the black poor, particularly black youth, by members of black culture are equally painful. The black elite and other critics often ignore the enormous obstacles that clutter the path of struggling blacks. If black youth choose to wear their clothes, and style their bodies, in ways that older blacks find offensive, then such offense may be interpreted as generational tension, or divergences in taste among the classes, but it should not be seen as an ethical deficiency among poor black youth.

And if their parents give them unique, unusual, fantastic, distinctive names, perhaps it does have meaning after all: to reach for equally fantastic and distinctive heights in the world, denied to their parents, that the children may yet fulfill. We should not allow *our* bigotry—and, as Howard Thurman pointed out, a bigot is a person who "makes an idol of his commitments"—to burden our brothers and sisters, who toil under almost unimaginable odds to make it from day to day. We should spare them our hang-ups, hates and hesitations. Perhaps there is perverse Afristocratic envy of the black young and poor who possess such distinctive names.

Maybe they have truly cast care for what others think of them to the wind and embraced with courage their freedom to explore their own bodies and create the meanings of their own names and fulfill their own destinies as best they can. That is a freedom all Americans, all humans, should enjoy. Even Bill Cosby, who, after all, gave each of his wonderful children names—not all of them conventional—that begin with E. When asked what they meant, he said they stood for excellence. Why can't poor parents enjoy the same freedom with their children?

Chapter Four

Family
Values

No longer is a person embarrassed because they're pregnant without a husband. (clapping) No longer is a boy considered an embarrassment if he tries to run away from being the father of the unmarried child (clapping). . . Ladies and gentlemen, the lower economic and lower middle economic people are not holding up their end in this deal. In the neighborhood that most of us grew up in, parenting is not going on. (clapping) In the old days, you couldn't hooky school because behind every drawn shade was an eye (laughing). And before your mother got off the bus and to the house, she knew exactly where you had gone, who had gone into the house, and where you got on whatever you have on, where you got it from. Parents don't know that today . . . 50 percent drop out, I'm telling you, and people in jail, and women having children by five, six different men. Under what excuse? "I want somebody to love me." And as soon as you have it, you forget to parent.

Grandmother, mother, and great grandmother in the same room, raising children, and the child knows nothing about love or respect of any one of the three of 'em (clapping) . . . If you knock that girl up, you're gonna have to run away because it's going to be too embarrassing for your family. And in the old days, a girl get pregnant, she had to go down South, and then her mother would go down to get her. But the mother had the baby. I said the mother had the baby. The girl didn't have a baby. The mother had the baby—in two weeks. (laughter) We are not parenting . . . Five, six children, same woman, eight, ten different husbands or whatever. Pretty soon you're going to have to have DNA cards so you can tell who you're making love to. You don't know who dis is; might be your grandmother. (laughter) I'm telling you, they're young enough. Hey, ya have a baby when you're twelve. Your baby turns thirteen and has a baby, how old are you? Huh? Grandmother. By the time you're twelve, you can have sex with your grandmother, you keep those numbers coming. I'm just predicting . . . Therefore, you have this pile up of these sweet beautiful things born by nature, raised by no one. Give 'em presents. You're raising pimps. That's what a pimp is. Pimp act nasty to you so you have to go out and get 'em something. Then you bring it back and maybe he or she will hug. And that's why pimp is so famous for them.

The timing couldn't have been worse: Bill Cosby had to cancel a couple of legs of his national tour to lecture poor black folk about their moral failures because news broke of allegations that Cosby had drugged and sexually assaulted a woman who considered him "a great friend and mentor."[1] Other family troubles Cosby has wrestled with over the years—including a daughter who abused alcohol and drugs and claimed Cosby was an absentee parent, and his battle to restore his image as America's Dad after a very public court case that revealed unsavory elements of his personal life, including allegations of an illegitimate child—offer sufficient reason to reflect on Cosby's moral standing and its impact on his recent crusade against poor parents. That is true because his attack is funded, in large measure, by the moral capital he has accumulated over the years. To be sure, Cosby, in principle, could be as wrong as two left shoes in the latest allegations he faces and still be dead right about the poor. But it would be a mistake to see Cosby's troubles, both recently and in the past, as unrelated to his arguments about the irresponsibility of the poor.

Cosby's comments also reflect the pressure blacks have historically felt to be morally exemplary in a way that white folk as a group have never faced. As a result of the incredible demand for black folk to prove our ethical worth, we have often adopted harder approaches to our family and race. We discipline our children more harshly, we judge each other less sympathetically, and we pull out all stops to prove to the wider, white world that we stomach no breach of the moral compact to be perfect. This often leads to just the sort of judgmental and angry attitudes as Cosby has expressed to the black poor, and arguably, within his own circle as well.

Since Cosby has taken to singling out poor families for special censure, his own family problems suggest that not only poor families have moral crises that warrant examination. At the very least, his travails should nudge him considerably toward humility and compassion, while they should cause the rest of us to find object lessons in the contrast between his pronouncements and his practice. It is hard not to conclude that Cosby has misspent his moral capital and, as I argued earlier, ranged far out of his analytical depth in misjudging the poor. Just when poor folk needed protection for the negative cultural downpour, Cosby came along, as the black elite have often done, to shower apocalypse instead of offering an umbrella. Contrary to what many of Cosby's defenders have claimed, there is nothing courageous in buffeting the vulnerable with bromides one has proven on occasion not to swallow oneself.

For legions of his admirers, it is difficult to swallow the notion that Cosby may have fouled up at all, or at least in any way that would suggest grave moral defect. In isolation, at least, the latest allegations strike most of his fans as unlikely to be true because they seem way out of character for Cosby. But then, there is the character of the accuser to consider as well. Andrea Constand, a 31-year-old former employee of the athletic department of Cosby's alma mater, Temple University, claimed that she had attended dinner at a Philadelphia-area restaurant with Cosby and a group of friends in January 2004. Afterward, at Cosby's invitation, she joined him in his suburban Philadelphia home.[2] Constand said after she complained to Cosby about her stress and tension, he gave her pills which made her dizzy and fall asleep. She admitted that her memory of the night's events was poor, but said that she definitely remembered Cosby fondling her. Constand claimed that after she awoke, her clothes were disheveled. She then allegedly drove herself home. Constand, a Canadian native who quit her job at Temple and returned home near Toronto three months after the alleged incident, didn't come forward to tell her story to the Canadian police until a year later, in January 2005. The Canadian police referred the charges to the Philadelphia police, and to the Cheltenham township police where Cosby's home is located. Constand told the police she took so long to press charges because of Cosby's fame, and because she was concerned about her job at Temple.[3]

Constand's father, Andy, said his daughter knew Cosby well, and that, "Indirectly, the incident was part of why she left Temple."[4] Constand's mother, Gianna, said that her daughter "enjoyed [Cosby's] friendship, his humor and his spirit," and that she "found him to be very sincere."[5] But Gianna says their relationship was strictly platonic. "Sometimes people make bad choices and obviously he did."[6] Andy says that his daughter "feels a sense of betrayal and feels justice has to prevail." He denied that his daughter's motivation was money. "We live a good life, have a nice house. I have four cars. We're not in it for the money. Justice has to be served."[7] Andy also explained his daughter's reticence to press charges. "Sometimes it takes a long time to build up the courage, especially when the person is universal and when a person is very famous. He (Cosby) was very good friends with my daughter and she is a very honest and decent person."[8] Those sentiments are backed up by Joan Bonvicini, coach of the University of Arizona women's basketball team that Constand played on more than ten years ago. "She's always been honest and upstanding. . . . I've never known her to lie."[9] Through his lawyer, Jack Schmitt, Cosby denied the allegations, saying they are "categorically false." Later his lawyer Walter M. Phillips, Jr., said that the charges are "pointedly bizarre because it's been a year since it allegedly happened, and she is coming forward. It will be vigorously defended."[10]

Another accusation was made in 2000, as the *New York Post* reported that Lachele Covington, a 20-year-old actress who had appeared several times on Cosby's CBS TV show, *Cosby*, filed a police report alleging that the comedian had put her hand under his T-shirt and guided it toward his sweatpants.[11] The *Post*, and several other media outlets, reported that a tabloid account of Cosby's alleged sexual misconduct went further: Cosby was accused by Covington in the *National Enquirer* of fondling her when they had dinner together at his East Side townhouse in New York City.[12] After drinks and dinner with the star, she asked for career advice, and Cosby is alleged to have responded, "There isn't anything you can't do if you put your mind to it."[13] Covington reported that Cosby said that when he wanted to think deeply, he used relaxation techniques, and seeking to demonstrate them, he allegedly moved behind her, rubbed her head, slid his hands down her arms, stopping short of her buttocks. Then, when Covington laid down to relax further, Cosby is alleged to have committed the troubling sexual acts.

Cosby's spokesman David Brokaw replied that "the story is not true. It did not happen. Mr. Cosby was not contacted by the police and the first he learned about this was from the *National Enquirer*."[14] (In the article, Brokaw did admit that Cosby had dinner with Covington, but denies anything inappropriate occurred.) Cosby threatened to sue the *Enquirer* for $250 million unless it retracted the story, but the tabloid stood by the story—and even threatened to counter-sue should Cosby proceed—noting that it included in its story Cosby's denial of Covington's allegations.[15] The police contacted the Manhattan district attorney's office, which declined to prosecute Cosby.[16] The complaint would only have resulted in a misdemeanor charge of sexual abuse in the third degree, similar in nature to Cosby lawyer Phillips's conjecture in the situation involving Constand that the charges, if pressed, would amount to little more than inappropriate touching.[17]

While we may never know if the most recent allegations are true, they prove that not even world-wide celebrity can protect one from the trials and tribulations that ordinary citizens endure. Of course, it's clear that fame and fortune often entice people to jealousy and diabolical schemes to soil one's reputation and to steal one's money by any means available. This may be the case with Cosby's accusers. On the other hand, the accusations could be true. Whatever the case, we should neither exult in Cosby's troubles (schadenfreude is an ugly trait), nor too quickly, nor automatically, ignore his conduct. (We should have learned something from other celebrities who have faltered, and if we're honest, from our own lives, our foibles, our downfalls, our weaknesses, our tawdry truths well-hidden behind manicured lawns or the pretending moral facades we erect.) Cosby has through his magnificent work and "clean" image earned the culture's benefit of the doubt, and in the case of Constand, the legal presumption of innocence until the proof of guilt. But as with any of us, what we reveal in public may not be all of what we are. Cosby has fiercely guarded his privacy, but on occasion, he has provided a rare glimpse into his family life, as he did when he addressed the traumas and conflicts surrounding one of his children.

In 1989, Cosby publicly discussed his daughter Erinn's struggles with drug and alcohol addiction. His hand had been forced by a *National Enquirer* article detailing his daughter's stay at a drug rehabilitation clinic for alcohol and cocaine abuse. The news, of course, was quite vexing for a man whose public image framed him as the premier American patriarch. He was still at the height of his fame as Dr. Cliff Huxtable, and the jarring contrast of his television authority and his personal struggles was poignantly drawn. "I always knew, of course, that Bill Cosby, actor and entrepreneur, is not Cliff Huxtable," *Washington Post* columnist William Raspberry wrote at the time. "Still it seemed to me that anyone who can be so convincing in his role as perfect dad must be an above-average father in real life."[18] The conflation of the two images, Cliff and Cosby, was seriously challenged when Cosby spoke to *Los Angeles Times* writer Lawrence Christon. "We have four other children," Cosby said. "This particular daughter appears to be the only one who is really very selfish. It isn't that we hang our heads or that we're embarrassed by this, because

we've been living with this person who knows that her problem isn't cocaine or alcohol. I think that she's a child who has
refused to take responsibility for supporting herself."[19]

Cosby told Christon that he had informed all his children
that they could become whatever they wanted if they pursued
higher education. Being equipped with an undergraduate and,
hopefully, a graduate degree, they would become, perhaps,
psychologists, anthropologists, engineers or artists. And
they'd never have to worry about how they'd pay rent or buy
food or a car, since it would all be provided along with a paid
vacation. Cosby and his wife Camille had set up a support system for their five children to dispense encouragement and
love while insisting they become educated. It was wonderful
and reasonable, but in Cosby's mind, his daughter bucked the
system.

> But since 14, Erinn has always said, "I have to be me."
> Fine. When she graduated high school, I said, "Obviously
> you have a better idea of what you wanna be." She's 23
> now. She's never held down a job, never kept an apart-
> ment for more than six months. She never finishes any-
> thing. She uses her boy friends. She wants the finer
> things but she can't stand anybody else's dirt, which is
> important. Developmentally, she's still around 11 years
> old. The problem isn't alcohol or drugs—at the rehab
> center her urine showed up negative. It's behavioral.
> She's very stubborn. It's painful, not to me and Camille,
> but to her. It's going to take her hitting rock bottom,
> where she's totally exhausted and at that point where she

can't fight anymore. Right now we're estranged. She can't come home. She's not a person you can trust. You think you're not a good parent because you don't answer the call. But you can't let the kid use you.[20]

Cosby's tough-love approach won applause. Calling Erinn a "loser of a daughter," Raspberry claimed that even as America learned a great deal from Cliff Huxtable, it might also glean lessons from real-life father Bill Cosby. "Parents are given to overestimating their role in their children's lives," Raspberry opined. "It is true that it is our responsibility to teach the basic values and to try to prevent as many of their childish mistakes as we can. But it is also true that our children are independent human beings, not printouts of our noble intentions." He concluded that there were "valuable lessons" in Cosby's tough-love approach, "chief among them the limits of what even the most loving of parents can do."[21] If that's true for a parent like Cosby, how much more true might it be for poor parents?

Despite his landmark television show, and despite writing the best-selling book *Fatherhood*, Cosby's relationship to his daughter reflected the tensions that beset millions of other families, rich and poor, suburban and inner-city, and black and white—and brown, red and yellow, too.[22] As it turns out, Cosby didn't discover his daughter's drug habit until she informed him.[23] Cosby checked Erinn into Rhode Island's Edgehill Newport Hospital and sought the advice of drug counselors and therapists for the proper response he should adopt. It was then that he decided that "tough love" was called for. "We love her and want her to get better, but we have to take a very firm, very tough stand that forces her to realize that no-one can fix her problems but her," Cosby said. "She has to beat this on her own."[24]

Erinn admitted that she began experimenting with drugs at an early age.[25] Her problems began at boarding school when her peers introduced her to marijuana, beer and vodka. When her parents insisted that she enroll at Spelman College—she took a year off before matriculating at the college her parents eventually blessed with an awe-inspiring contribution of $20 million—Erinn partied hard and eventually dropped out of school.[26] At nineteen, she headed to New York to work as a waitress and continued her drug use before retreating to Rhode Island. When she left rehab, she fell back into her bad habits and began once more to take drugs.[27] Cosby admitted that "he was at his wit's end"—a position many parents come to—and told *Redbook* magazine that parents "have a dream of how to raise a child then all of a sudden they see it being crushed."[28]

But perhaps his family situation was a bit more complicated than good parent and bad child. When Erinn read what her father had to say about her to Christon in 1989, she was pained, but didn't speak out until three years later. "All that stuff is his perspective," Erinn claimed. "He was not there. . . . I had already hit my rock bottom without [my parents'] knowing about it. The only reason they knew I was doing drugs is because I told them. These aren't things that are abnormal in any other family, but because of who I am, it's a big deal."[29] But she couldn't hide the hurt she felt when she read her father's comments. "I think it's really awful that he can say something like that, that makes him look like a saint and me look like a piece of shit. I didn't use my boyfriends, they used me."[30] Erinn admitted that her parents had expectations that "didn't fit my goals." She also warned against conflating the Huxtables and the Cosby family. "The average family, if they're not divorced, has a mother and father who come home every day. Mine didn't. . . . When I'd see him, it was always about school. It wasn't like, 'Let's talk, Dad. . . .' We never were stable. During the week, you'd go to school, then you're off on the weekend to wherever he was working."[31]

As a result, Erinn got very close to her grandparents, who offered love and care. After graduating from a Quaker boarding school and attending, and then leaving, Spelman—"I don't like being in an environment with one race," she said, while also detesting the efforts of sororities to recruit her and the spite of jealous classmates—she returned to Manhattan and continued her drug abuse. But where Cosby dismissed his daughter's problem as behavioral, she saw in her drug use a quest for her father's love. "I found myself surrounded by the wrong people. I used to live with wanting the . . . validation, especially from my dad, because he wasn't there. I guess I wasn't feeling confident, so you get involved with drugs."[32]

Erinn said that in treatment at the rehabilitation center, she owned up to many of her weaknesses and, equally important, discovered that she didn't need her father's validation, a prospect that, ironically, may have infuriated him more. "I think that's what made him even more mad." Although her parents were invited to join in family therapy, she claims they "never showed up. . . . I thought, 'Who were the best people to go to when you're crying out for help . . . ? He never had any interest in what I was doing. . . . Even the people at the rehab center were surprised, because they thought my parents would really want to know." Despite the troubles they had been through, and despite talking mostly by phone—Erinn moved to Miami in the early 1990s—she still contended in 1992 that she and her parents loved each other.[33]

Erinn's move to Miami wasn't motivated only by the desire to escape family troubles and a history of drug abuse, but also by the constant specter of paparazzi angling in trees outside her window for a shot—and a failed marriage in 1990. She was also trying to put behind her the memory of a tragic event that sent her to therapy: an alleged November 1989 sexual assault by boxer Mike Tyson when she was twenty-three years old. Erinn claimed that she and a female friend met the pugilist at a New York nightclub in the company of one of Erinn's male friends. At 11:30 P.M., the foursome headed off in Tyson's car to talk, and ended up at his New Jersey home for what she was told was a get-together. She felt safe because she was with friends, it wasn't too late, and when they arrived at Tyson's home, several cars were parked outside. But once inside, there was no one there; the cars obviously all belonged to Tyson. The boxer invited his guests to look around, and when Erinn stopped in a room to ask about boxing memorabilia, Tyson left the room. "I was still looking. I heard the door lock, and I turned around and the next thing I knew I was on the ground," Erinn claimed. "He was groping."[34] Erinn said that Tyson kept her face to the floor, holding her down by the arms and covering her mouth. "He didn't say anything to me basically. It was a lot of struggling and at one point I was able to scream. I had been trying to scream all the time. I was fighting for my life. I was terrified and I knew I had to do something. I am not going to sit there and let this guy do this."[35]

Erinn said that when a female member of Tyson's household staff heard Erinn's scream, she knocked on the door, prompting the boxer to let Erinn up, and she quickly ran away. Once downstairs, Erinn said she told her girlfriend she wanted to leave, even as she claimed that Tyson offered her and the household staff member money to keep quiet. When Erinn arrived at her parents' home in New York, where she was living, she told them what had happened and they pledged to handle it. A couple of weeks later, Erinn claimed that Tyson confronted her in the same club, angry that she had told her parents and outraged that part of the agreement they allegedly extracted from him was to attend therapy for a year—an agreement Erinn claimed Tyson didn't keep.[36] Tyson was asked to leave the club. For a long time, Erinn did not speak publicly about the alleged incident, even when Tyson was on trial in 1992 for allegedly raping beauty contestant Desiree Washington, a silence she regretted. "I knew and I believed her. It stays with you. Seeing him every day on TV, I get angry. It is always going to be there. . . . I wish I had possibly gone to the police and pressed charges and maybe this would have prevented the whole thing from happening. At that time I was scared . . . and really didn't want to deal with it."[37] Tyson denied the claim and his lawyer, Alan Dershowitz, issued a statement, saying that "Erinn Cosby's three-year-old allegations are demonstrably false. We are reliably informed that Mike Tyson and Erinn Cosby were never alone in the same room together, and there are a number of witnesses who would so testify."[38] Erinn finally came forward after a former boyfriend threatened to sell the story to a tabloid if he wasn't paid off. When she refused, the *National Enquirer* ran the story in April 1992, under the headline, "Bill Cosby's Daughter—Mike Tyson Tried to Rape Me, Too!"[39] When asked to comment, Cosby declined, saying through a spokesman, "It's a family matter."[40]

Out of Erinn's tragedy came some good: She appeared on a few talk shows, including *Donahue*, to give her side of the alleged Tyson assault, which forged a renewed relation with her father. "After I did *Donahue*, my dad thanked him for making it easier for me to say what I had to say, and was very proud of the way I came across. I think for the first time . . . he's beginning to understand something. He has a lot of pride, and he's not one to tell me, 'Oh, Erinn, I'm really proud of you.' He'll have eight other people tell me before he would."[41]

Erinn's struggles with alcohol and drug abuse point to internal issues she needed to confront, since, as both she and her father concluded, her problems grew less from addiction than from the personal choices she made. And her rebellion may have indeed called for the tough-love measures that Cosby sought to apply. It also appears that, at crucial points in her story, Erinn sought the love and affection of a father who, contrary to his public image, was endlessly absent and forbiddingly distant. Of course, that is often the price paid by the children of any prominent figure. But it seems that Cosby's unwillingness to own even part of her drug drama—and his insistence that Erinn's problems were wholly self-created, despite her contention that her abuse of alcohol and drugs was in part an attempt to fill in the void left by her father's absence—suggest Cosby's inability to believe that anything he did might have contributed to his daughter's actions. This in no way relieves Erinn of responsibility for her actions, but it need not be an either-or proposition, so that Cosby fails to come to grips with the notion that actions he took—or, as it were, didn't take—may have made his daughter more vulnerable to her demons. To own up to one's direct, or even indirect, influence in another's fate or fortune, without assuming undue praise or scorn for either, is a sign of moral maturity.

If Cosby found it difficult to attend therapy with his daughter, as she claims, it might have stemmed from the fear of losing absolute parental authority in a therapeutic setting, which demands all participants be equal partners in struggling toward wholeness and truth. The therapeutic setting might encourage an empathy that one otherwise resists, or is incapable of achieving alone. While Cliff Huxtable may have been more willing to acknowledge his culpability while demanding responsibility from his child, Bill Cosby appears to have been incapable of such an admission. And if what Erinn says is true, that Cosby found it nearly impossible to tell her that he was proud of her, and it's evident that he was, then he may have been plagued by the syndrome of *the difficult admission*—of love, of pride, of longing, of regret, of grief, of pain, of whatever emotion claims one's attention—that affects so many parents and partners.

It would be too easy to overinterpret, and hence misinterpret, the relation between Cosby's apparent difficulties in his family life and his current assault on the poor. After all, he has been remarkably generous in giving millions to black colleges and causes. But it would not be contradictory to suggest that Cosby's resistance to viewing shared responsibility as a mode of moral survival has an effect on how he has held the poor accountable for their plight without calculating the role of other factors—structural racism, economic inequality, public policy decisions and the like, factors I address in the last chapter. And neither would it require dime or pop psychology to conclude that the social scold possesses an unshakable belief in his correctness, an admirable trait in forging one's path in the world when few others believe in you, as Cosby did in his early comedy career, but a less desirable feature as one tries to understand and address social phenomena like poverty. A lot more empathy—the kind that may have been helpful in his dealings with Erinn, a privileged child—is surely called for when addressing a population of severely underprivileged folk.

Happily, Erinn's relationship with her parents improved considerably; in October 1998, *Jet* magazine reported that Erinn wed Michael Canaday, an internal medicine physician, in a private ceremony at her parents' Philadelphia home.[42] And she has taken an active part in the "Hello Friend" foundation the Cosbys established in memory of their murdered son, Ennis, to help children with learning differences.[43]

If Cosby was able to reconcile with Erinn, the failure to
come to successful terms with another woman claiming to be
his daughter led to a trial in court and perhaps Cosby's most
embarrassing episode: the allegation that he fathered a child
out of wedlock—a claim he denied, but which forced him to
confess his adultery. In a tragic confluence of sordid events,
on the day Cosby lost his beloved son, Ennis, a doctoral student in education at Columbia University, in a racially
charged murder in Los Angeles, Autumn Jackson, a twenty-
two-year-old woman who claimed to be Cosby's illegitimate
daughter, demanded on the phone that the comedian pay her
millions so she wouldn't sell her story to the tabloid *Globe*.
Two days later, Jackson and an acquaintance, Jose Medina, a
fifty-one-year-old writer, were lured from their Los Angeles
base to the New York offices of Cosby's lawyer to sign what
they believed was a multimillion-dollar settlement. They
were arrested on the spot for extortion. Jackson had begun
her extortion efforts in November of 1996, after she placed a
call to one of Cosby's representatives saying she had run out
of money. (Cosby had been sending her money for years.)
Cosby arranged for Jackson to receive $3,000, but that didn't
satisfy her, and she demanded more money in exchange for
her silence.[44] Jackson and Medina eventually concocted a
scheme to extort $40 million from Cosby, but after he refused
to pay, Jackson lowered the price to $30 million, and, ulti-
mately, to $24 million.[45]

Initially, Cosby and his spokesman David Brokaw
"unequivocally and absolutely" denied that Jackson was his
daughter, saying they had a birth certificate to prove their

claim. Brokaw admitted that Cosby had paid Jackson's educational expenses, as he had for numerous young people, but that he didn't know how Cosby chose scholarship recipients or even how Jackson had been selected.[46] Brokaw was even more emphatic in dismissing Jackson's claim and suggesting Cosby's ease in denying paternity. "This woman is claiming to be his daughter, and she tried to extort $40 million from him, and she's now in custody, so what's the implication. Obviously, if Bill Cosby allowed the process to unfold as he has, then he is comfortable with what he's maintaining, which is that he's not the father."[47]

Eventually, however, it leaked out that Cosby had had an affair with Jackson's mother. At Jackson's trial in a Manhattan Federal District Court in July 1997, Cosby was forced to admit to a "single sexual encounter" in Las Vegas in the early '70s with a fan named Shawn Thompson.[48] Later, Cosby said that Thompson visited him and showed the star a child's picture. "Doesn't she look like Ensa?" she asked Cosby, referring to one of his daughters. "This is your daughter." Cosby's reply was short and simple. "I said, 'That's not my daughter,' and that was it."[49] (Thompson claimed that she had no other lovers besides Cosby at the time and that Jackson was born nine months after their fling.) Cosby says that Thompson promised to keep quiet about their tryst to spare Mrs. Cosby any embarrassment. (He eventually told her in the early '80s.) Later, however, according to Cosby, Thompson constantly "borrowed" money from Cosby with an implied threat of telling Camille, a threat Thompson denied making. Over the years, Cosby gave Thompson more than

$100,000, either in cash or by checks in the names of friends whom he would reimburse. "Obviously, with the threats going and going," Cosby said in court, "I just didn't want her to have any sort of evidence that she could say, 'Well you paid this to me.'"[50]

Cosby testified that, despite his troubles with Ms. Thompson, he made an effort to support Autumn with her educational and living expenses, even though he was careful to point out to her that he wasn't her father. "Autumn, I will tell you this: I am not your father, I will be for you a father figure—a father figure—but I am not your father."[51] Robert M. Baum, one of Jackson's defense attorneys, was barred by Judge Barbara S. Jones from eliciting testimony on the issue of paternity. He was granted permission by the judge to try to prove that Autumn believed she was Cosby's child, hoping to explain Autumn's actions as "a lawful negotiation of her rights as a daughter."[52] To bolster his claim, Baum told the jury that when Autumn was a child, her mother Shawn shared with her a secret as she watched a Saturday morning cartoon. "You know who that man is who you are watching on TV?" Shawn asked Autumn. "The voice of Fat Albert? That man is Bill Cosby. He's your father."[53] Baum seemed to imply that Cosby had sent mixed messages to Autumn: On the one hand, he denied being her father, and on the other hand, he appeared to behave in a way that suggested he was. For example, Cosby admitted in court that he told Autumn he loved her, and he spent time with her—like the time Cosby described taking a high-school-age Autumn to the tap-ing of an episode of *The Cosby Show* in New York, and placing her photo on a piece of furniture on the set so that she could view it when she watched at home. Cosby made her feel special and encouraged. "You will see this picture of you, and this is to inspire you to go and become somebody."[54]

Cosby also admitted that he had scrapped taking a paternity test in Chicago several years before the trial began because he feared that the results would leak out to the tabloids. (Before the start of the trial, Cosby had once again declined to take a paternity test, but after it was finished, he offered to take the test, and gave his blood, but Autumn refused to participate.)[55] In an interview outside of court, Baum cited Cosby's decision to forgo the paternity test, and his admission that he loved Autumn, as factors reinforcing Autumn's belief that Cosby was her father. Baum said that "under the circumstances, where he's paying for everything and the mother is saying, 'He's your father,' how could she believe anything else?"[56] Baum contended that Autumn kept her secret until she became desperate, until she was homeless and living in a car—and that only after making repeated requests to Cosby for more money did she attempt to sell her story, believing, in Baum's words, that "it is the only property I have to sell in order to survive."[57]

But Cosby would have none of it; his actions recall his "tough-love" approach to his troubles with Erinn. After Autumn dropped out of college, and sought more money from him, Cosby went off. "I was upset," Cosby confessed in court. "And I said to her, 'I'm tired of you. I'm tired of your mother.

You and your mother have never given me a happy moment for what I've given.'"[58] Cosby offered to pay for college and living expenses if Autumn found a part-time job to help herself, an offer he framed tersely: "take it or leave it."[59] It was then that Jackson came up with her scheme, in cahoots with Medina, to extort Cosby for millions, and placed several calls to Cosby and his representatives. They also wrote letters to several of the companies for whom Cosby endorsed products, calling attention to his alleged fathering of an illegitimate daughter in an effort to embarrass him with the corporations who paid him as much for his wholesome image as for his enormous talent. The letters, to CBS, Kodak, Phillip Morris, the owner of Jell-O, two publishers of Cosby's books, and even President Clinton, misspelled Autumn's first name and charged that Cosby was a "Deadbeat Father. . . . Autum is left in the Cold, Penniless and Homeless."[60]

Cosby spoke in court about his embrace of "the moral values" and "the family values" in his vast body of work, including his commercials, signaling how potentially damaging Jackson and Medina's actions were. "They come to me," Cosby said, in reference to the companies that had signed him to endorse their products. "Kodak is family, family pictures, family children. The pudding is family. Ford, car, family."[61] That's when Cosby instructed his lawyers to contact the FBI and to snag Jackson and Medina, who were eventually convicted of extortion, conspiracy and crossing state lines to commit a crime. A third man, Antonay Williams, with whom Autumn eventually had twin boys (delivered in prison), cooperated with the authorities and was given probation.[62] When her daughter was sentenced to serve twenty-six months in prison, Autumn's mother Shawn protested, "This child is facing long years for phone calls and letters, when all they really were were a cry for help." She said that Cosby should "run as fast as he can to the judge and ask for leniency for her."[63]

Although no one excused Jackson's behavior, some critics offered sympathetic portraits of Jackson while criticizing Cosby for failing in his parental obligations.[64] One of the most thoughtful and balanced takes on the entire affair was provided by *New York Times* columnist Bob Herbert. Readily conceding that Jackson's behavior was "stupid, preposterous, pathetic, and no doubt illegal . . . [and] also—intentionally or unintentionally—profoundly cruel" (since it coincided with Ennis's death), Herbert let on that "you cannot escape the queasy feeling that this [trial] is something that should not be happening. This is unnecessary."[65] Herbert argued that Cosby's claim that he "unequivocally and absolutely" was not Autumn's father was too strong in light of his admitted affair with Shawn Thompson. Herbert argued that while the court ruled that the legal proceedings wouldn't worry with the question of Cosby's paternity, "you would have to be a cold fish indeed to believe it is not relevant to Autumn Jackson. There seems to be no doubt that Ms. Jackson has long believed that she was Bill Cosby's daughter, and that must have been a torment."[66] Herbert said that Jackson must have been "hurt and confused" when at age nine, she saw *The*

Cosby Show become a cultural phenomenon and Cosby, her father, at least in her mind, become America's dad. As Herbert poignantly wrote:

> It must have been alternately exciting and unbearably depressing. Autumn Jackson would sit in front of the tube on Thursday nights and laugh with the rest of the country at the idealized antics of the Huxtable family. And then she would go to bed with the inescapable thought that her father, the greatest of them all, cared more for his TV children than for her. Bill Cosby may not be Autumn Jackson's father. But it was Autumn's desperate fantasies about the perennially absent Mr. Cosby that drove her to make the ludicrous demands that landed her in such deep trouble. . . . [Y]ou wonder if there isn't room somewhere in this entertainment for some measure of mercy. What she did was wrong. But is it necessary to send her off to a stretch in a Federal penitentiary? You wonder what purpose that would serve. And you toy incessantly and uneasily with the most disturbing of thoughts: What if Bill Cosby really is her father?[67]

As with Erinn, Cosby's lack of empathy proved strong—an empathy, by the way, that need not have meant that he was willing to cavalierly dismiss Jackson's responsibility, only that he might have, as Herbert argued, placed himself in her spot, one that, for all we know, he was responsible in part for creating as her potential biological father. Cosby's claim over the last several years is that he, and not Autumn or her mother, took a blood test to settle the matter once and for all, but that ignores the context in which he was finally willing to offer proof: *after* Autumn was ordered to prison; *after* she had suffered for most of her life believing that he was her father; *after* her repeated efforts to forge a permanent bond with him were frustrated; *after* Cosby twice reneged on taking a paternity test; and *after* the portrayal of her as *merely* a horrible opportunist and extortionist was set in the minds of those who had no sympathy for her. What she did was surely atrocious, harmful and, in many ways, self-destructive. But the question hangs over Cosby's head, put there by a thinking public and stated by Herbert: What if Cosby really is Autumn's father?

If he is, it wouldn't make what Jackson did any less unsavory, but it would mean that Cosby failed to honor his obligation to be a good parent. It would mean that he put his child through untold suffering and, against the Bible's regulations, tempted his child to do wrong by withholding from her not his money but his abiding presence and the ministry of time. It would mean that he caused her psychic anguish, helped to spark in her brutal self-doubt and confusion, and, perhaps, contributed to her moral instability. Jackson should have been held responsible for her actions, which means she should have been placed in a structured environment with institutional support to confront the error of her ways. Some deem a prison sufficient; I think a halfway house, with reduced time for seeking to complete her education, plus psychological counseling, would have been better. But Cosby should not so easily get off the hook if he is indeed Jackson's father. Given his eagerly down-putting speeches delivered to the poor for their terrible parenting, he would deserve to be held in lower esteem for his potential parental offenses. Since we may never know whether or not he is her father, it may be that he will have to endure a lifetime of skepticism about this most primal of parental responsibilities: acknowledging the child you make and acting in a healthy, productive fashion toward your seed. That is, after all, what Cosby in much meaner terms has demanded of the poor. Why not expect him to at least do the same?

*   *   *

The danger in making class-based assessments of character is that we associate wealth and resources, or at least style and status, with superior moral achievement. If wonderful families like Cosby's can struggle, and if a man of Cosby's stature can stumble, then all of us can. (We shouldn't make the mistake of characterizing the life of a family unit by measuring its worth with too short a moral yardstick, a point that Cosby should remember, even as we shouldn't forget that Cosby and his wife and children stand as a testament to the beauty and power and unimaginable generosity of the black family, despite the troubles they have encountered.) All families, whether rich or poor, can, and often do, suffer from poor moral choices, or from the inevitable strife of the clashing personalities of its members, or from generational tension. To be sure, poor families are more vulnerable in particular ways to troubles from which well-to-do families are exempt: the lack of healthcare, childcare, nutrition, cash reserves, credit and money for education. But the ethical plagues that Cosby sees emanating from poor homes and parents are widely shared in all communities. In holding this view, one need not believe that poor families should be spared critique or rigorous examination, but such assessments must be fair minded and balanced, and rooted in the desire for uplifting change to occur. I have no doubt that in his heart of hearts Cosby has the desire to see the poor thrive; but there can be little doubt that the method of verbal assaults he has adopted is counterproductive to his stated goal. Criticism is one thing; condescension and condemnation are another.

Moreover, the bitter attacks Cosby has launched dishonor the incredible strength of character of millions of poor blacks who have never cheated on their wives and never had babies and not taken care of them (and, in fact, have often reared children not from their own flesh). Indeed, if the black folk who support Cosby's contentions about the poor were honest, especially those who say we should finally air our dirty laundry and be done with the protective secrecy that only seals our moral doom, they would have to admit that much of the moral miasma plaguing black America comes from the top, not the bottom.

The truth is that the black elite, and in some cases the black masses, have always taken the poor to task for their poor parenting. But in some instances, the elite and the middle classes, and the working classes, have defended the poor and noted the obstacles they had to surmount to be successful parents. We can get a flavor of such sentiment in the 1914 publication *Morals and Manners Among Negro Americans: A*

Social Study Made by Atlanta University, Under the Patronage of the Trustees of the John F. Slater Fund, a report growing out of an annual conference studying Negro problems held at Atlanta University.[68] Edited by W.E.B. Du Bois and Augustus Granville Dill, *Morals and Manners* captures turn-of-the-century beliefs about the moral and religious condition of black America by recording the responses to a questionnaire distributed nationally to preachers, teachers, social workers, skilled trade workers (contractors and builders, bricklayers, tailors, painters, blacksmiths, dressmakers, cigar manufacturers, harness makers, stationary engineers) and professionals, including physicians, dentists, lawyers and others. The answers to questions about good manners, sound morals, cleanliness, personal honesty and the rearing of children, among other subjects, are categorized by the thirty states of the respondents. The responses to the condition of parenting in the early 1900s may as well have been snatched from the mouths of contemporary observers, parents and critics on every site of the ideological spectrum.

In Alabama, it is noted that the "better families look after children well," while others, the less well to do obviously, "are somewhat neglectful." Another says that generally speaking, "the rearing of children is well done, tho many fail thru ignorance and lack of character." A respondent from the District of Columbia agreed, sounding like a modified version of Cosby, saying that "[b]etter classes of colored people rear their children properly. Among the lower elements the children are not reared properly."[69] And, in a clear example of how things hardly ever change for the poor, one observer says that the "children are neglected in many cases from the lack of facilities to rear them properly, inadequate schools, necessity of the parents to work and spend little time in the home."[70]

Another Alabama observer says that "[f]our fifths of the children are improperly reared" because the "parents in equal numbers have never had the proper training themselves." This is a kinder version of Cosby's quip that he blamed the children for their bad habits of speaking until he heard their parents. In Arkansas, it was the granting of too much freedom and the shifting of responsibility onto the shoulders of children at an early age that hurt them. "There is a tendency to permit children to have too many liberties before they are really able to see for themselves or really know what are the consequences that result from too early taking upon themselves the responsibility which belongs to mature years and I believe the parent is wholly in error."[71] In Georgia, a respondent echoes what seems to be the perennial claim among each generation of black folk: "I do not think that parents are quite as strict with their children as they were when I was a child." Another Georgia resident thinks that structural factors, such as the need for the mother to work outside the home, always a necessity in black families, prevent the poor from doing as good as job as they might. "Not much care is taken along this line. Many mothers work out and children are left a great deal to themselves."[72]

But in Illinois, an observer thinks that it isn't just poor black families who have trouble with their children. "Some of our best citizens hardly know what their children are doing."[73] In Kentucky, it's the lure of pop culture that is ruining neglected children, a trend that the PTA fearlessly combats by helping untutored mothers. "Altho many of our children are neglected and allowed to run to the moving picture shows and public dances at night unaccompanied, yet the 'Parent-Teachers' Association' is making a winning fight to give assistance to incompetent mothers."[74] An Ohio resident agrees, suggesting that "our curfew can hardly keep them off the street at night," and that their "entertainment is left too much for their selection," while another Ohioan says that there "is too much laxity," that children "are not taught to obey their parents and superiors," and that "they are allowed to go and come too much at will without reporting to superiors; to visit pool rooms, saloons, dances and places of cheap notoriety."[75]

In Mississippi, the theme of my-generation-is-better-than-yours crops up again, as a respondent claims that parenting is not attended to as carefully "as in former years. Parents of the second generation after slavery do not seem to be so expert in that art as their ex-slave parents."[76] And to flip the class code and to give pride of place to the unlettered, but more experienced, black parent, a Missouri observer notes that some of "the best women we have in morals and education, are the poorest housekeepers. . . . They are not the equal of the older people in rearing children."[77] In citing the loss of respect for the older generation, a claim that is evergreen in black culture across time, a New Jersey observer says that even though most "of the parents are rearing their children well," they fail to, "in many cases . . . teach them respect for elders and reverence for God." In Texas, apocalypse and utter hopelessness appear to reign, as one respondent says that parenting is "a complete failure. Lost almost without remedy. Indeed, a sad state of affairs as the children are permitted to run the streets at will." In the same state, an opposite viewpoint emerges from a respondent who sees the virtues of parents, community and teachers working together, claiming that parenting receives "great attention among the people of our race and every school is supported by strong mothers' clubs who go side by side with teachers in the welfare of the children."[78] Another Texas observer lauds the work of male parents and the church, saying that the "Father's Club is doing a grand work," and that "[p]astor and people alike have united to see that the children are trained in the home and that good instruction is gently given to them." Finally, a Mississippi observer notes the incredible moral strength and encouraging example of poor black parents who transmit values and a love of learning against the odds. "It is really pathetic to see the sacrifices the humble Negroes are making to educate their children. There is very little companionship; while the parents work and strive to improve their children's condition, they very often take them in their confidence and talk with or advise them to live honestly and uprightly."[79]

It should be apparent from these few citations that black folk have always engaged, sometimes cantankerously, sometimes caustically, at other times compassionately, but always vigorously, in a dialogue about black parenting. (And if one were to take early twentieth-century criticisms of black youth on face value, it was the generation of blacks that Cosby praised in his speech, the generation that included Dorothy

Height and Kenneth Clark, that appeared to be headed for hell in a handbasket wrapped in bows. That should provide a cautionary tale about too easily assuming that our youth are morally distinct from older generations, which, though now lauded, were once condemned.) Elitist diatribes were often mixed in with homegrown strategies aimed at uplifting poor black parents and their children from their difficult circum-stances. There was no shortage of assault on the moral lapses of poor blacks, but there was, too, some recognition that the black elite have no superior grasp of morality. The themes that occupy black life now—how well we're attending to our children, how much of pop culture they should consume, the role of religion in their values education, the training that poor parents need to succeed, the economic and social barriers that prevent their flourishing—have been a consis-tent worry in black life for at least a couple of centuries. The styles that we now adopt to address the black poor—whether edifying and encouraging or demoralizing and demeaning—were just as visible in black communities a century ago. And the modes of discourse we evoke to enforce our moral views—religious address or spiritual refer-ence, noble racial didacticism, commonsense cultural rationalism, folk wisdom and the like—were vibrantly used in the early 1900s.

While Cosby has described the lethal moral seizures in black America in terms of class and age—he has lambasted the poor and the young for quite some time now, and I engaged his arguments in Chapter Three—it is also clear that on some issues, including the themes of his speech and this book, there may be as much a *genre* divide as a generational one. There were blacks of an earlier generation, for instance, as is evident in observations from *Morals and Manners*, who laid full responsibility for the poor on their shoulders, while today folk like Cosby flow steadily in their wake. Then there were folk who emphasized structural elements that might help explain why poor parents had a tough time of it—mothers going to work outside the house, poor workers struggling to make ends meet, the hostile racial and economic conditions of the times. The same is true for certain social analysts today. There were people a century ago who railed against the evils of popular entertainment, just as there are today critics of the consumption of hip-hop and rap; there were also folk in earlier decades who celebrated the joys and consolations of secular music and, like their contemporaries, drew from it sustenance for their lives. In homage to Sterling Brown—who divided the black character types in American literature into seven categories: the contented slave, the wretched freeman, the comic Negro, the brute Negro, the tragic mulatto, the local color Negro and the exotic primitive—I want to suggest seven types of black folk in the cultural imagination who straddle generational lines in their interests, identities and insights: ghettocentrists, gangstas, griots, gamers, gospelers, gentries and gayz.

Ghettocentrists hold that the ghetto, the inner city, the local black neighborhood, is the source, the *locus classicus*, of authentic black identity and supplies important standards, norms, habits, traits and behaviors for black community. In the past, this category included writers like Richard Wright and James Baldwin, and it now includes athletes like Allen Iverson, hip-hoppers from KRS-ONE to Nas, and millions of ordinary residents as well.

Gangstas believe that the lifestyle and ideology of the outlaw, the rebel and the bandit challenge the corrupt norms of the state, the government, and the rule of law in society. In the past, it has included Harlem gangsters like Ellsworth "Bumpy" Johnson and Leroy "Nicky" Barnes and the characters of writers like Chester Himes and Donald Goines. Today, it includes rappers NWA, Notorious B.I.G. and 2Pac, and thousands of small-time hoods, gang bangers and anonymous thugs.

Griots believe in the obligation to preserve cultural memory, racial practice and ethnic solidarity. They argue that the transmission of cultural habits, moral traits and racial wisdom are critical to the flourishing and survival of black culture. In the past, this included cultural nationalist Marcus Garvey, educator Mary McCleod Bethune and writer J. A. Rogers, and in the present, it includes intellectuals Maulana Karenga and Haki Madhubuti and rappers Chuck D. and Talib Kweli.

Gamers include folk who hustle in a variety of guises— bank employer, local entrepreneur, underground economist— and who seize the metaphor of gaming, prominent in arcane social and philosophical theory, to explain and extend the trickstering tradition in black culture. They are all united by "getting over." In the past, this included leaders such as Booker T. Washington and entrepreneur Madame C. J. Walker, and in the present, it includes entrepreneurs Russell Simmons and Sean "P. Diddy" Combs.

Gospelers represent the spiritual renewal and religious vitality of black culture. They prize the virtues of moral suasion and decent living as the antidote to personal failure and existential fear. There is a premium on inner peace, spiritual *and* social transformation, and, especially these days, material security, signifying the split soul of religious piety. In the past, this genre included Mahalia Jackson, Martin Luther King, Jr., and C. L. Franklin, and today, it includes Kirk Franklin, Yolanda Adams, T. D. Jakes, Louis Farrakhan, Jesse Jackson, Charles Adams, Jeremiah Wright, Freddie Haynes, Lance Watson, Rudolph McKissick, Calvin Butts and Carolyn Knight.

Gentries are the black aristocrats, the black elite, the Afristocracy, who embody the ideals, norms, behavior and performance of proper society, with a dash of uplift thrown in for good measure. As a class, they both love and loathe black folk, accounting for the ethical schizophrenia of their activities, from helping the poor to haranguing them. In the past, this included the Dobbs and Bonds of Atlanta and the Walkers of Memphis; today, it includes any Negro included in Lawrence Otis Graham's *Our Kind of People*.

Gayz are the aggressively, progressively gay, lesbian, bisexual, transgender presence in black America who gain the political meaning of their identity by fighting both racism in gay communities and homophobia in black life. Gayz challenge the monolithic conception of black identity while forging solidarity in the fight against the terrors of race and class. In the past, this category included James Baldwin and, more recently, the late Audre Lorde, and today it includes Barbara Smith, Randall Kenan, E. Lynn Harris, Keith Boykin and Meshell Ndegeocello.

These types embody some ways that black folk throughout our history have responded to the critical issues of black identity, social struggle and political organization. They also suggest how we have gathered our individual and collective resources to combat racism and other social plagues. Since these types are neither rigid nor pure, there has been quite a bit of traveling back and forth between categories, but I think they still capture major intellectual, social and political orientations in the culture. Perhaps in picturing black culture and identity through these categories, we can understand the persistence of certain beliefs in black culture that trace an ideological, even sociological, vein, and perhaps a class-based one as well, challenging strict precepts about generational difference. To be sure, the generational differences among the types are crucial and should be paid attention to—for instance, contemporary griots may have a more complex vision of the means to transmit black values than their predecessors. But the consistency of orientation may nonetheless be highlighted, and prove useful, as we engage historical arguments about the organization of black life and thought.

For our purposes, these types suggest that the relentless attempt to tag the current black generation, especially its poor and most vulnerable members, as somehow unalterably alienated from the mainstream of black life, and, most important, from the best traditions of our history, is in fact inaccurate. So much of the criticism endured by young and poor black folk revolves around their alleged ethical estrangement from the black moral mainstream in history. And yet, if we see that types of black people have consistently behaved or thought in a certain fashion—and this without casting an essentialist frame to the proceedings, but offering instead a nuanced, historical exploration of cultural continuity—we may dispense with the vindictive use of history against the black poor and young, such as the one Cosby has appealed to in his recent remarks. In its place, we can offer more sophisticated and subtle analyses of cultural traits and racial behaviors that have roots in antecedent practices. These types point to the heterogeneity of black culture and suggest that internal racial conflicts between different kinds of black folk have as much to do with current clashes over how we view the poor, for instance, as do simple differences in age and time. If nothing more, the existence of these types gestures toward discovering more complex explanations for black behavior beyond the clichés and stereotypes that plague the discussion.

If Cosby's discussion of the poor has been hampered by such clichés and stereotypes, and a failure to recognize the racial and cultural continuities suggested by these types, his apparent ignorance of the vast body of literature on the lives of the poor, or his deliberate rejection of its claims, especially about obstacles poor parents face, is even more problematic, and even depressing. It would take a gargantuan act of will to overlook the work of William Julius Wilson, Michael Katz, Robin D. G. Kelley, Elijah Anderson, Katherine Newman and literally hundreds of other scholars who have intelligently and in great detail specified the barriers poor parents face, from dwindling public capital to lethal public policies, including welfare reform, and the obstacles we have known

about for decades, including social demobilization precipi-
tated by structural changes in the economy—for instance, the
shift from manufacturing to service industries, the heightened
technological monopoly of labor, and the disappearance of
work.[80] Cosby has shown no familiarity with the depressing
statistics that make life hell for the poor, for instance, that
more people die younger in Harlem than in Bangladesh, that
nearly 25 percent of black America is poor, and that the min-
imum wage has plummeted by nearly 35 percent since 1968.[81]
And what of the best-selling books that document the plight
of the working poor, those citizens who rise every day out of
commitment to the work ethic but who are repaid with wages
that place them below the poverty line? Surely Cosby read
Barbara Ehrenreich's masterly journalistic exposé of the cruel
predicament of the working poor, *Nickel and Dimed*, or David
Shipler's sobering portrait of the same population, with a title
as austere and elegant as the subject it describes, *The Working
Poor*, whose opening lines should haunt Cosby and all of us:
"Most of the people I write about in this book do not have the
luxury of rage. They are caught in exhausting struggles. Their
wages do not lift them far enough from poverty to improve
their lives, and their lives, in turn, hold them back. The term
by which they are usually described, 'working poor,' should be
an oxymoron. Nobody who works hard should be poor in
America."[82] Even Cosby's attacks on single black mothers
contain an irony: Their numbers have actually gone down. In
1970, for black females between ages fifteen and seventeen,
there were 72 pregnancies per 1,000, while in 2000, there
were 30.9 per 1,000.[83] Despite his defenders' suggesting that

Cosby has a right to blast the poor because he was one of them, a crucial distinction must be made: Cosby was a poor *child*, not a poor *parent*. Even though there are numerous liabilities of being poor as a child, one of them isn't shouldering moral responsibility and social stigma for one's plight, a regular occurrence for poor parents.

There was a time when Cosby was much better informed and much more compassionate about the poor, earlier in his career, when he wasn't yet so far from poverty's orbit that he could fly off into rage against its victims. In an interview, Cosby painted a poignant portrait of what it was like to be poor.

> I think whites should begin to understand how personally destructive poverty is. Drive through Harlem sometime; if a cat's got no bread, he's just not going to look good. He'll look bad enough not having a job and having no money coming in; but if he comes out of a one-room apartment with three or four brothers, and his father has no job, how can he *possibly* look good? And when you're poor, nobody wants to have anything to do with you. . . . The point is: The poorer you are, the uglier you are. And that poverty creeps into every part of black people's lives: poor education, poor housing, poor sanitation, poor medical care and, as a result of all these, poor jobs. . . . But the truth of the matter is that no parent can command a kid's respect if the parent doesn't have a strong game going for himself—if the father doesn't have a job. The kid will hear his mother chewing the old man out

because he's not working. Or he'll hear them both moaning and groaning because there's no money coming in. . . . If the kid's working and the old man isn't, he's not the father, man; he's just an older guy who can beat you up . . . because he's bigger and stronger, but he certainly isn't anybody you can use as an example of what you want to be when you grow up. . . . Men on relief should be taught skilled jobs. That's only half of it, though, because it isn't enough just to teach skills. We must also make sure there are jobs available to use the skills.[84]

That's the Cosby we need to revive: a critical, clear, compassionate analyst, perhaps even an informal ethnographer, of the lives of the poor. We need not pity the poor, nor should we deny the huge problems among the parents of the black poor, but we should never lose sight of the colossal barriers they face just to get up in the morning, just to put one foot in front of the next, just to make ends meet. What we need more of is the relentless effort to help lift the poor from their condition even as we enable them to respect themselves and support their families through the hard work for which they are often given little credit. In this era of family values, we must learn to value all families. As Cosby's family troubles prove, one need not be poor to experience failure or setback, and as the lives of so many poor folk suggest, you need not be wealthy to act decently in society and to love, and be loved, at home.

Chapter Five

Shadow Boxing with a Scapegoat?

(or, Do White People Matter?)

*I heard a prize fight manager say to his fellow who was los-
ing badly, "David, listen to me. It's not what's he's doing to
you. It's what you're not doing." (laughter).*

*We cannot blame white people. White people (clapping) . . .
white people don't live over there. They close up the shop early.
The Korean ones still don't know us well enough. . .they stay
open 24 hours (laughter). . .Brown Versus the Board of
Education is no longer the white person's problem. We've got to
take the neighborhood back (clapping). . . Now look, I'm telling
you. It's not what they're doing to us. It's what we're not doing.*

*   *   *

Ever since Bill Cosby pilloried the poor, he has been praised for at long last breaking the silence about black pathology and the failure of lower-class blacks to see that their miserable lot is all their doing. Blaming white folk is a game that black folk have got to give up, and fast, before lacerating denials of our self-imposed downfall take all the wind from our cultural sails. For Cosby, self-initiative, not systemic solutions, is the way to black salvation. But taking Cosby seriously can only mean the continued frustration of all good people in the quest to figure out the causes of black suffering. It's not that taking responsibility for oneself is in any way damaging to the poor, and, in fact, it is quite a good thing for them, and for all of us, to do. It is, rather, the heartless rider to such a belief that is the problem: the illusion that by assuming such responsibility the problems of the poor will disappear. It's no sweat off Cosby's back if he turns out to be wrong; but it may bring greater social stigma to the poor, and threatens to plunge those who buy Cosby's argument deeper into regretful self-loathing because they believe they haven't solved the riddle of their poverty. In truth, Cosby's position vividly revives the embarrassment over the bad behavior of the poor that the black elite have felt for more than a century. Cosby says he doesn't care what whites think, but in truth, his embarrassment suggests he cares a great deal.

Cosby's position is dangerous because it aggressively ignores white society's responsibility in creating the problems he wants the poor to fix on their own. His position is especially disingenuous because he has always, with two notable exceptions, gone soft on white society for its role in black suffering. Now that he has been enshrined by conservative white critics as a courageous spokesman for the truth that most black leaders leave aside, Cosby has been wrongly saluted for positions that are well staked out in black political ideology. This false situation sets him up as a hero and a dissenter, when he is neither. Self-help philosophy is broadly embraced in black America; but black leaders and thinkers have warned against the dangers of emphasizing self-help without setting it in its proper context. It creates less controversy and resistance—and, in fact, it assures white praise—if black thinkers and leaders make whites feel better by refusing to demand of them the very thing that whites feel those leaders should demand of their followers, including the poor: responsibility. Like so many black elite before him, Cosby, as a public figure who has assumed the mantle of leadership, has failed in his responsibility to represent the interests, not simply demand the compliance, of the less fortunate.

It should surprise no one that Bill Cosby has let white folk off the hook for the problems of black America. Cosby, as we've seen, has never been comfortable in confronting white society over the legacy of white supremacy. His emphasis on color-blind comedy, and his retreat from social activism, were as much about avoiding the discomforts of race—including, oddly enough, the responsibility to represent as a fortunate black the interests of other blacks—as they were about overcoming racism. That's the case because deciding to "work white" meant that the white audience, his bread and butter, must never be toasted. "People have to like you if you're going to be a comic," Cosby said in 1969. "After a cat establishes the fact that he's funny, 40 percent of the pressure is eased up on him because, when he walks out, people already like him."[1] Cosby's likability extended to *The Cosby Show* in large part because he refused to put white folk on the spot by speaking about race at all. Sut Jhally and Justin Lewis, in their empirical study of *The Cosby Show*, point out a disturbing consequence of the show's success: that it made white America believe that everything was fine in black America, that racism was no longer a bother and that whites wouldn't have to wrestle with their role in a society that was still plagued by racial inequality. As Jhally and Lewis write:

> Our argument is, in essence, a simple one: programs like *The Cosby Show* encourage the viewer to see the real world through rose-tinted spectacles. . . . [T]he viewers' ability to distinguish the TV world from the real one does not prevent them from confusing the two. *The Cosby Show*, we discovered, helps to cultivate an impression, particularly among white people, that racism is no longer a problem in the United States. Our audience study revealed that the overwhelming majority of white TV viewers felt racism was a sin of the past; *The Cosby Show*, accordingly, represented a new "freedom of opportunity" apparently enjoyed by black people. If Cliff and Clair can make it, in other words, then so can all blacks. The positive images of blacks promoted by shows like *Cosby* have, therefore, distinctly negative consequences by creating a conservative and

comfortable climate of opinion that allows white America to ignore widespread racial inequality.[2]

Not only did *The Cosby Show* encourage whites to be racially oblivious (*Cosby* debuted halfway through Ronald Reagan's rule and, like the president, the comedian possessed the uncanny ability to make millions of citizens feel very good about being American, an easy enough feat since they were joined at the hip of nostalgic patriarchy, Cosby as Father, Reagan as Grandfather, a partnership fueled by racial amnesia), but it also shifted the blame for poor blacks who weren't like the Huxtables onto the poor themselves. Henry Louis Gates, Jr., argues that the images on *The Cosby Show*, much like those on the controversial early '50s series *Amos 'n' Andy*, took on a life of their own in the culture and reinforced harmful conservative political beliefs.

> This helps to explain why "Cosby" makes some people uncomfortable: As the dominant representation of blacks on TV, it suggests that blacks are solely responsible for their social conditions, with no acknowledgment of the severely constricted life opportunities that most black people face. What's troubling about the phenomenal success of "Cosby," then, is what was troubling about the earlier popularity of "Amos 'n' Andy": it's not the representation itself (Cliff Huxtable, a child of college-educated parents, is altogether believable), but the role it begins to play in our culture, the status it takes on as being, well, truly representative. As long as *all*

blacks were represented in demeaning or peripheral roles, it was possible to believe that American racism was, as it were, indiscriminate. The social vision of "Cosby," however, reflecting the miniscule integration of blacks into the upper middle class (having "white money," my mother used to say, rather than "colored" money) reassuringly throws the blame for poverty back onto the impoverished.[3]

That's a point that Cosby sorely needs to remember.

It's a point Cosby might have easily grasped nearly thirty years ago, when he wrote his 1976 doctoral dissertation, or before that, nearly forty years ago, when he hosted a 1968 television special, *Black History: Lost, Stolen, or Strayed?* These two documents, along with an interview Cosby did in *Playboy* magazine in 1969, are the rare exceptions when Cosby took off the gloves, and the blinders, to discuss race in public with candor and discernment.[4] In Cosby's career, none of these three performances have garnered anything near the attention paid to his albums, TV series or books. They are radical departures from his color-blind catechism, which explains, perhaps, their relative obscurity in his corpus. I've already taken up his dissertation, which bluntly engages the obstacles to black educational achievement, earlier in the book; his provocative, race-conscious narration in *Black History*, though it packs a rhetorical wallop (when I saw this as a ten-year-old in school, it was high octane fuel to study black culture, and take pride in myself, even more), and while doubtless an expression of his views at the time, was scripted for him to read.

But Cosby is totally unfettered in his *Playboy* interview, parts of which I've discussed already, and it is here that one finds a reflective soul who was much more willing than he is today to hold white America accountable for its numerous sins against his brothers and sisters.[5] It is tempting to classify Cosby's remarks as merely a reflection of the racial times in which they were hatched, but that is unlikely, at least not as a primary explanation for their existence, since Cosby so diligently guarded his color-blind bona fides even then. It is more likely that this was an aspect of Cosby's identity that he routinely suppressed, both in private in mixed-racial company and in a public composed of whites of every ideological stripe, but that he chose, at this moment, to reveal to the open-minded, liberal white readers of a men's magazine.[6]

Cosby's interlocutor, Lawrence Linderman, asked Cosby about his comedy routines, his role on *I Spy*, and black stereotypes. Linderman wondered whether Cosby agreed with Black Panther leader Eldridge Cleaver's belief that a civil war was in the offing if black demands for equality went unheeded. "A lot of black men feel that way, and I can't say they're wrong, because America's resistance to giving the black man a fair shake is almost unbelievably strong," Cosby replied. "And when black people keep butting their heads against the stone wall of racism, there are those who feel they *have* to become violent."[7] Cosby suggested that there could be no denying that there should be equality in America, but that the obstacle to equality lay not in black people themselves, as Cosby now contends, but in white society. "[T]he white man doesn't want us to have it," Cosby said, "because then he'll be giving up a freedom of his—to reject us because of color. I really think that black people could march until the end of the world and the majority of whites still wouldn't want to give up what they see as their precious right to be racists." Of course, some may decide that Cosby felt as he did then about white resistance because the legal barriers to black equality remained, but that is inaccurate, since by the time of his *Playboy* interview, all the major civil rights legislation from the '60s had already been passed: the 1964 Civil Rights Act, which made discrimination illegal in public places, such as restaurants, hotels and theaters; the 1965 Voting Rights Act, which gave black southerners the right to vote; and the 1968 Civil Rights Act (the Fair Housing Act), passed in the wake of Martin Luther King, Jr.'s, assassination, which outlawed housing discrimination.

It was King's assassination that drove Cosby to conclude that "the nonviolent approach appear[s] irrelevant to many black people." Cosby believed that nonviolence was "as meaningful today as when [King] was alive," even as he understood the disavowal of the philosophy by activists like Stokely Carmichael, a complexity of thought that shows in Cosby's mapping of the black ideological landscape. "I don't think people can arbitrarily be put into neat categories of violent or nonviolent. I can tell you that I *don't* believe in letting black people get pushed around when they're in the right. If a lot of black people no longer believe in nonviolence, it's because they've lost all faith and trust in white men." That loss of faith, alas, seems to have had little to do with the black failure to take advantage of increasing opportunities and everything to do with the persistence of structural, and, yes, systemic, barriers to progress. Cosby even believed that "[m]any intelligent and educated black people are tired, just tired, of being noble, of not striking back," a statement that may have revealed Cosby's own frustration with his color-blind ideals and his political noninvolvement. (In fact, earlier the same year, another reporter noted Cosby's "remarkable self-control—at what cost in self-repression, tension and future grief, who can say?")[8]

Cosby made a remarkable comparison, one also made by King a year earlier in a little-known sermon, between the condition of blacks and those citizens of the world interred in concentration camps.[9] Cosby believed that many whites secretly hoped that blacks would renounce nonviolence so that a law could be produced to "quietly march us off into concentration camps until we learned that this is *their* country." When Linderman countered that most whites think that the "concentration camp theory is a myth," Cosby elaborated.

Look, it's possible to have concentration camps in Chicago—or in almost any large city—by simply blocking off the ghetto, putting barbed wire around it and not letting anybody in or out. This isn't going to happen until we give the whites a little more of a reason for putting us in a concentration camp, but it isn't too far away. . . . Farfetched as it may sound, black people will actually go to war if they're driven to it: Not *all* black people, but the ones who feel they're willing to give up their lives in order to mess up this country, to bring America to its knees.[10]

Linderman asked Cosby whether such a war could be averted and he bluntly replied, "That's up to the white man. He's at the point now where he will either have to allow the black man his civil rights or try to wipe him out." Cosby expertly mapped the escalating methods of black dissent called into being by staunch white resistance: singing, sit-ins and marching; enduring beatings, burnings and bombings; the assassinations of black leaders; and the sparking of urban rebellions. When Linderman evoked Malcolm X's famous application to black struggle of the adage that the squeaky hinge got the oil—that only black violence could get white America to respond—Cosby proved to be Malcolm's metaphoric match, and perhaps even more emphatic in his blistering indictment of the genocidal intentions of the white establishment.

I really think that, all along, the white man has been oiling the hinge with the secret intention of slamming the door. And when he finally slams it shut for good—and has his genocidal war—he won't have to worry about the squeak anymore. What will be left won't exactly be a country, but at least the place will be well run. Except that America will have to find someone else to dance to its music. The Mexicans will folk-dance for a while, and then Puerto Ricans, and then the Chinese people will be dancing; but soon enough, *that* squeaky-hinged door will be slammed shut, too—and padlocked.[11]

Cosby spoke powerfully about how racist white leaders foment tension between the races. He argued that the easy access to guns heightened racial tensions—"The way I look at it is that guns are sold to protect whites against blacks"— especially between blacks and poor whites, since the "leaders of bigotry have got to keep the poor, ignorant white cat really upset and nervous, so that their friends the gun manufacturers can sell him some guns and maybe even some bazookas as well." Cosby wasn't sure whether race war could be prevented, but if that prospect was to be strengthened, it rested in amassing black political power, such as had occurred in Cleveland and Gary, Indiana, with the election of the nation's first black mayors. But Cosby admitted that these politicians would most likely be hamstrung by white boards of directors and city planners who would block the path of racial progress. Cosby also revealed that most blacks don't trust black politicians who are beholden to white interests. He colorfully explored the "field nigger" versus "house nigger" dichotomy, perhaps most famously employed by Malcolm X as a way to distinguish between blacks on plantation fields, who had the fate of the race in mind, and those in the house with the master, who made his interests, not the well-being of blacks, the highest priority.

Cosby was equally eloquent about the misleading belief among some critics that the immigrant experience cast a chastising lens on blacks who failed to match the achievements of citizens who hailed from foreign shores. Cosby anticipated some of the arguments made by contemporary scholars about how ethnic Europeans are remade as white Americans in the crucible of race, while blacks continue to be excluded from the privileges of white skin in the mainstream.

> When the French, Poles and Czechs come off the boat, they're welcomed to America, "the land of the free, the home of the brave." The Statue of Liberty welcomes them, but it doesn't welcome the man who was *born* here—the black man. There's no lamp lit for him; so the black man has to climb up there and light it himself. . . . If all these European countries are so groovy, then how come when their guys get off the boat, they turn out to be bigots?[12]

For Cosby, the "unkept promises and half-truths" of whites to blacks have issued in a "justifiable distrust" of white America. He argued that it was just for black folk to run their own organizations, "even at the risk of alienating white friends," since true white friends would understand the need for racial autonomy.

Although Cosby has recently urged an almost blind devotion to self-help strategies while leaving aside concern for structural factors, he encouraged a vastly different approach years ago. When Linderman posed to Cosby the results of a poll suggesting that "most white people believe there's no real difference in the way they grow up and the way blacks grow up—and conclude that blacks themselves are totally responsible for all their social and economic problems"—a statement that very much reflects Cosby's current mindset, showing that he's only now caught up to what white folk believed thirty-five years ago, the same white folk he deemed as hurtful to black interests—Cosby sang a different tune.

> I find it hard to believe that white people don't know what life is like for the average American black. Did his mother have to pay more than $200 for a couch that costs white people $125? A guy in the slums buys a car for $150 and has to pay $400 a year insurance on it. The ghetto supermarkets sell food you can't find anywhere else; did you ever eat green meat and green bread? How many winters have white people spent with rats scurrying around their apartments at night, with windows boarded up but not keeping out the cold, and with no heat? Try to get a ghetto slumlord to fix up an apartment and you'll know what frustration and bitterness is.[13]

Not only did Cosby call out the extraordinary shortsightedness, and unfairness, of whites' believing that black folk had caused their own problems, but he discerned as well that "most black people have finally discovered they've been deluding themselves." In answer to Linderman's terse, "About what?" Cosby brilliantly summarized the insight of many blacks torn between fighting for justice and acknowledging the bone-deep refusal of whites to accept them. The civil rights movement under King's leadership had forced racism "out into the open, so the world could see it." It was then that blacks "found out that most whites just didn't *want* them to have a growing place in America's future." That realization, Cosby says, was the seed of blacks' finding salvation in their own race, and "we turned to ourselves for help, as we had to." Building a haven to nurture a proud black identity was crucial to these self-help measures. For Cosby, many blacks had begun to go to necessary extremes to bolster their identities and to reject

> white power, white imperialism and . . . [t]he main white value—greed. Through greed, whites have been fooled into thinking that freedom for black people means they'll lose their jobs, their homes, even the clothes off their backs. Certain ideas have been laid on the white man to exploit his greed, and the windup is that whites, because of greed, think all black men are lazy and shiftless and everything else represented in racist stereotyping. But this has all been the result of lies, and white people now have to listen to the truth: Freedom, for any man, is a *need* like food and water. The black man needs his freedom and he is determined to get it—now. If white America chooses to withhold equality from the black man, the result is going to be disaster for this country. But if whites allow the black man the same civil rights they themselves take for granted, then they're *really* in store

for a shock: this country will turn into the coolest and grooviest society the world has ever seen.[14]

Cosby's intelligent and unsparing dissection of white supremacy, a rare public gesture by this color-blind figure, offers stirring testimony against his present refusal to hold white society responsible for its role in black suffering *at all*, or more than perfunctorily, in asides that serve as begrudging concessions and preludes to more attack. ("And please don't give me anything about systemic racism," Cosby said in a Detroit stop on a national Blame-the-Poor Tour billed as *A Conversation with Bill Cosby*. "Yes, it's there, but why is your mouth not working?")[15] Cosby's ill-tempered insistence that the poor not blame white folk for their troubles appears to be at once a caricature of how the black poor think of their condition and a flat disavowal of the history he so eloquently covered in his *Playboy* interview.

The black poor, like most black people, have a more sophisticated and perhaps more complex understanding than we might imagine about how they have come to be poor and what they must do about it. Few studies of the black poor portray them as endlessly griping about "the white man," and when they do, they understand "the white man" not literally but rather in metaphoric terms, as a symbol of the myriad forces that have helped to determine their plight. Many black poor, as we have seen, share some of the same values that motivate the mainstream—hard work, when they can get it; the desire for their children to prosper; the dream of upward mobility; and the soulful embrace of decent living. If they know, as most of them surely do, that they have kept their values and made every effort to climb out of the endless pit of poverty, they may sadly conclude that they are cursed, with social scientists and critics right there to confirm their suspicions, while no amount of corrective theology will remove its trace completely from their souls, especially in this age of the gospel of prosperity. (The gospel says, "If you're blessed and favored, you'll be prosperous, and showered with material goods, and if not, you're praying and living wrong," another way to blame the poor for their plight, except now it's more lethal because it's under God's signature.) Or they may believe that they are blessed *because* they're poor, adjusting to their inevitable plight and seeing in it, defensively, for their salvation and sanity, the design of The Spirit, which, in some cases, is nearly as bad as feeling cursed. Or they see that they are the victims of forces beyond their control but against which, with God's help, or with the help of more secular consolations, they are pledged to fight, if not for themselves, then for their children's sake.

Those poor who arrive at the latter conclusion (and it is the bulk of them, it miraculously seems), even if they are taunted by the lure of the first two options, have already mobilized a keen sense of self-determining action. Too often, some of them take on conservative beliefs about why they are poor as a kind of wish fulfillment: If they conform to the narrative that hard work leads to success, despite the contrary testimony of their lives and those of many of their friends, they may strike the existential lottery and get out of the ghetto. Ironically, the more desolate their condition, the more determined some poor people are to strictly abide by such beliefs, because they are so desperate for it to be true. They are even willing at times to sacrifice their survival skepticism, the instincts that screen errors and lies, in the hope that they can trade distrust of their own instincts for rewards—of upward mobility and material security. Given the war on the poor being fiercely waged in the culture, the moral counternarratives, the ones that admit to continuing obstacles and that proclaim their worth not because they're poor but because they have managed to remain human in inhuman circumstances, wither on the vine. Cosby's blaming of the poor for failing to take the blame for their lives (though in truth many more poor people than should already do) and for blaming, instead, the white man, deprives the poor of a reasonable, empirical explanation for their plight and keeps them from connecting to a venerable legacy of social action, both of which were symbolized in Cosby's *Playboy* interview.

What, then, has led Cosby to withdraw his kindly countenance from the poor and to offer them, instead, a menacing scowl, while rejecting the explanations he offered in his *Playboy* interview? As far as I can tell, there are two factors. First, he is embarrassed by how poor black folk behave. Cosby's embarrassment is widely shared among the black elite and harkens back a century to when black aristocrats promoted a philosophy of racial uplift to prove to racist whites that blacks were human—a favorite Cosby theme. As a result, upper-class blacks became moral cops: They policed poor black communities from the pulpit, the lectern, the convention floor, and the fraternity and sorority hall, damning the pathologies they believed were ruining the reputation of the race. Cosby's views are little more than an update of this mode of racial reckoning. Second, Cosby seems to have departed in fatal ways from the hard-won racial wisdom about the individual traits and societal forces that influence one's economic and social standing. There is often a critical ideological balance in black communities that colors our beliefs about poverty— about what explains why some people are born poor but escape, while others remain trapped. Cosby's beliefs tap into complex views held by blacks about the causes of poverty that we will need to explore before situating his comments.

The philosophy of racial uplift, dating back to the nineteenth century, rests on the belief among black elites that the lower classes of black folk had to be roped in before their moral lapses gave white folk even more reason to repress black life. Indeed, the tensions between the black elite and the working classes and poor folk that I describe in Chapter 4 grow out of the philosophy of racial uplift. Black aristocrats took to chastising poor black folk in a variety of venues, including schools, churches and community and fraternal organizations, seeking to inculcate in their loose charges the Victorian values to which they subscribed and which they hoped would win them acceptance from the white majority. The ultimate goal of racial uplift philosophy was to prove to white folk that the black race had made significant progress in reaching the goal of true civilization. Ironically, many of these whites would never themselves meet the strict standards advocated by many black aristocrats, and neither would they have to prove themselves worthy of the very requirements they imposed on black life, thanks to one of the more gleaming hypocrisies that composed the immoral backbone of white supremacy.

Racial uplift, however, wasn't a simple affair, and had at least two prongs.[16] The first prong, a more interesting and organic vision of racial help that was obscured rather quickly by its more elitist interpretation, extended from the folk religion of slaves and touted personal, spiritual and, at points, social transcendence of earthly suffering. Education and theological resistance to white supremacy were viewed as crucial to black liberation and the social uplift of black folk from the pits of political degradation. This vision of uplift was prominent in the aftermath of slavery and during Reconstruction. The second prong protruded from the efforts of black elites to promote what historian Kevin Gaines says was "self-help, racial solidarity, temperance, thrift, chastity, social purity, patriarchal authority, and the accumulation of wealth. . . . Amidst legal and extralegal repression, many black elites sought status, moral authority, and recognition of their humanity by distinguishing themselves, as bourgeois agents of civilization, from the presumably undeveloped black majority; hence the phrase, so purposeful and earnest, yet so often of ambiguous significance, 'uplifting the race.'"[17]

Within black female religious circles the notion of racial uplift was translated into what religious historian Evelyn Brooks Higginbotham calls the "politics of respectability."[18] Black female religious elites sought to transmit middle-class values to the black masses to bolster notions of self-help and to win the approval and respect of white America. The politics of respectability "equated public behavior with individual self-respect and with advancement of African Americans as a group. They felt certain that 'respectable' behavior in public would earn their people a measure of esteem from white America, and hence they strove to win the black lower class's psychological allegiance to temperance, industriousness, thrift, refined manners, and Victorian sexual morals."[19] While black religious women also attacked the failures of the American political system to provide racial equality for blacks, they were equally adamant about fussing at poor blacks for failing to adopt middle-class lifestyles. Black women also formed clubs and sororities to ensure the racial uplift of the black masses, pursuing their goals within a male-dominated culture whose elitist leadership had imposed yet another set of expectations on women to be moral exemplars for the masses and respectful of male privilege.[20]

Black elites also used the press to lob rhetorical bombs at the black poor, some of which rival Cosby's assault for color and cruelty. *Chicago Defender* editor Robert S. Abbott repeatedly called out from his pages for the uncouth black masses, newly migrated from southern cities and hamlets, to behave in more appropriate, that is, restrained, middle-class fashion. A series of cartoons that ran in the *Defender* in the 1920s and 1930s capture in their titles the efforts of the black elite to shame the black poor into behaving better: "Folks We Can Get Along Without" and later "Folks We Must Live Without."[21] The *Defender* warred against the black masses in editorials like the one entitled "THE NIGGER," where the term, according to the writer, was justly applied to the "handkerchief heads that are coming to this city from many of the southwestern states," blacks who talked loud, exhibited brash behavior and wore shabby clothing.[22] In New York's *Amsterdam News*, a columnist complained that young blacks who claimed they had "no chance" to make it in the white world should "deport [themselves] with greater decorum and decency on street cars" and quit acting "like so many jungle apes." After noting that the young black used "the street car" as "his stage and he is the star performer," and after observing young black men issuing catcalls to black and white girls, playing musical instruments, using profanity and appearing in "the car in full monkey regalia and strut[ting] as though they were the princes of the jungle," the writer concluded that "What we need among us is about five million funerals."[23]

From the beginning, these internal tensions in racial uplift thinking, between its more populist, resistive leanings and the elitist shadow cast by black aristocrats who became the public face of the philosophy, have defined the ambivalence black folk feel toward racial uplift. There is great enthusiasm among the masses for racial uplift that embraces and encourages the rank and file; in turn, there is among this group well-deserved skepticism about the chiding that comes down from well-positioned, well-heeled, well-appointed blacks who seek more to appease white folk than to relieve the suffering of blacks. Of course, the black elite have historically found great refuge in the private observance, and public performance, of their civility; such civility is not only an argument in defense of their humanity but it is, as well, an argument against the behavior of those (poor) blacks thought to undermine their positions and privileges among whites. To be sure, there was, and is, not a strict line of class affiliation keyed to even elitist views of racial uplift; some poor blacks embrace such views in the hope that they might actually approach the dignity promised, which means, of course, unhealthy doses of self-abnegation, given that the price of admission to such fraternity is the conscious rejection of the identity they have inherited or invented. And in some cases, the black elite commit class suicide and reach beyond the limits of their circles to embrace the masses—Martin Luther King, Jr., comes readily to mind.

With Cosby, the Afristocracy has reclaimed the most harmful, hurtful dimensions of its racial uplift role—which, ironically enough, has always ridden down on the masses of black folk, so perhaps it should be re-baptized as racial castdown—and spoken in its most virulent voice about the poor. While it is clear that Cosby's mean-spirited attacks are of a piece with the most vicious elements of racial uplift philosophy, they might have as easily veered toward the redemptive elements of uplift: focusing on elements of mass black culture that enable black folk to resist their oppression, transcend their suffering and transform their pain. Instead, Cosby has added to their misery. As were his most prickly predecessors, Cosby is so obviously embarrassed by the masses of black folk that he has taken to insulting and, truly, intimidating them, from a bully pulpit that stretches across the media and extends into arenas across the nation. Besides wanting white folk to think of black folk as human, Cosby's intent appears also to be to get rid of the scourge of unwashed masses whose language, thinking, behavior, clothing and bodies are irre-

deemably offensive. Of course, there is ample cause for concern, even alarm, about some younger blacks and the poor,
but the answer to their condition is surely not a beloved
father figure firing missiles at them from an ideological
launchpad located in the white media, operating from within
a worldview more easily associated with uncaring quarters in
the mainstream than with healing traditions of black social
movement and self-criticism. Rather than encounter the
problems of the poor, or the conditions that offer them limited options, which often, yes, lead to poor choices, Cosby
blasts them in condescending anger. He has, in his most
recent comments, ceased being curious, or courageous, about
the sources of poverty and surrendered to a cynical reactionary politics that, as William Ryan said in 1971, blames
the victim.[24]

In our society, according to sociologist Joe Feagin, there
are three ways to explain the causes of poverty: the individualistic, which blames the poor for their poverty; the structural, which emphasizes economic and social forces; and the
fatalistic, which isolates factors like bad luck, chance and ill-
ness.[25] Since the myth of romantic individualism still strongly
grips the culture, it is unsurprising that the individualistic
explanation for poverty is most widely favored. In this view,
people are poor because they lack thrift, are lazy and have
loose morals and other character defects.[26] Neither should it
be surprising that those with greater status in society, for
instance, those who are white, older and have higher
incomes, are drawn to individualistic explanations of poverty,
while those with lower status, those who are black, younger

and with lower incomes, stress structural elements, although they often cling tightly as well to individualistic explanations.[27] This testifies to the apparent hegemony the individualist account enjoys across the culture, even among the working class and poor themselves. In contrast to this pattern, structural accounts of poverty's origins fluctuate according to group membership, personal experience and the social climate at any given time. Instead of displacing individualistic explanations, structural forces compete for a hearing alongside the dominant ideology. In times of crisis, however, whether a severe economic downturn or racial rebellion, there is greater tolerance and support for structural explanations.[28] Perhaps this is so because big social crises are bound to affect folk we know to be decent and hardworking and thus we are more sympathetic to redistributing wealth and implementing social welfare initiatives than might otherwise be the case. Also, traumatic snags in the social fabric created by visible racial unrest or cultural disquiet remind us that there is greater work yet to be done to knit us together as "E Pluribus Unum." They also underscore how our thinking about who deserves relief from social suffering is as much a matter of trust as it is a matter of objective calculation.

As a group, blacks are only slightly less likely to single out individualistic factors as the cause of poverty than whites, but at the same time, blacks embrace structural explanations much more forcefully. Much more than whites, who favor individualist explanations in greater numbers, blacks embrace both explanations of poverty.[29] This intriguing simultaneity of beliefs among blacks challenges flat either-or thinking, and may suggest why black views on the causes of poverty are more complex than usually allowed for. It also gives the lie to folk like Cosby who labor under the mistaken assumption that most blacks, even the poor, don't understand that, to some degree, in some cases, personal factors play a role in poverty, even if that role is much slighter than those who would like to lay the entire burden on the laps of the poor prefer to believe. Most black folk, it seems, are already quite willing, even when it's not in their interest, or even especially relevant, to take account of individual responsibility in computing what must be done to explain or relieve their poverty. The need, therefore, for loud lectures about hard work and personal initiative is vastly overplayed and, in many cases, those lectures are vainly repetitive, more an instance of the lecturer needing to prove he is willing to take the poor to the woodshed than a case of the poor forgetting their obligation to do as much as they can to forsake indigence. (The presumption of rational self-identification is key here, too, since most folk don't want to be poor, and if we can imagine ourselves as them, and vice versa, we must presume that they would act exactly as we would to escape poverty. This view was succinctly stated by Malcolm X when he said, "I'm the man you think you are. . . . If you want to know what I'll do, figure out what you'll do. I'll do the same thing—only more of it.")[30] Thus, when black folk support social intervention on behalf of the poor, such as redistributive measures, and when they accent structural features of poverty, or fatalistic elements like poor health or bad luck, they must not be seen as doing reflexively what comes naturally to blacks. Such views slight the complex moral and social landscape black folk occupy, including the poor. Eschewing simplistic or reactionary thinking, they often sort through the causes of poverty and combine them in a fashion that is more complicated and honest, and certainly more humane, than their most vicious critics.

When blacks lean toward structural explanations of poverty, emphasizing low wages, severe underemployment, racism and poor schooling, there is at work what may be termed *formal empathy*, or the principled identification with the difficulties and struggles of the majority of blacks beyond the boundaries of one's individual experience. Even if one is socially stable and economically secure, one nevertheless opts to take account of the forces that fail the masses of blacks— economic inequality, racial hierarchy, social dislocation, environmental devastation, material deprivation, restructured work and the like—in explaining why so many are poor. Formal empathy neither discounts nor exaggerates the role of personal responsibility in an explanation of poverty; instead, it relates individual initiative to the possibility of its achievement in a world where inequalities remain entrenched. Any calculus of social desert, or blame, must rest on a just tabulation of the forces that bolster or blunt the drive to move beyond one's difficult circumstances. To suggest that the lack of personal initiative is the source, and not the consequence, of poverty, is to confuse cause and effect. This is another way of saying that formal empathy insists on tracing onto the moral landscape the anatomy of social responsibility, a matter I will elaborate shortly.

Social science research on the "underdog perspective" suggests that gender (women are more likely than men to view structural causes of poverty as crucial) and household income (those with lower incomes are clearly inclined to invoke structural factors) play a significant role in shaping beliefs about the causes of and solutions to poverty.[31] When one throws race into the mix, there is clear evidence that experience of oppression increases the likelihood of pointing to structural features to explain personal and social status. Even those citizens with greater education seem to have more awareness of the variables that create inequality and, generally speaking, have greater compassion for the poor and socially vulnerable.[32] One might also use education to get at contrasting beliefs about poverty by focusing on how people explain to themselves the social-psychological factors that determined their success in formal schooling and work. When one compares "internal and external self-explanations" for educational and employment success and applies them to beliefs about poverty, there are interesting racial differences.[33] Internal self-explanations stress social-psychological variables having to do with ability (talent, intelligence and skills) and effort (desire, dedication, motivation), while external self-explanations involve social-psychological variables that have to do with opportunities (family background and other life circumstances) and luck (fate and chance).

For whites, as might be expected, resort to internal self-explanations strengthens beliefs that individualistic elements cause poverty, while adopting external self-explanations leads to an emphasis on structural factors.[34] This suggests that whites view their personal situations and those of others in a similar fashion. The appeal to internal self-explanations reflects the embrace of the dominant ideology of individualism and makes it more likely that its advocates will stress personal responsibility to the strongest degree in blaming people for their own poverty. The use by whites of external self-explanations suggests a willingness to cut across the dominant ideological grain and to underscore the role of structural factors in accounting for poverty. The difference between the two tells how whites view the causes of poverty. As sociologist Matthew Hunt argues, when "whites say, 'I made it because of me,' they tend to view the society as an open system in which people have similar chances, personal responsibility is the rule applied to everyone, and poverty gets explained in the terms of internal/individual-level factors. Similarly, when whites believe they have been held back by outside, external forces . . . they also assume that similar . . . barriers in society must exist for others (e.g. the poor)."[35]

For black (and brown) people, on the other hand, there are huge differences. The use of internal self-explanations by blacks underscores for them the role of structural, not individualistic, elements in the cause of poverty. External self-explanations, on the other hand, increase the likelihood of individualistic, not structural, explanations for poverty. There appears to be a dramatically different understanding of the relationship between personal experience and causal explanations of status in black communities than in white ones. As Hunt suggests, one reason for this might be that black experience is conditioned by class and caste. For blacks who are

gainfully employed, this results in a halfway house of thinking: "they are better off than the abject poor but still relatively disadvantaged compared with middle-class whites,"
suggesting that they are in a unique position to understand
both "their relative success and the importance of beliefs in
internal, individual sources of advancement" and the "relative disadvantage and the continuing significance of external,
environmental barriers to equality with whites."[36] Thus, for
blacks, internal self-explanations flow "from a sense of having
worked hard and having made sacrifices to achieve personal
success and the status that gainful employment brings,"
although, unlike whites, who generalize from their personal
experiences to the poor, employed black folk have more complex views that are shaped by their racial status.[37] As a result,
even when employed blacks explain their success by internal
elements like hard work, talent and dedication, they also realize they have had to surmount structural barriers in the
process, leading them to believe that other black folk face
similar obstacles. Thus, internal elements are but one factor
in explaining success. Black folk often understand the role of
both internal and external factors, and thus, "assuming personal responsibility, or saying 'I made it because of me,' does
not preclude—indeed it can increase—the acknowledgment
that structural barriers exist in society."[38]

It is clear from social science research that many black folk
are capable of sustaining two apparently contradictory views:
recognizing that individual responsibility for personal destiny
is enormously important to the culture, while at the same
time acknowledging the structural barriers that prevent both

social justice and self-realization. Most successful black folk appear to recognize that while they have worked hard, applied themselves diligently and taken advantage of every opportunity to enhance their God-given talents, other black folk may not be as fortunate as they are in laying claim to their educational and employment aspirations. The sensitivity among gainfully employed black folk to the plight of less fortunate members of the race contrasts with the beliefs of most whites, who lean far too heavily on individual responsibility as the nearly exclusive determinant of social status. Since the bulk of blacks embrace structural explanations for poverty while leaving room for personal agency—and while the black poor themselves often seek to exercise to the best of their ability individual responsibility in the midst of incredibly difficult circumstances—it stands to reason that prominent and fortunate blacks have a responsibility to acknowledge that complexity while putting forth arguments that defend the most vulnerable of the race. This holds even for conservative members of the race. Although newfangled black neoconservatives have often forgotten this lesson, black conservatives from the past were more willing to acknowledge structural barriers while emphasizing personal initiative.

Bill Cosby has forsaken these insights, the result of centuries of struggle, to embrace in his public comments a callous disposition to the poor that resembles the most extreme and acid views promulgated by some conservative white critics. Cosby has clearly spurned formal empathy and embraced almost exclusively an individualistic framework, leaving behind the close attention to structural features—poor housing, terrible classrooms and tough neighborhoods—that he so ably explored in his *Playboy* interview. Just as in his comedy Cosby has consistently sought to appeal to a white audience, his recent views certainly play to the preference among most whites to explain their situation and, therefore, the situation of all others, in terms of initiative and personal responsibility. Cosby undoubtedly is aware of the conservative cultural and moral values that are widely shared in most black communities, even among the poor, a fact that not only contradicts the image his public harangues present—that most poor blacks have lost their moral compass—but also suggests that calls for personal responsibility are ethically redundant. It is not that such calls are not useful, and to a large degree predictable, given that, in a certain view of these matters, the train of moral enlightenment glides on tracks of sheer repetition. But that is different from dissing an entire group of folk—a fact that is hardly mitigated by Cosby's insistence after his attacks that he doesn't mean *all* poor black folk, the verbal equivalent of a "wink-wink" to the knowing—for not possessing the very thing he knows is abundant, a moral sensibility that is far richer than their material circumstances.

Cosby's views of the black poor are so bent out of shape by his apparent aggravation that he is led to deny the rigid racial realities that make it extremely difficult, and in some cases impossible, for poor black folk to flesh out their desires to be educated, gainfully employed and free from the despotic empire of want and penury. There is significant disadvantage still to black skin in an American culture that proclaims the virtues of individualism while denying to blacks, *as a group,* the means to fulfill their individual potential. Not only does Cosby discount the white racial privilege he so honestly confronted in his *Playboy* interview, but he underplays the persistent racism that affects blacks of every class level, but especially poorer blacks. To adapt an old saying in black America in explaining the relative impact of social forces, if well-to-do blacks have a cold, then poor blacks surely have pneumonia. The reason Cosby can be relatively dismissive of structural racism may have to do with his *relative* freedom from the constraints of social prejudice as a globally recognized celebrity, and his failure to fully account for the structural economic injustice faced by poor people may have something to do with his freedom from want, and from the severe psychological and personal penalties it imposes on the most vulnerable. While most of us are disturbed by self-destructive behavior among poor folk, we must also have a clearer grasp of the social and economic landscape for the poor, and what extreme poverty does to individuals trapped in situations of acute desperation.

None of this suggests a black disinterest in responsibility, but it does suggest a widening of our understanding of just what responsibility is, who has it, and how it functions in a more complex vision of social justice for *all* Americans. I suggest that we hold in mind several dimensions of responsibility, summarized in the dynamic, reciprocal relation between three interrelated types of responsibility: *personal* and *social responsibility*, *moral* and *intellectual responsibility*, and *immediate* and *ultimate responsibility*. Personal responsibility involves the individual's being accountable for her actions and acting in a moral fashion that is helpful to herself and to the members of her family, community and society. Social responsibility involves the society's exercising collective accountability to its citizens by acting, through agencies (social services, psychological services and the like), institutions (schools, religious organizations, government and the like), and spheres (private and public employment and the like) to enhance their well-being, especially the most vulnerable. To speak of personal responsibility without understanding its relationship to the social order is to miscalculate what we may reasonably expect from human beings in a given situation. On the other hand, to speak of social responsibility without factoring in the roles and duties of individuals is to misjudge the extent of accountability we can reasonably expect from our society.

Moral responsibility involves self- and other-regarding behavior that aims to realize the good intentions, and maximize the just actions, of persons and societies. Intellectual responsibility involves the exercise of mental faculty for the purpose of self-development and the development of society. To speak of moral responsibility without understanding its constitutive relation to the intellectual goals, and possibilities, of individuals and societies is to misjudge what we can reasonably expect from either. To speak of intellectual responsibility without understanding the ethical ideals and moral properties that constitute and govern intellectual pursuit—and the social conditions that make it possible—is to miscalculate the relation of thought to behavior.

Immediate responsibility involves persons and societies acting accountably to address issues, ideas and problems in the present time and environment. Ultimate responsibility involves persons and societies acting accountably to address issues, ideas and problems with an eye on their personal and social impact in the long run. There is another meaning as well: Ultimate responsibility involves assigning culpability for actions, and consequences, that may appear to lie with particular individuals but that in fact is determined by larger and perhaps more distant (in time) forces. To speak of immediate responsibility without figuring in ultimate responsibility in both senses is to minimize the role of more distant and daunting factors that shape the choices at hand. To speak of ultimate responsibility, in both senses, without understanding how immediate responsibility may still alter personal and social outcomes is to posit a determinism that dishonors individual effort and social transformation.

These meanings of responsibility should be kept in mind as we make demands for the poor to be more responsible. Too often we fail to give them credit for how they are already being personally and morally responsible, given the conditions they confront in the home, in the neighborhood, in the school and in society. We have at the same time failed to calculate, or to as aggressively demand, social responsibility toward the poor. And with both targeted and indiscriminant assaults on the poor, and Cosby fits the latter bill, we have failed to act in an intellectually responsible fashion to use the wealth of research we have at our disposal to relieve, rather than reinforce, their suffering. And we surely haven't used our resources to retard the personal and collective demons that gnaw at the souls and flesh of the poor. Neither have we

accepted our ultimate societal responsibility for the problems—racism, class and caste prejudice, with all of their
attendant ills, which the poor didn't invent—they grapple
with daily. As with Cosby, we have given far too much
emphasis to the personal responsibility of the poor without
speaking of our social, intellectual, moral and, yes, ultimate,
responsibility to the poor. This is more than a philosophical
category mistake; it has fatal consequences for how we view
the poor and what resources we are willing to place at their
disposal to more fully enable them to escape their plight. Our
irresponsibility in this matter far outweighs whatever irresponsibility we might impute to the poor.

We have acted, as a society, in an intellectually and
morally irresponsible fashion when we assign too much
weight to personal responsibility of the poor without figuring
out whether they can even respond honorably and reasonably
with the resources at hand to the challenges they face, challenges rooted in finite factors that have in large part been
constructed by, and in, the social order. But perhaps one of
the biggest disservices, and one of the greatest acts of intellectual irresponsibility, is to believe (and to demand the poor
believe it too) by assuming personal responsibility, the poor
could in any significant way alter their social plight. As
Bishop T. D. Jakes said in response to Cosby's comments:

> Mr. Cosby's comments now stir blacks to ask whether
> we are strong enough to be publicly vulnerable.
> Unquestionably, we care about and take responsibility
> to shape the futures of our beloved children. It is a chal-

lenge. Within those challenges, some believe racism is not a factor. But if credentials, performance and good grammar could end bias and injustice, Danny Glover would have no trouble hailing a cab in New York. If brains and competence always earned their due, women in corporations would not find a glass ceiling, and the Jewish community would never trip over disrespect. While black education and eloquence are critical, they alone don't ensure access to the American dream. Conditions for blacks are drastically improved; and as overt racism recedes, blacks increasingly have the light to more clearly distinguish our self-inflicted wounds from the social bruising of our bludgeoned history. But while black introspection is crucial to healing, it is one-half of the solution. The greater solution is for all Americans to look inside and root out the lingering attitudes and bias that continue to fuel injustice.[39]

The poor cannot erase the blight of white supremacy by behaving better, no matter what advocates of racial uplift or personal responsibility like Bill Cosby suggest. Assuming personal responsibility cannot remove vicious structural barriers to economic mobility. Exercising personal responsibility cannot prevent the postindustrial decline in major northeastern cities, nor can it fix the crumbling infrastructure that continues to keep the poor, well, poor. Being personally responsible can't stop job flight, structural shifts in the political economy, the increasing technological monopoly of work, downsizing, or outsourcing, problems that middle-class folk, who are presumed

to be more personally responsible than the poor, face in abundance these days. As historian Robin D. G. Kelley observes:

> The reality is, all the self-help in the world will not elimi-
> nate poverty or create the number of good jobs needed to
> employ the African American community. Multinational
> corporations control 70 percent of world trade, and about
> one-third of world trade consists of transfers within the
> 350 largest global corporations. Rather than merely
> exploit Third World labor to extract or cultivate raw
> materials, increasingly we have witnessed the export of
> whole production processes as corporations seek to take
> advantage of cheaper labor, relatively lower taxes, and a
> deregulated environment. . . . Well-paying jobs made
> possible by decades of union struggle disappeared. By
> 1979, for example, 94 percent of the profits of the Ford
> Motor Company and 63 percent of the profits from Coca-
> Cola came from overseas operations. Between 1973 and
> 1980, at least 4 million U.S. jobs were lost to firms mov-
> ing to foreign countries. And during the decade of the
> 1970s, at least 32 million jobs were lost as a result of
> shutdowns, relocations, and scaling back operations.
> Moreover, the economy we are dealing with is not only
> global and transnational but depends on state interven-
> tion to help keep it afloat—a state, by the way, we fund
> with our tax dollars.[40]

And, in an act of supreme intellectual and moral irresponsibility, we have as a society—hence, we have been socially

irresponsible as well—enlarged the myth of individualism that holds that most folk who make it in our culture have done so on merit and talent alone, that they have been personally responsible, denying that they have also benefited from skin color, social class and gender preference, social forces that put individuals of predictable pedigree in the right place at the right time either to enhance their innate gifts or to have their mediocre skills overlooked in a social order that favors them despite their deficits. And many black folk who have climbed upward are morally and intellectually irresponsible when they benefit from affirmative action—not because they lack talent, but because they possess it but have been historically denied the opportunity to exercise it—and then blast the black poor who have not received the slightest benefit from this measure of compensatory justice. Moreover, huge corporations benefit from their own variety of welfare, as do the rich in the form of untold subsidies and tax breaks. We hold the poor immediately responsible for mastering their domain, and yet society bears the ultimate responsibility for making their social environment a cruel obstacle course of severely limited options while virtually assuring their failure with poorly arranged alternatives to their suffering. This is not to deny the need for the poor to exercise personal responsibility; it is simply a demand that we not be intellectually and morally irresponsible by overemphasizing its role in removing the barriers they confront, barriers that have a relationship to their ability to thrive. To paraphrase Dorothy Day, the great Catholic social activist who spent her life working with and loving the poor, but not pitying them, we must work toward a world in which it is easier for the poor to behave decently.[41]

Cosby's rabid insistence on personal responsibility to the exclusion of every other variety of responsibility has predictably won him plaudits from black and white conservatives, from Walter Williams, Thomas Sowell and Star Parker to the *National Review*'s Jonah Goldberg and assorted online ideologues. Of course, Cosby was widely celebrated by black columnists of every ideological stripe for his views about personal responsibility, while only a few of them insisted on broadening the view to include at least a nod to social responsibility. For the most part, the black press, and blacks in the press—with the notable exception of a few online writers like William Jelani Cobb, *Time* magazine's Christopher John Farley, and the *Village Voice*'s Ta-Nehisi Coates—did little more than rubber-stamp Cosby's opinions, evoking unsettling memories, if not in tone then at least in effect, of their elitist kin from the last century.[44] As disappointing as the capitulation of the black press was— and, quite frankly, so was the fawning, or silent, surrender of most black intellectuals, pundits and public figures, even those who might have openly disagreed with a celebrity of lesser wattage, or one not so beloved in the race—it is perhaps the affirming signal that Cosby's vicious assaults send to equally vicious right-wing interests that is most damaging. Cosby's insistence on self-help lets society off the hook, including governmental bodies, segments of private industry and certainly racist quarters of the culture that have like vultures picked at the bones of the black suffering that they, or their ideological predecessors, helped to impose. It is intellectually irresponsible for Cosby to spout his gospel of self-help and personal responsibility without paying strict attention to the social forces that have pulverized the black families he now attacks in terms that are, he unapologetically admits, "vulgar."[42]

In the aftermath of his comments, Cosby has been heralded by the white folk, including conservatives, he claims not to care about. But the dead giveaway that Cosby truly cares about what whites think is his contention during his speech that "The white man, he's laughing, got to be laughing." I think it is Cosby's embarrassment for the poor in the sight of "the white man" that has caused him to go off on the poor. As a result, Cosby has been embraced by white pundits and critics. Not only have they heaped praise on his head, but they have heaped scorn on the black poor, and other black leaders, in the name of the freedom to emote that Cosby's comments gave rise to. As Jonah Goldberg stated in the *National Review*:

Conservatives have long argued that the best thing for the black community is, in the late Pat Moynihan's celebrated (though misunderstood) phrase, a policy of "benign neglect." Most people faced with the choice of sinking or swimming will swim. And there's no reason to believe, conservatives argued, that blacks wouldn't swim like anybody else if they had to. Many immigrants come to this country far poorer than the average poor black but still work their way into the middle class, because they bring with them a set of values our society tends to reward. They also usually have an ethnic social network waiting for them, which helps them get on their feet. Why should blacks be any different? If blacks were cut off without a dime from the federal government, non-racist conservatives argued, blacks would develop individually and as a community, the habits and institutions necessary for as decent a life as anybody could expect—much as they had, ironically, during segregation. That's not an argument for segregation, of course, but for the sort of self-help blacks relied on before the government started "helping" them. As countless callers to black radio point out, that self-help involved shaming those who were letting the rest of the community down. . . . Bill Cosby knows the answer, and he should be congratulated for shaming those who deserve—and need—to be shamed.[43]

In Goldberg's eyes, Cosby's politics of shame, glimpsed in his relentless assaults on poor blacks, represent an exemplary moral, and political, response to poverty, when in fact Cosby's approach, as we've seen, is much more deeply rooted in destructive class politics than most critics seem to realize. What is clear is that Cosby's stance has emboldened white conservative interests in their public attacks on poor blacks. Cosby thinks that such unsolicited—but, surely, it can't be claimed, unforeseen—support may be the price he has to pay to get a hearing in the culture. "If I have to make a choice between keeping quiet so that conservative media does not speak negatively, or ringing the bell to galvanize those who want change in the lower economic community, then I choose to be a bell ringer," Cosby said in a statement. "I think it is time for concerned African-Americans to march, galvanize and raise the awareness about the epidemic to transform our helplessness, frustration and righteous indignation into a sense of shared responsibility and action."[44]

The effect of white conservatives on Cosby's thinking is unmistakable, especially as he lashes out at leaders and thinkers with a more complex vision of how one truly helps the poor. "The poverty pimps and the victim pimps keep telling the victim to stay where they are," Cosby told an audience in Detroit in January 2005. "You're crippled, you can't walk, you can't get up, you can't do this, you can't do that. And I'm saying, you'd better get up." That quip so pleased conservatives that it made both *The O'Reilly Factor* and *Hannity & Colmes* on the Fox News Network.[45] Of course, if Cosby were willing to actually explore the social responsibility for the suffering of the black poor, and to stop telling a narrow truth about them, such a statement might signal the possibility of helpful, hopeful dialogue—and put to rest his need for off-the-cuff ranting and raving. Even a Cosby defender, Pulitzer prize–winning columnist Leonard Pitts, had to admit that "it's much easier for a black multimillionaire to dismiss white people's opinions than it is for a black man or woman living paycheck to paycheck."[46]

Many in the black community have come to Cosby's aid, suggesting that his "airing dirty laundry," even at the risk of offending the poor, was both a valiant departure from tradition and a necessary safeguard of just the sort of free speech that might help us confront grave social crises. I, for one, applaud the move away from quarantining black discourse in supposedly private black quarters, which were ostensibly open to most black folk but in truth were relatively closed and antidemocratic spaces. What was usually meant by hashing things out in private was gatherings of the leaders of black organizations, or on the convention floors, platforms and meeting halls of groups to which the masses of blacks were not necessarily invited. Open, democratic, honest dialogue is best. That, for sure, is not what is occurring with Cosby's tirades; they are one-sided, intimidating displays of rhetorical bluster and misdirected passion that have the effect of quelling, not sparking, true, robust, open-ended, just and democratic conversation. Besides, these same folk failed to defend the producers of the film *Barbershop*, which, it was believed, soiled the reputation and savaged the images of Martin Luther King, Jr., and Rosa Parks. No one claimed that the charges about King—that he had extramarital affairs—were wrong. Most folk simply argued that such charges should not be irresponsibly portrayed in a film piped to sections of a white world that looked to seize on any negative information about a beloved black leader, in fact, the most beloved leader of all, to justify their racist attacks. The message seems to be that while it's horrible, perhaps even racist, to pounce on King's reputation and image, it's just fine to beat up on poor blacks in an equally "irresponsible" fashion.

Other black critics argue that Cosby said the right thing, but at the wrong time in the wrong place. Others say that Cosby was saying little more than what we hear regularly, in equally unvarnished manner, in the barber's chair or on the street corner. I think a more accurate analogy is that Cosby is like the person who sounds good to himself singing in the shower but, when he hits the stage, he's lost all the conditions that made his song soar: the claustrophobic acoustics of a confined space; the protection of privacy; the guarantee of a positive, if subjective, assessment of one's skill; and the lack of a critical audience to offer feedback. Henry Louis Gates, Jr., asked why "the huge flap over Bill Cosby's insistence that black teenagers do their homework, stay in school, master standard English and stop having babies? Any black person who frequents a barbershop or beauty parlor in the inner city knows that Mr. Cosby was only echoing sentiments widely shared in the black community."[47] Except most brothers in the barber's chair aren't invited to appear on CNN to spread their views, and neither does that qualify them to take a position—or, for that matter, to be offered one—on Professor Gates's black studies faculty at Harvard.

While white conservatives embraced Cosby's comments lashing out at poor blacks, the same conservative establishment pilloried his wife, Camille, when she bravely penned an op-ed in the aftermath of their son Ennis's murder by an immigrant from the Ukraine. Camille Cosby, who, like her husband, earned a doctorate in education from the University of Massachusetts, was as blunt as her husband, except her righteous indignation and impassioned reasoning were directed at white racism.

I believe America taught our son's killer to hate African-Americans. After Mikhail Markhasev killed Ennis

William Cosby on Jan. 16, 1997, he said to his friends, "I shot a nigger. It's all over the news." . . . Presumably, Markhasev did not learn to hate black people in his native country, the Ukraine, where the black population was near zero. Nor was he likely to see America's intolerable, stereotypical movies and television programs about blacks, which were not shown in the Soviet Union before the killer and his family moved to America in the late 1980s. . . . Yes, racism and prejudice are omnipresent and eternalized in America's institutions, media and myriad entities. . . . Ennis William Cosby was shot and killed in a middle- to upper-middle income, predominately white community. The misperception immortalized daily by the media and other entities is that crimes are committed in poor neighborhoods inhabited by dark people. All African-Americans, regardless of their educational and economic accomplishments, have been and are at risk in America simply because of their skin colors. Sadly, my family and I experienced that to be one of America's racial truths. Most people know that facing the truth brings about healing and growth. When is America going to face its historical and current racial realities so it can be what it says it is?[48]

Predictably, Mrs. Cosby's comments were met with harsh resistance from the white conservative press, and from some black conservatives. Although she wasn't nearly as visible as her husband in his crusade, Mrs. Cosby did respond briefly in writing to the critiques of her commentary, insisting that "racism is at the heart of America's past and present histories, and all of us have been stung by it." Then she made a structural link that her husband had made in his *Playboy* interview, but which he had wholly neglected in his comments about the poor. "America's institutions have a fundamental responsibility to be just, unprejudiced and truthful to all of its people." She wrote that racism "continues to divide our country; therefore, constructive dialogue and action are needed for America to have a healthy populace." Mrs. Cosby also stated that the "focal point [of my article] was institutional racism— that is, entities in both the public and private sectors which have practiced, influenced and sustained biased values that Black people are inferior."[49]

Camille Cosby's provocative essay set off quite a different media firestorm than the one that blazes around her husband. It was, too, a much more courageous commentary than the one offered by Bill Cosby. Camille Cosby's commentary was surely much more likely to offend deep-pocketed private and public interests in the white mainstream. Camille Cosby's views cut across the amnesia and dishonesty that fuel the continued distortion of race in America. And she used her perch as one of the wealthiest and most beloved black women in the nation to identify with the masses of black folk, including the poor, fighting the vicious legacy of white supremacy. And her insistence on the social responsibility the country owes to its citizens to educate them about racism, and to confront its brutal consequences in American life, was especially powerful. Unlike her husband in his recent comments, Camille Cosby sought to speak directly to the sources of so much suffering among black folk in the country.

One of the most dishonest effects of elevating Cosby as a spokesman of black interests is that conservative commentators pretend that he is the first prominent black leader to call for personal responsibility. By being portrayed as distinctive in his views, Cosby is made morally exceptional, and hence viewed as an exemplar to the masses of black folk and our leaders and used to chide those who haven't caught on to the need for personal responsibility. One conservative white columnist praised Cosby's bravery for airing dirty laundry while decrying the "complete breakdown of leadership within the [black] community," claiming that folk like Al Sharpton, Louis Farrakhan and Jesse Jackson have "spent the past 20 years telling the black community that their problems are due to the white man keeping them down." He asked, when "was the last time any of those men looked within the black community and said there is a problem?"[50] Black conservative activist Star Parker asked, "If Cosby's appeal for personal responsibility among African Americans is not news for black leadership, then one must ask why this leadership opposes every reform that attempts to recognize these points, turn back government and return choice and responsibility to black citizens."[51] Farrakhan, of course, has been promoting a gospel of black self-help for decades, and while he assaults white supremacy, he recognizes the virtue of black folk, including the black poor, assuming responsibility for their destinies. After all, the call for a million men to converge on Washington, D.C., a decade ago rested on the argument that black males should take greater responsibility in their homes and communities. Sharpton has constantly applauded the virtues of hard work and self-determining action for black folk. And Jesse Jackson is in a long list of leaders who have understood the dynamic relationship between personal and social responsibility.

It may be because many black leaders and thinkers have been unwilling to blame black people, especially the black poor, for their problems, even as they value personal responsibility—and social, intellectual, moral, immediate and ultimate responsibility as well—that their contributions are so easily ignored. At their best, black thinkers and leaders have rarely isolated self-help philosophy from a simultaneous damning of the white supremacy that makes it necessary. Marcus Garvey, the Jamaican-born activist who organized and led the Universal Negro Improvement Association (UNIA), the largest black nationalist movement in the nation's history, emphasized political resistance and a brand of self-reliance that might have made Emerson proud. Garvey deplored the systemic racism that prevented blacks' flourishing.[52] Acknowledging that black folk are treated equally to whites "nowhere in the world, with few exceptions," Garvey argued that "there should be an equitable distribution and apportionment of all such things, and in consideration of the fact that as a race we are now deprived of those things that are morally and legally ours, we believe it right that all such things should be acquired and held by whatsoever means possible." At the same time, Garvey and the UNIA promoted "self-help and self-reliance," eschewing slavish dependence on other races, with the admonition that "[p]rayer alone is not going to improve our condition, nor the policy of watchful waiting," thus encouraging black folk to take their destinies into their own hands.[53]

W.E.B. Du Bois, an advocate of engaged thought and aggressive social action, agreed in principle with Garvey's move to join sustained resistance to white supremacy and racial self-help. Du Bois linked self-help to self-regard, and to the willingness to associate with other blacks, cautioning blacks against "affront[ing] our own self-respect by accepting a proffered equality which is not equality, or submitting to discrimination simply because it does not involve actual and open segregation; and above all, let us not sit down and do nothing for self-defense and self-organization just because we are too stupid or too distrustful of ourselves to take vigorous and decisive action."[54]

Martin Luther King, Jr., the most valiant freedom fighter of the twentieth century, argued that "if first-class citizenship is to become a reality for the Negro he must assume the primary responsibility for making it so."[55] King contended that the Negro "must not be victimized with the delusion of thinking that others should be more concerned than himself about his citizenship rights." King was quick, however, to insist that black folk "must continue to break down the barrier of segregation," and to "resist all forms of racial injustice." Nonviolent social resistance was the collective expression of black self-help, as King urged black folk to "take direct action against injustice without waiting for other agencies to act."[56] At the same time, King insisted that one of the "sure signs of maturity is the ability to rise to the point of self-criticism."[57] King admitted that some blacks had "lost that something called *initiative*," and that some had used their oppression to excuse mediocrity. But King anticipated the racist use of his words, concluding that the "only answer that we can give to those who through blindness and fear would question our readiness and capability is that our lagging standards exist because of the legacy of slavery and segregation, inferior schools, slums, and second-class citizenship, and not because of an inherent inferiority."[58]

Finally, Jesse Jackson, the most gifted social activist and public moralist of our times, has consistently over his forty-year career in public service sought to eradicate racism and economic inequality while preaching a gospel of self-help. As head of Operation PUSH, and then the Rainbow/PUSH Coalition, Jackson has encouraged his followers to reject alcohol, teenage sex, and drugs ("get the dope out of your veins and hope in your brains"); to war against misogynistic lyrics and violence in hip-hop culture; and to become deeply involved in their children's education. In the 1970s, Jackson launched the Push for Excellence (EXCEL) program, devoted to bridging generational and cultural gaps by bringing together parents, students and teachers in pursuit of educational excellence across the nation. Over five hundred public school districts invited Jackson to help them implement his program. When Jackson appeared on *60 Minutes*, the program recorded his intriguing mix of self-help philosophy, down-home vernacular, and folksy-country-preacher-meets-big-city-activist as he chided and challenged his black listeners in a speech.

You know, I look at a lot of these theories that many social workers come up with, like, "Now the reason the Negro can't learn is his Daddy's gone, his Momma is piti- ful, there's no food in the refrigerator, it's rats all in his house . . . and that's the reason he can't learn." Then we go to school and the teacher—standing there reeling the guilties—says, "These poor and pitiful Negroes got all these trials and tribulations. Now I have to stand up here and teach them how to read and write and count." Well, if we can run faster, jump higher and shoot a basketball straighter off of inadequate diets, then we can read, write, count and think off of those same diets. The challenge is mobility.[59]

Nearly two decades later, after a murder outside of his kitchen, the shooting of his grocer across the street, a triple murder down the block and the burglary of his house while his mother-in-law was present, Jackson launched what he termed a "victim-led revolution," which brought together a network of local churches to provide mentoring to first-time offenders who had no family to guide them. Jackson has also worked tirelessly to erase social injustice and the structural inequalities that prevent blacks and other poor people from enjoying the opportunity to exercise their full citizenship. Jackson, for example, appeared before the National Press Club in 1994 to criticize President Clinton's budget plans, which, during a widely touted economic recovery, slashed crucial programs for young people, the working classes and the poor.

The third year of recovery [and the] unemployment of African Americans is going up, not down. Unemployment for America generally is down to 6.4 percent. For African Americans, [it's] 13 percent and rising. Race rhetoric is offensive. Race discrimination is deadly. Young African Americans who drop out of school [are unemployed at a rate of] 43.5 percent. For those who played by the rules, high school graduates, unemployment [is] 25 percent. Young African Americans who have some college suffer an unemployment rate [of] 18 percent. College graduates [are] unemployed [at] 11.3 percent. And this is the third year of the recovery. We need a plan for jobs in this country. The president hails the recovery and the jobs being created. But in January alone, major companies announced 100,000 new lay-offs. The jobs that are going are generally better than the jobs that are coming. One in seven jobs last year was provided by a temporary help company. We need an urban policy and an economic development plan. Instead, we are going the other way. This year's budget features high visibility cuts in urban programs. Bus and subway fares will go up as mass transit subsidies are slashed. Libraries will close. The young and old will be left in the cold as home heating aid is cut. The crisis in affordable housing, [is] met by slashing [the] public housing budget $3 billion. Badly funded training programs for disadvantaged young people [are] eliminated to pay for a badly funded training program for disadvantaged workers.[60]

Jackson's latest venture, termed the Wall Street Project, combines his fight for equality with the intent to democratize capital, an extension of his belief that black folk and other oppressed peoples must demand a fair share of the economy. Jackson contends that "urban America has been redlined," and since the government hasn't offered tax incentives for inner-city investment, as it has "in a dozen foreign markets," it is time to boost the economic health of black America by encouraging major financial forces to take the ghettos seriously. "Clearly, to break up the redlining process, there must be incentives to green-line with hedges against risk," Jackson says. "When you place a car dealership or a drugstore or a movie house in these areas, you increase the tax base for the school—that enhances the quality of life. We've been so preoccupied with getting the government to behave in a fair and democratic way, we were not able to focus on the private sector where most of the jobs are, where most of the wealth and opportunities are."[61]

Many leaders have had far more understanding than Cosby has shown for the complex variables that make, and keep, folk poor. That is why it is probably best that he explore his gifts for comedy and leave the social analysis and race leadership to those better suited to the task. If nothing else, Cosby's ventures into the realm of social criticism prove the nontransferability of genius; one's position must be earned in every sphere or else it amounts to little more than concession, or, worse yet, a handout to the fortunate. Cosby's celebrity has given him a big platform, but he must be much more responsible with his gifts and positions in talking about the poor than he has yet been.

Even as Cosby further victimizes the poor, he seems to be a victim himself, of compassion fatigue, or what Barack Obama has gracefully termed an "empathy deficit."[62] Cosby does appear to have a crushing lack of spiritual empathy—not to be confused with maudlin emotion, or pitying affirmation, but a willingness to be kept awake in another's bed of pain before lashing them for being morally asleep. It may be that Cosby has grown weary because he has tried to shoulder more than he can carry, or, perhaps, once he saw that the problems of the poor were deeper than his generous pockets and the will of the state, he got angry *at* them, instead of *with* them. It may do him good to recall that only a handful of black people in history have ever possessed his material blessings, but most blacks have, nevertheless, through faith, or a belief in themselves and one another, conquered slavery and apartheid and self-hate with a spiritual abundance that trumps rational deliberation and common sense.

Perhaps the most damaging consequence of Cosby's war on the poor is that they are left less defended and much more vulnerable to rebuff, even by folk—policy analysts, public policy makers, politicians—who might be sitting on the fence wondering what to do about the poor, and who now get a huge cue from Cosby that it's just fine to leave them to sink or swim for themselves. In that sense, Cosby, much more than the poor he castigates, is supremely irresponsible. He has been given to talking about Jesus in his shrill sermons to, and about, the poor. Cosby lambastes the poor for "asking Jesus to do things for you. And you can't keep saying that God will find a way. God is tired of you . . . Well, you probably gon' let Jesus figure it out for you. Well, I got somethin' to tell you about Jesus. When you go to the church, look at the stained glass things of Jesus. Look at 'em. Is Jesus smiling? Not in one picture. So, tell your friends: Let's try to do somethin'. Let's try to make Jesus smile." What, indeed, would make Jesus smile? The answer is simple: If we "love mercy, do justly and walk humbly with thy God" as the prophet Micah says—and if we "love thy neighbor as thyself" as Jesus says—it would bring a smile to the Lord's face. I think that the notion that God helps those who help themselves sounds good but is little more than the theological attempt to sanctify American individualism.

The gospels, on the other hand, emphasize our collective responsibility as a community, out of which individual responsibility and standing flow. Jesus' commitment to the poor is foundational to the gospels, and is a central tenet of the Christian faith. Beyond that, compassion for the poor is the hallmark of true civilization, sacred or secular. Cosby and the rest of us must learn that lesson and do as Jesus did. In fact, in his first public appearance, Jesus read from the prophet Isaiah and used his words to sum up his mission, one that all of us, believer and unbeliever alike, might adapt. As it reads in Luke 4:16–21 of the Revised Standard Version of the Bible:

And he came to Nazareth, where he had been brought up; and he went to the synagogue, as his custom was, on

the sabbath day. And he stood up to read; and there was
given to him the book of the prophet Isaiah. He opened
the book and found the place where it was written,

"The Spirit of the Lord is upon me,
because he has anointed me to preach good news to
the poor.
He has sent me to proclaim release to the captives
and recovering of sight to the blind,
to set at liberty those who are oppressed,
to proclaim the acceptable year of the Lord."

And he closed the book, and gave it back to the attendant, and sat down; and the eyes of all in the synagogue
were fixed on him. And he began to say to them, "Today
this scripture has been fulfilled in your hearing."

It is left to those of us who have managed to do well, those
of us who, in the words of faith, are blessed, to help fulfill
Jesus' words. Obviously Cosby has forgotten a crucial concept
Jesus advocated: "From everyone to whom much has been
given, much will be required."[63]

Perhaps we should turn to another legendary black figure
with Philadelphia connections, W.E.B. Du Bois, for just such
compassion and insight.

Above all, the better classes of the Negroes should recognize their duty toward the masses. They should not forget
that the spirit of the twentieth century is to be the turning of the high toward the lowly, the bending of
Humanity to all that is human; the recognition that in

the slums of modern society lie the answers to most of our puzzling problems of organization and life, and that only as we solve those problems is our culture assured and our progress certain. . . . So hard has been the rise of the better class of Negroes that they fear to fall if now they stoop to lend a hand to their fellows. . . . This is especially true in a city like Philadelphia which has so distinct and creditable a Negro aristocracy; that they do something already to grapple with these social problems of their race is true, but they do not yet do nearly as much as they must, nor do they clearly recognize their responsibility. Finally, the Negroes must cultivate a spirit of calm, patient persistence in their attitude toward their fellow citizens rather than of loud and intemperate complaint. A man may be wrong, and know he is wrong, and yet some finesses must be used in telling him of it. . . . [I]t will not improve matters to call names or impute unworthy motives to all men. Social reforms move slowly and yet when Right is reinforced by calm but persistent Progress we somehow all feel that in the end it must triumph.[64]

"Niggas Come in All Colors"

Let me tell you something, your dirty laundry gets out of school at 2:30 every day, it's cursing and calling each other "nigga" as they're walking up and down the street. They think they're hip. They can't read; they can't write. They're laughing and giggling, and they're going nowhere.

Long before his most controversial speech, Bill Cosby gave another address that suggests he possessed precisely the sort of humor and wordplay against which he has recently raged. Speaking to the Congressional Black Caucus's first national gathering in 1971, Cosby took his turn at the lectern after a fiery oration by the late, great Ossie Davis, Jr. After a few introductory comments, he jumped to the heart of his remarks.

"I think that all you niggas need to," he said, half tongue-in-cheek, and the audience erupted in laughter for nearly half a minute before he could finish his phrase, "check yourselves out."[1] Cosby let the laughter die down a bit, but once he was rolling, like the good comedian he is, he rode the wave some more.

"So I say good evening, niggas, because . . . that's what a lot of you gon' be when you leave the room." There was more laughter and applause from his well-heeled black audience. But he wasn't finished.

"And I mean the white people sittin' there, too. . . . Niggas come in all colors."

Cosby was not only flaunting convention and bringing into his august crowd the word "nigga"—and it was that blackened version he smoothly, effortlessly deployed, not its derisive mainstream white pronunciation—but he was flowing in the vernacular, ebonicizing his pronunciation, inflection and intonation throughout.

Cosby vowed that he would support the Caucus for the rest of his life, interestingly enough, because he was tired as a black entertainer of carrying the load that black leaders should shoulder.

"The black establishment for too long has been the entertainers," Cosby said. "And black entertainers very seldom get a chance to enjoy what da white entertainers have—that is to be able to go out on da Riviera wit' sunglasses and float around on a raft. No, 'cause you know if you saw a picture of me out there on the Riviera wit' my sunglasses on, you'd say, 'Look at that nigga, and we up here struggling.'" The crowd responded uproariously, knowingly, since this was a prime moment of racial reciprocity: A black speaker was reveling in the privileges of inside communication without the need to explain that he didn't mean "nigga" in a hateful way. Neither did he have to explain himself to blacks who thought it was demeaning for a black person to use the "N" word. In fact, he didn't seem to care at all.

Cosby went on to say that the black entertainer must still entertain, even as black folk had to get themselves together. Speaking to the black political and social elite, Cosby took more liberty, even swearing at the podium with a convincing display of transgression against the solemnity of the occasion celebrating black leadership.

"And da people still have to get an ass-kickin' to go out and vote."

Cosby claimed that "ain't but one person together, and that's Ossie Davis, just left here. Poured his heart and soul into a beautiful speech so you could make da sign and give a half-hour handshake to each other and den walk out and still be a nigga." More laugher still.

Cosby hit a prescient theme, telling the black folk they couldn't blame other folk for their plight: White entertainers with a black sound, like Joe Cocker, couldn't be held accountable when black folk refused to support black entertainers like Ray Charles. And they couldn't blame Jews for opening stores in the black community, especially since they lacked the skill to do so themselves.

"Ain't but seven of you in this place can run a store," Cosby claimed, to tremendous laughter and applause. It seems they were willing to concede their inabilities, at least for the night, or, at the very least, for the moment. Cosby stormed on, saying that young black folk must be looked after, underlining the need to get off of drugs.

"It's got to start with the young, too. Our young kids takin' drugs today. They were takin' 'em yesterday. Only reason why everybody knows about it now is 'cause white kids are involved heavily."

Cosby drew to a close and reminded his audience once again who they really were, despite their status and standing in the community.

"So when you leave here, depends on just how long it's goin' to take you before you go back to bein' a nigga." More laughter, and applause, and recognition that Cosby was doing serious race-work in his comments. His vernacular, his liberal use of "nigga" and his pointed communication to folk he loved were all recorded and distributed to a wider audience on Motown's Black Forum label.

It is more than ironic that Cosby begrudges the same freedoms to the young folk of today. Times have definitely changed, circumstances have been hugely altered, but the persistent freedom of black folk, especially artists and leaders, to open their mouths and speak with all the spirit and spunk their people love them into, is what he could take for granted. Perhaps he should think about extending that same freedom to those he castigates for cursing and saying "nigga," both of which he did that night.

Acknowledgments

First, I want to thank the millions of poor, black, struggling folk whose lives are an inspiration to me, and who, I hope and pray, feel the love and respect I have for them reflected in my book.

As usual, I want to thank the wonderful Liz Maguire, my brilliant editor and intellectual partner with whom I also share a marvelous friendship. I am grateful to Chris Greenberg who has truly gone beyond the call of duty in so many ways. I want to thank Christine Marra for her care of the book, Brian Mulligan for his super design, and Anna Kaltenbach for her expert editing skills.

I want to thank God for God's love which sustains me, and for such wonderful friends, colleagues and family. I am thankful to my friends for giving me encouragement and support: Carolyn Moore-Assem, without whose insight and help I couldn't have begun, or finished, this book; J.Van, for being magnificent, smart as a whip, and for the shout-outs, love and encouragement; to Robin Kelley, Deidra Harris-Kelley, and Elleza, for your support, and your brilliance and commitment to freedom; to Farah Jasmine Griffin, for your brilliance and your generosity of spirit; and to Susan Taylor and Khephra Burns, for your love and encouragement, your genius and your unwavering support.

I want to thank my colleagues in the Africana Studies and Religious Studies Departments at the University of Pennsylvania—especially Tukufu Zuberi, a brilliant scholar and soulful public intellectual, and Ann Matter, a brilliant scholar and loving, nurturing mentor. I am grateful to the tremendous help, far, far beyond the call of duty, provided by: Gale Garrison, Carol Davis, Onyx Finney, Marie Hudson, Cheryl Graham-Seay, Valerie Walker, Darlynn Lee, Susan Cerrone, Cybil Csigi, Joyce Roselle and Pat Johnson. And for her magnificent, expert and incredible research assistance, I am grateful to LaTeisha Moore. It has been great being part of the Penn family.

Finally, I want to thank my family, including my wonderful mother Addie, my stalwart brothers Anthony, Everett, Jr., Gregory and Brian, and my many nieces and nephews. I also want to thank my children, Michael Eric Dyson, II, Maisha and Cory Daniels, and Mwata Dyson, to whom this book is in part dedicated. And last, but surely not least, I want to thank the Rev. Marcia Louise Dyson, without whose steady love and deep devotion none of this—books, writing, lecturing, reading, preaching and more—could ever take place.

Notes

Preface

1. "Rainbow/PUSH Coalition Holds 33rd Annual Conference in Chicago," *Jet*, July 26, 2004, p. 4.

Introduction An Afristocrat in Winter

1. Felicia R. Lee, "Cosby Defends His Remarks About Poor Blacks' Values," *New York Times*, May 22, 2004, p. B7.
2. There is a precedent of appellations seeking to capture the black elite. Nathan Hare speaks of the Black Anglo-Saxons, whereas William Jelani Cobb writes about the Afrostocracy. I have over the years preferred Afristocracy, emphasizing with the "i" the connection to the term African American culture. See Nathan Hare, *The Black Anglo-Saxons*. 2nd ed. (Chicago: Third World Press, 1992).
3. William Julius Wilson, *When Work Disappears: The World of the New Urban Poor* (New York: Knopf, 1996).
4. Elizabeth Warren and Amelia Warren Tyagi, *The Two-Income Trap:*

Why Middle-Class Parents Are Going Broke (New York: Basic Books, 2003).

5. Kanye West, sound recording "All Falls Down," *College Dropout*, Roc-A-Fella Records, 2004.

6. Hebrews 11:13 (King James Version).

7. 1 Kings 19:4 (King James Version).

Chapter One Speaking of Race—Or Not

1. Mel Watkins, *On the Real Side: Laughing, Lying, and Signifying—The Underground Tradition of African-American Humor that Transformed American Culture, from Slavery to Richard Pryor* (New York: Simon and Schuster, 1994), pp. 489–495. Redd Foxx and Moms Mabley would eventually gain a wider (and "whiter") audience, but their blue style and insider racial humor kept them for years working the black chitlin' and club circuit.

2. Ronald L. Smith, *Cosby: The Life of a Comedy Legend* [Updated version] (Amherst, N.Y.: Prometheus Books, 1997), p. 43.

3. "'Raceless' Bill Cosby: Comedian Excludes 'Color' Reference from Repertoire," *Ebony*, May 1964, p. 131.

4. Dan Goodgame, "'I Do Believe in Control': Cosby Is a Man Who Gets Laughs—and Results—by Doing Things His Way," *Time*, September 28, 1987, p. 62.

5. Richard Zoglin, "Cosby, Inc.: He Has a Hot TV Series, a New Book—and a Booming Comedy Empire," *Time*, September 28, 1987, p. 59; Smith, *Cosby*, p. 46.

6. Stanley Karnow, "Bill Cosby: Variety Is the Life of Spies: For the First Time, a Negro Stars in a TV Series—and He Won't Sing, Dance or Play the Second Banana," *The Saturday Evening Post*, September 25, 1965, p. 87.

7. Zoglin, p. 59.

8. Karnow, p. 86.

9. "Color Him Funny," *Newsweek*, January 31, 1966, p. 76; C. H. Simonds, "Primarily a Guy," *National Review*, October 4, 1966, p. 1008.

10. "The Spy," *Newsweek*, December 14, 1964, p. 51.

11. Karnow, p. 88.

12. "Color Him Funny," *Newsweek*, January 31, 1966, p. 76.

13. Simonds, p. 1008.

14. "Color-Blind Comic," *Newsweek*, May 20, 1968, p. 74.

15. Thomas B. Morgan, "I Am Two People, Man," *Life*, April 11, 1969, p. 76.

16. "'Raceless' Bill Cosby," p. 131.

17. "Color Him Funny," p. 76. One can't help but read Cosby's statement against the most famous formulation of black folk being viewed as a problem, authored by W.E.B. Du Bois sixty-one years earlier: "Between me and the other world there is ever an unasked question: unasked by some through feelings of delicacy; by others through the difficulty of rightly framing it. All, nevertheless, flutter round it. They approach me in a half-hesitant sort of way, eye me curiously or compassionately, and then, instead of saying directly, How does it feel to be a problem? they say, I know an excellent colored man in my town. . . . At these I smile, or am interested, or reduce the boiling to a simmer, as the occasion may require. To the real question, How does it feel to be a problem? I answer seldom a word." *The Souls of Black Folks* [A Norton Critical Edition, Edited by Henry Louis Gates, Jr., and Terri Hume Oliver] (New York: W. W. Norton, 1999), pp. 9–10.

18. Ibid.

19. In Cosby's case, this not only applied generally to his career, but quite specifically to his role on *I Spy*. "At the outset, according to show-business insiders, Cosby was slated to play the familiar Negro role of second banana to the white star, Bob Culp. But as the drive for civil rights gathered momentum, the image of a Negro as a full-fledged costar began to look better and Cosby's part in *I Spy* was gradually upgraded." Stanley Karnow, "Bill Cosby: Variety Is the Life of Spies: For the First Time, a Negro Stars in a TV Series—and He Won't Sing, Dance or Play the Second Banana," *The Saturday Evening Post*, September 25, 1965, p. 88.

20. "I Spy: Comedian Bill Cosby Is First Negro Co-Star in TV Network Series," *Ebony*, September 1965, p. 65.

21. "'Raceless Bill Cosby," p. 131.

22. Ironically enough, *I Spy* producer Sheldon Leonard sought to protect Cosby's character from the stereotype of the hypersexed stud. "I am not going to feed the concept that a Negro only responds to the sex drive. We want him to have girls, but there has to be sweetness and dignity in it." *Newsweek*, "Color Him Funny," January 31, 1966, p. 76. Obviously, Culp worked free of both sexual stereotype and the compulsion to make his sexual encounters sweet and dignified. The point is that even under ostensible equality—and an artistic environment allegedly free of the constraints of color—Cosby's character still bore the inescapable burden of race.

23. Smith, *Cosby*, p. 74. Cosby was emphatic about not wanting to get the white girl, either. "Now don't get it wrong. It was my decision right from the start to play it that way. As long as I'm on the screen, whether television or films, I will never hold or kiss a white woman. Hey, our black women have just nothing to look forward to in films, nothing to identify with . . . tell me, how often do you see a black man falling in love and making love with a black woman? So as it is, I want to be seen only with our women—not Chinese or Filipino women, not yellow, green, pink, or white. Just our women, black ones." Smith, *Cosby*, pp. 74–75.

24. Faith Berry, "Can 'Just for Laughs' Be Real for Blacks?" *New York Times*, Dec. 7, 1969, p. D23.

25. Ibid.

26. Ibid.

27. Ibid.

28. Smith, *Cosby*, p. 150.

29. Ibid.

30. Ibid.

31. Cosby was also raked over the coals by critic Andrew Sarris in the *Village Voice* for his performance alongside Raquel Welch in the 1976 film *Mother, Jugs and Speed*. Sarris accused Cosby of doing "a Stepin Fetchit imitation." Smith, *Cosby*, p. 136.

32. Karnow, p. 88.

33. Lawrence Linderman, "Playboy Interview: Bill Cosby—A Candid

Conversation with the Kinetic Comedian-Actor-Singer-Entrepreneur," *Playboy*, May 1969, pp. 74, 76.

34. Smith, *Cosby*, p. 69.

35. Gerald Nachman, *Seriously Funny: The Rebel Comedians of the 1950s and 1960s* (New York: Pantheon Books, 2003), pp. 583–584.

36. For an insightful study of *The Cosby Show*, see Sut Jhally and Justin Lewis, *Enlightened Racism:* The Cosby Show, *Audiences, and the Myth of the American Dream* (Boulder: Westview Press, 1992). For another very smart take on the show, and on black television in general, see Herman Gray, *Watching Race: Television and the Struggle for Blackness* [With a New Introduction] (Minneapolis: University of Minnesota Press, [1995] 2004), pp. 79–84. For a brilliant study of black television in relation to the civil rights and black power struggles, see Christine Acham, *Revolution Televised: Prime Time and the Struggle for Black Power* (Minneapolis: University of Minnesota Press, 2004). Also see Sasha Torres's fine study, *Black, White, and in Color: Television and Black Civil Rights* (Princeton: Princeton University Press, 2003).

37. Zoglin, p. 60.

38. "Life with Bill Cosby: Pretty Wife, Camille, Swept Along by Husband's Swift Rise from Obscurity to Stardom," *Ebony*, September 1966, p. 40.

39. Linderman, "Playboy Interview: Bill Cosby," p. 82.

40. Brad Darrach, "Cosby!" *Life*, June 1985, p. 37.

41. Alvin Poussaint, "The Huxtables: Fact or Fantasy?" *Ebony*, October 1988, p. 74.

42. Ibid.

43. Lynn Norment, "The Cosby Show: The Real-Life Drama Behind Hit TV Show About a Black Family," *Ebony*, April, 1985, p. 30.

44. During slavery, the shrewd use of stereotype was a way that blacks used negative appraisals of their identities by white owners to their advantage. As historian Ira Berlin writes, "In the very stereotype of the dumb, brutish African that planters voiced so loudly, newly arrived slaves found protection, as they used their apparent ignorance of the language, landscape, and work routines of the Chesapeake to

their own benefit. Observing the new Negroes on one Maryland estate, a visitor was 'surprised at their Perseverance.' 'Let an hundred Men hew him how to hoe, or drive a Wheelbarrow, he'll still take the one by the bottom, and the Other by the Wheel.' Triumphant planters had won the initial battle by gaining control over Chesapeake society and placing their imprint on the process of production, but slaves answered that the war would be a long one." Berlin, *Many Thousands Gone: The First Two Centuries of Slavery in North America* (Cambridge, Mass.: The Belknap Press of Harvard University Press, 1998), p. 120.

45. Cosby would surely disagree with Henry Louis Gates, Jr., on his views of *Amos 'n' Andy*. Gates says that one "of my favorite pastimes is screening episodes of 'Amos 'n' Andy' for black friends who think that the series was both socially offensive and politically detrimental. After a few minutes, even hardliners have difficulty restraining their laughter. 'It's still racist,' is one typical comment, 'but it was funny.' The performance of those great black actors—Tim Moore, Spencer Williams and Ernestine Wade—transformed racist stereotypes into authentic black humor. The dilemma of 'Amos 'n' Andy,' however, was that these were the *only* images of blacks that American could see on TV. The political consequences for the early civil rights movement were thought to be threatening. The N.A.A.C.P. helped to have the series killed." Gates, "TV's Black World Turns—But Stays Unreal," *New York Times*, Sunday, November 12, 1989, p. 40.

46. "Died," *Newsweek*, December 2, 1985, p. 104.

47. For a discussion of the cultural and racial context in which Wayans's show and other black series either flourished or floundered on the Fox network in the 1990s, see Kristal Brent Zook, *Color by Fox: The Fox Network and the Revolution in Black Television* (New York: Oxford University Press, 1999).

48. Alison Samuels, "Cosby in Winter," *Newsweek*, November 3, 2003, p. 62.

49. For instance, see Alison Samuels, "We Are Losing . . ." *Newsweek*, March 17, 1997, p. 58.

50. Michael Eric Dyson, *I May Not Get There With You: The True Martin Luther King, Jr.* (New York: Free Press, 2000).

51. Mos Def, sound recording, *Black on Both Sides*, Rawkus Records, 1999.

52. "Compared to What," written by Gene McDaniels, on the sound recording *Swiss Movement* by Les McCann and Eddie Harris, Atlantic Records, 1969.

53. *New York Times*, Sunday, November 12, 1989, p. H1.

54. Ibid, pg. 40.

55. "Color Him Funny," p. 76.

56. Morgan, p. 78.

57. Tiger Woods, Media Statement, cited in Jay Nordlinger, "Tiger Time: The Wonder of an American Hero," *National Review*, April 30, 2001, p. 41.

58. Morgan, p. 78; Nachman, pp. 572–573; Smith, p. 46.

59. Smith, p. 70.

60. "I Spy," *Ebony*, p. 66; Smith, pp. 70–71.

61. Lawrence W. Levine, *Black Culture and Black Consciousness: Afro-American Folk Thought from Slavery to Freedom* (New York: Oxford University Press, 1977).

62. Quoted in Nachman, p. 573.

63. Du Bois, *Souls*, p. 11.

64. Nachman, p. 572.

65. Cited in Mel Watkins, *On The Real Side*, p. 503.

66. Smith, p. 57. The italics are found in the first edition of Smith's book, published in 1986 by St. Martin's Press; in the second edition, the italics are removed. I have kept them because I think they accurately convey Cosby's frustration.

67. For instance, when Chris Rock's comedy stirred controversy among African Americans, and led to the charge of his "stereotyping" black culture, "Rock and his supporters [said] the controversy misses the point of his art, which turns images upside down in the interest of promoting new thinking in America." Kevin Chappell, "Bigger, Better, and Hotter! Chris Rock Talks About Fame, Controversy and the Challenge of Being No. 1," *Ebony*, October 1999, p. 163.

68. Mark Dowie, *American Foundations: An Investigative History* (Cambridge, Mass.: MIT Press, 2002), pp. xvi, xxi–xxiii, 7, 12.

69. A.S. Doc Young, cited in Smith, p. 92.

70. Smith, p. 75.

71. Ibid., p. 168.

Chapter Two Classrooms and Cell Blocks

1. Lawrence Linderman, "Playboy Interview: Bill Cosby—a Candid Conversation with the Kinetic Comedian-Actor-Singer-Entrepreneur," *Playboy*, May 1969, p. 73.

2. Ibid.

3. Richard Zoglin, "Cosby, Inc.: He Has a Hot TV Series, a New Book— and a Booming Comedy Empire," *Time*, September 28, 1987, p. 59.

4. Ibid.

5. Ibid. In the acknowledgments to his doctoral dissertation, Cosby thanks Damerell, who, he says, "guided me in the writing of the technical and creative components of my television research."

6. Howard Fuller, "The Struggle Continues," *Education Next*, Fall 2004, pp. 27–28.

7. Alec Klein, "A Tenuous Hold on the Middle Class," *Washington Post*, December 18, 2004, p. A1.

8. Mary Pattillo-McCoy, "Black Picket Fences: Privilege and Peril among the Black Middle Class," in Dalton Conley, Editor, *Wealth and Poverty in America: A Reader* (Malden, Mass.: Blackwell Publishing, 2003), p. 106.

9. Klein, p. A1. "Vital Signs," *The Journal of Blacks in Higher Education*, Autumn 2003, p. 73.

10. "Black Middle Class: Getting Squeezed," *The Middle Class Squeeze*, Rep. George Miller, Committee on Education and the Workforce Democrats, July 15, 2004, Issue # 8, www.house.gov/georgemiller; "Vital Signs," p. 73.

11. Klein, p. A1.

12. Ibid.

13. "Black Middle Class: Getting Squeezed" and "Vital Signs," p. 73.

14. "Vital Signs," p. 73.

15. Linda Darling-Hammond, "The Color Line in American Education: Race, Resources, and Student Achievement." *Du Bois Review* 1:2 (2004), p. 214.

16. Jonathan Kozol, *Savage Inequalities*, p. 3, cited in Darling-Hammond, p. 215.

17. Kozol, pp. 236–237, cited in Darling-Hammond, p. 25.

18. "The Racial Wealth Gap Has Become a Huge Chasm That Severely Limits Black Access to Higher Education," *The Journal of Blacks in Higher Education*, 2005, pp. 23–25.

19. Gary Orfield, *Schools More Separate: Consequences of a Decade of Resegregation* (Cambridge, Mass.: The Civil Rights Project, Harvard University, 2001).

20. Orfield, cited in Darling-Hammond, p. 217.

21. William Henry Cosby, Jr., *An Integration of the Visual Media Via Fat Albert and the Cosby Kids into the Elementary School Curriculum as a Teaching Aid and Vehicle to Achieve Increased Learning*, University of Massachusetts, September 1976, p. vi.

22. Ibid., pp. 3, 4, 5.

23. Cited in "Bill Cosby and the Politics of Race," in Michael Eric Dyson, *Reflecting Black: African-American Cultural Criticism* (Minneapolis: University of Minnesota Press, 1993), p. 85.

24. Cosby, p. 8.

25. Ibid., p. 11.

26. Ibid., pp. 11–12.

27. "Vital Signs," Autumn 2003, p. 73.

28. "The State of the Dream 2004," report by United for a Fair Economy, 2004, p. 16.

29. "Vital Signs," Autumn 2003, p. 73; "State of the Dream," p. 17.

30. See Janet Duitsman Cornelius, *When I Can Read My Title Clear: Literacy, Slavery, and Religion in the Antebellum South* (Columbia: University of South Carolina Press, 1991).

31. Among the voluminous research, see J. L. Dillard, *Black English: Its History and Usage in the United States* (New York: Random House,

1972); William Labov, *Language in the Inner City: Studies in the Black English Vernacular* (Philadelphia: University of Pennsylvania Press, 1972); Geneva Smitherman, *Talkin and Testifyin: The Language of Black America* [1977] (Detroit: Wayne State University Press, 1986); John Baugh, *Black Street Speech: Its History, Structure and Survival* (Austin: University of Texas Press, 1983); Geneva Smitherman, *Black Talk: Words and Phrases from the Hood to the Amen Corner* (Boston: Houghton Miflin, 1994); Salikoko S. Mufwene, John R. Rickdord, Guy Bailey and John Baugh, Editors, *African-American English: Structure, History and Use* (New York: Routledge, 1998); Theresa Perry and Lisa Delpit, Editors, *The Real Ebonics Debate: Power, Language, and the Education of African-American Children* (Boston: Beacon Press, 1998); John Rickford and Russell John Rickford, *Spoken Soul: The Story of Black English* (New York: John Wiley & Sons, Inc., 2000); Lisa J. Green, *African American English: A Linguistic Introduction* (Cambridge: Cambridge University Press, 2002); Marcyliena Morgan, *Language, Discourse and Power in African American Culture* (Cambridge: Cambridge University Press, 2002); and Sinfree Makoni, Geneva Smitherman, Arnetha F. Ball, Arthur K. Spears, Editors, *Black Linguistics: Language, Society, and Politics in Africa and the Americas* (New York: Routledge, 2003).

32. James A. Harrison, "Negro English." *Anglia* 8 (1884), p. 232, cited in Shelley Fisher Fishkin, *Was Huck Black? Mark Twain and African-American Voices* (New York: Oxford University Press, 1993), p. 42.

33. James Baldwin, "If Black English Isn't a Language, Then Tell Me, What Is?" in *The Price of the Ticket: Collected Nonfiction 1948–1985* (New York: St. Martin's/Marek, 1985), p. 650.

34. Cited in Candace Murphy, "The Cosby Sweater Has Unraveled; Cosby has unraveled some woolly memories the past few months by lambasting African-American parents for their parental failures," *Oakland Tribune*, August 8, 2004.

35. Ta-Nehisi Coates, "Ebonics! Weird Names! $500 Shoes! Shrill Bill Cosby and the Speech That Shocked Black America," *Village Voice*, May 26–June 1, 2004.

36. Bill Cosby, "Elements of Igno-Ebonics Style," *Wall Street Journal*, January 10, 1997, p. A10.

37. Ibid.

38. Lawrence Linderman, "Playboy Interview: Bill Cosby—a Candid Conversation with the Kinetic Comedian-Actor-Singer-Entrepreneur," *Playboy*, May 1969, p. 175.

39. Ibid.

40. Jonathan D. Rockoff, "Phonics Called Helpful to a Point: Many Md. Educators Favor Comprehensive Approach," *Baltimore Sun*, January 14, 2005.

41. Elizabeth Chin, *Purchasing Power: Black Kids and American Consumer Culture* (Minneapolis: University of Minnesota Press, 2001).

42. Ibid., p. 9.

43. Ibid., p. 129.

44. Ibid., pp. 60–61.

45. Ibid., p. 60.

46. "I Spy: Comedian Bill Cosby Is First Negro Co-Star in TV Network Series," *Ebony*, September 1965, p. 68.

47. Stanley Karnow, "Bill Cosby: Variety Is the Life of Spies," *The Saturday Evening Post*, September 25, 1965, p. 88.

48. Edward Sorel, "The Noble Cos," *The Nation*, September 6, 1986, p. 243.

49. National Public Radio, *Talk of the Nation*, July 7, 2004.

50. Richard Hofstadter, *Anti-Intellectualism in American Life* (New York: Alfred A. Knopf, 1963).

51. Ibid., pp. 3–4.

52. Ibid., p. 6.

53. Les Christie, "Endangered: The American Reader," *CNNmoney*, July 12, 2004, http://money.cnn.com/2004/07/09/news/bookreading.

54. Vladimir I. Chuprov, "Youth in Social Reproduction." *Russian Social Science Review*, September-October 1999, vol. 40.

55. Seon-Young Lee, Bonnie Cramond, and Jongyeun Lee, "Korean Teachers' Attitudes Toward Academic Brilliance." *National Association for Gifted Children*, Winter 2004, vol. 48.

56. Walter E. Houghton, "Victorian Anti-Intellectualism." *Journal of the History of Ideas* 13:3 (June 1952), pp. 291–313.

57. Signithia Fordham and John Ogbu, "Black Students' School Success: Coping with the Burden of 'Acting White,'" *The Urban Review* 19:3, pp. 176–206.

58. Henry Louis Gates, Jr., "Breaking the Silence," *The New York Times*, Section 4, p. 11; "Transcript: Illinois Senate Candidate Barack Obama," *Washingtonpost.com*. http://www.washingtonpost.com/we-dyn/articles/A1975-2004July27.html.

59. Philip J. Cook and Jens Ludwig, "Weighing the Burden of 'Acting White': Are There Race Differences in Attitudes Toward Education?" *Journal of Policy Analysis and Management*, Spring 1997, pp. 256–278.

60. "'Acting White': Is It the Silent Killer of the Educational Aspirations of Inner-City Blacks?" *The Journal of Blacks in Higher Education*, Autumn 1997, p. 94.

61. Ibid.

62. Douglas Massey, Camille Z. Charles, Garvey Lundy and Mary J. Fischer, *The Source of the River*, cited in Tim Wise, *Affirmative Action: Racial Preference in Black and White* (New York: Routledge, 2005), p. 146; "Vital Signs," *Journal of Blacks in Higher Education*, Winter 2003/2004, p. 65.

63. "Vital Signs," *Journal of Blacks in Higher Education*, Winter 2003–2004, p. 65.

64. Massey et al., cited in Wise, p. 146.

65. Karolyn Tyson, William Darity & Domini Castellino. *Breeding Animosity: The "Burden of Acting White" and Other Problems of Status Group Hierarchies in Schools*. Paper # SAN04-03, September, 2004. Also see Paul Tough, "The 'Acting White' Myth," *New York Times Magazine*, December 12, 2004.

66. Ibid.

67. Ibid.

68. "Vital Signs," Autumn 2004, p. 73.

69. "The State of the Dream 2004: Enduring Disparities in Black and White," *United for a Fair Economy*, January 2004, p. 20.

70. Ibid.

71. *Cellblocks or Classrooms? The Funding of Higher Education and Corrections and Its Impact on African American Men*. Justice Policy Institute, August 28, 2002.

72. Michael Eric Dyson, *Why I Love Black Women* (New York: Basic Civitas Books, 2003), p. 202.

73. For claims of genocide, see Robert Staples, "Black Male Genocide: A Final Solution to the Race Problem in America," *Black Scholar*, no. 3 (May-June 1987). For claims about young black males as an endangered species, see the essays in Jewelle Taylor Gibbs, editor, *Young, Black, and Male in America: An Endangered Species* (Dover, Massachusetts: Auburn House Publishing Company, 1988).

74. Gibbs, *Young, Black, and Male in America*.

Chapter Three What's in a Name (Brand)?

1. Diana Crane, *Fashion and Its Social Agendas: Class, Gender, and Identity in Clothing* (Chicago: University of Chicago Press, 2000).

2. Shane White and Graham White, *Stylin': African American Expressive Culture from Its Beginnings to the Zoot Suit* (Ithaca, N.Y.: Cornell University Press, 1998).

3. Ibid., p. 92.

4. Ibid., p. 93.

5. Ibid., p. 155.

6. Ibid., p. 154.

7. Ibid., p. 163.

8. Ibid., p. 222.

9. Ibid., p. 222.

10. Willard B. Gatewood, *Aristocrats of Color: The Black Elite, 1880–1920* (Fayetteville: University of Arkansas Press, 2000 [1991]), p. 187.

11. Ibid., p. 203.

12. White and White, p. 239.

13. Ibid., p. 229.

14. Ibid., p. 240.

15. Robin D.G. Kelley, "The Riddle of the Zoot: Malcolm Little and Black Cultural Politics During World War II," *Race Rebels: Culture, Politics, and the Working Class* (New York: The Free Press, 1994), pp. 161–181; White and White, pp. 254–256.

16. Crane, p. 187.

17. Ibid., p. 189.

18. "Hot Clothes," *American Demographics*, quoted in Crane, p. 191.

19. Crane, p. 191.

20. Ibid. Of course, I am not arguing that "ghetto chic" or "ghetto couture" is unproblematic: The black youth who drive its creation are surely not rewarded—either through wide cultural notice or in monetary measure—for their inspiration. And neither am I arguing that these youth are immune to the consumptive fetishes that mark the cultural landscape. But that is the point: These youth are part of consumer cultures that rest, in part, on the stimulation of desires for material products that can be, well, all-consuming. But black youth are no different in this regard than the rest of us, if it is true that they are more vulnerable because of their tenuous economic standing in society. Nevertheless, even given their limitations and conditions, black youth have helped to shape the consumptive desires of millions through their ingenious innovations in fashion and style.

21. C. Shilling, cited in Alexandra Howson, *The Body in Society: An Introduction* (Cambridge, UK: Polity Press, 2004), p. 111.

22. Howson, *The Body in Society*, pp. 110–111.

23. Rufus C. Camphausen, *Return of The Tribal: A Celebration of Body Adornment—Piercing, Tattooing, Body Painting, Scarification* (Rochester, Vt.: Park Street Press, 1997), p. 16.

24. Ibid.

25. D. Altmann, cited in Howson, p. 111.

26. See Margo DeMello, *Bodies of Inscription: A Cultural History of the Modern Tattoo Community* (Durham: Duke University Press, 2000), pp. 174–177.

27. Ibid., p. 6.

28. Alice Walker and Pratibha Parmar, *Warrior Marks: Female Genital Mutilation and the Sexual Binding of Women* [Reprint Edition] (New

York: Harvest Books, 1996).

29. Ibid., pp. 21, 27, 29, 41.

30. I realize, as proved by Larry Koger's book *Black Slaveowners: Free Black Slave Masters in South Carolina, 1790–1860* [Reprint] (Columbia: University of South Carolina Press, 1995), and as Edward Jones's Pulitzer Prize–winning novel, *The Known World* (New York: Amistad Press, 2003), illustrates, that some blacks owned blacks during slavery. I am suggesting that poor, despised, subjugated blacks never owned other human beings. In the use of "Shaniqua" and "Taliqua" here, I intend the same class division Cosby suggested, but with a different interpretation: I am arguing that the poor black in slavery was never in a position, as were aristocratic blacks, to do the greatest damage to other blacks.

31. Ira Berlin, *Many Thousands Gone: The First Two Centuries of Slavery in North America* [Reprint] (Cambridge, Mass.: The Belknap Press of Harvard University Press, 1998), pp. 95–96; 149–150; Stephen Wilson, *The Means of Naming: A Social and Cultural History of Personal Naming in Western Europe* [Reprint] (London: Routledge Press, 1998), p. 309.

32. Ibid., pp. 95–96; 149–150; Wilson, ibid.

33. Wilson, p. 309.

34. Wilson, p. 308.

35. As Wilson writes, the question of who named the slaves—owners or blacks themselves—is "not easy to answer. Slaves who were bought would already have names but these could be changed. The naming of children born on plantations depended on the policy of the owners and also on what category of slave they belonged to: house or field slaves. Some owners and/or their wives clearly named their slaves. Humorous, classical or religious names may betray this control, or aspects of the pattern of naming. Few names were duplicated on the Chesapeake Bay plantations in the mid-eighteenth century and names were not usually transmitted within families.

"Other owners allowed slave parents to name their offspring, and we have seen that they might pick African names or imitate those of the master's family. More significantly, names were passed on within slave families. Slavery was not conducive to family life. . . . And some owners were reluctant to part families. It was liberal owners, who thus fostered slave families, who also left the naming of children to their parents." Wilson, p. 312.

36. Wilson, p. 312. There is proof that the significance of naming lasted far beyond slavery. In the rural South, there was often a big celebration attending the naming of an infant, and before that, rituals of recognition of the importance of birth for the expectant mother and unborn child, suggesting the transformation of time and space in black rural communities around family and female bonding. "Before the birth, the women quilted, sewed, had slumber parties, and developed a sisterhood group around the expectant mother. They met at her house and prepared it for the new arrival. Once the baby was born, they danced, sang, toasted the new mother with iced tea, and reminisced about old times, especially the last birth before this one. Much time was spent thinking of a name for the child and celebrating its meaning, which more often than not reflected family ancestors and traditions.

"Naming celebrations had their own peculiarities and functions. People came from all over to find out for whom the child was named. The name was often announced throughout neighborhoods, in churches, and at the local schools. Relatives and friends visited to see if the name suited the child's physical, intellectual, and emotional characteristics. The naming ceremony had dancing and singing. Community members brought food, and the new parents and older siblings had the opportunity to tell well-wishers how excited they were about the new baby and how his or her name continued family traditions." Valerie Grim, "African American Rural Culture, 1900–1950," in R. Douglas Hurt, Editor, *African American Life in the Rural South, 1900–1950* (Columbia: University of Missouri Press, 2003), pp. 1112–1113.

37. Berlin, p. 173.

38. Berlin, Ibid.; Wilson, p. 309. As Wilson points out, by the nineteenth century, that number had dropped to only one percent, signaling the erosion of the older generation's influence and the successful incorporation, acculturation and, indeed, assimilation, of the African

slave to American life, at least at the level of naming practices.

39. Berlin, p. 173.

40. Ibid., p. 174; Wilson, p. 310.

41. Wilson, p. 310.

42. Ibid.

43. Peter Wood discusses this in *Black Majority: Negroes in Colonial South Carolina from 1670 Through the Stono Rebellion* (New York: Knopf, 1974), pp. 185, 182, respectively, cited in Leslie M. Harris, *In the Shadow of Slavery: African Americans in New York City, 1626–1863* (Chicago: University of Chicago Press, 2003), p. 36.

44. Wilson, p. 311. For a discussion of the "Big" designation, see Betty M. Kuyk, *African Voices in the African American Heritage* (Bloomington: Indiana University Press, 2003), p. 42.

45. Wilson says that more sons were named for their fathers because owners usually recognized "uterine ties" and as a result paternal ties were "much more vulnerable." Also, he suggests, "there may also have been a traditional patrilineal sense" operating as well. Wilson, p. 312.

46. Berlin, p. 240.

47. Ibid.

48. Berlin, p. 321.

49. Wilbert Jenkins, *Climbing Up to Glory: A Short History of African Americans During the Civil War and Reconstruction* (Wilmington, Del.: SR Books, 2002), p. 154.

50. Stanley Lieberson and Kelly S. Mikelson, "Distinctive African American Names: An Experimental, Historical, and Linguistic Analysis of Innovation," *American Sociological Review* 60:6 (December 1995), p. 930.

51. Wilson, p. 314.

52. Ibid.

53. Ibid.

54. Ibid.

55. Ibid.

56. Ibid., pp. 314–315.

57. Ibid., p. 315.

58. See Lieberson and Mikelson, p. 932, for claims of the relation

between black power, black nationalism, distinctive black culture and unique names. According to Wilson, a study by Jerrilyn McGregory ("Aareck to Zsaneka: New Trends in African American Onomastics," *Proceedings of the XVIth International Congress of Onomastic Sciences* [1990], pp. 389—396) that examined unusual names in Indiana found that "one quarter of girls' names were distinctive in 1965, but 40 per cent by 1980. Boys' names remained more traditional from the custom of naming them after fathers, but here too there was a clear trend towards distinctive Black names. McGregory relates this development to the disillusionment which followed the 'success' of the Civil Rights movement." Wilson, p. 315.

59. *Jet*, June 31, 1993.

60. Lieberson and Mikelson, p. 930.

61. Ibid.

62. Ibid., p. 931.

63. Ibid., p. 933.

64. Ibid., p. 934.

65. Ibid.

66. Ibid., pp. 935–936.

67. Ibid., p. 936.

68. Ibid., p. 937.

69. Ibid., p. 939.

70. Cathy M. Jackson, "Names CAN Hurt!" *Essence*, April 1989.

71. Clifford Thompson, "Inventing Our Names, Our Selves: African Americans' Personal Names," *Commonweal*, March 24, 1995.

72. Ibid.

73. Ibid.

74. On ABC TV's newsmagazine *20/20*, black reporter Jami Floyd did a piece that took off on Bertrand and Mullainathan's study, which is discussed in the text that follows. Floyd assembled a group of black professionals who didn't believe that their unique black names would prevent them from getting a job. Floyd put twenty-two names to the test, and had the group post two identical resumes each on popular job Web sites: one with their real name, the other with a white-sounding name. Predictably, the white-sounding names got the nod at least 17

percent more than their unique black names. During the piece, Floyd interviewed conservative essayist Shelby Steele, who, predictably, laid into the unique black names and blamed the folk who bore the names, not the society that courts prejudice against them. "I think it's a naiveté on the part of black parents to name their children names that are so different than American mainstream names. It suggests to people outside that community who hear those names a certain alienation, a certain hostility." Steele argued against giving kids unique black names. When Floyd asked Steele, "So, you're telling black folks, don't name your child DeShawn or Laquita?" Steele replied, "Yes." Floyd said, in response to Steele's answer, "Name your child John or Robert or James or William," and Steele replied, "I'm saying don't name your son Latrell. Don't do that. He's going to live 50, 60 years in the future. Give him a break, call him Edward." Thus, Steele concedes the argument to dominant culture's bias, and counsels no resistance at all on the part of parents or other blacks to such bias. Fortunately, Floyd also interviewed sociologist and author Bertice Berry, who argued that when black folk who have power have unique or unusual names, folk learn to say them. "We've learned to say Condoleezza. And you just can't get more ghetto than Condoleezza. . . . We hear Leontine and you think opera. But it's 'Leon-tine,' 'Colin'; when they are associated with power and wealth, we learn them." See transcript, "The Name Game: Can a Name Hold You Back in Job Search?" *20/20*, August 20, 2004.

75. Marianne Bertrand and Sendhil Mullainathan, "Are Emily and Brendan More Employable than Lakisha and Jamal? A Field Experiment on Labor Market Discrimination," Chicago Jobs Council.

76. Kendra Hamilton, "What's In a Name? Study Shows That Workplace Discrimination Begins Long Before the Job Seekers Show Up for an Interview," *Black Issues in Higher Education*, June 19, 2003.

77. Bertrand and Mullainathan.

78. Robert J. Barro, "What's in a Name for Black Job Seekers?" *Business Week*, November 3, 2003, p. 24.

79. Ibid.

80. Ibid.

Chapter Four Family Values

1. "Woman Makes Groping Allegations Against Bill Cosby: Cosby's Lawyer Says Claims Are 'Categorically False,'" January 20, 2005, NBC10.com. For the claim of being a "great friend and mentor," see Jonathan Kingstone and Ian Robertson, "Bill Cosby 'A Mentor' to Accuser," *Toronto Sun*, January 22, 2005.

2. Jonathan Kingstone and Ian Robertson, "Bill Cosby 'A Mentor' to Accuser," *Toronto Sun*, January 22, 2005. Constand's name was first used in this Canadian paper, and not in American papers, which have usually observed a ban on naming accusers/alleged victims in their news accounts of cases.

3. Brodie Fenlon, "Cosby Denies Assault; Woman Claims She Was Drugged, Fondled in Star's Home," *The Ottawa Sun*, January 21, 2005, p. 5.

4. "Family Defends Woman's Groping Allegations Against Bill Cosby: Cosby's Lawyer Says Claims Are 'Categorically False,'" January 21, 2005, NBC10.com.

5. Kingstone and Robertson.

6. Ibid.

7. Ibid.

8. Ibid.

9. Maryclaire Dale, "Cosby Lawyer Asks Why Accuser Took So Long," *Seattle Post-Intelligencer*, January 21, 2005.

10. Ibid; "Woman Makes Groping Allegations Against Bill Cosby." In the end, district attorney Bruce Castor decided not to file criminal charges against Cosby.

11. Mark Stamey, Murray Weiss and Andy Geller, "Actress' Bombshell: Cos' Rubbed Me the Wrong Way," *New York Post*, March 2, 2000, p. 14.

12. Ibid; Michael Starr, "Cosby: Tabloid Lied," *New York Post*, March 8, 2000, p. 81; Mark Armstrong, "Cos Cracks 'Enquirer,'" March 8,

2000, Eonline.com; "Cosby Threatens to Sue Tabloid over Sexual Abuse Story," March 7, 2000, Cnn.com; "Cosby Wants Retraction," *Chicago Sun-Times*, March 8, 2000, p. 52.

13. Stamey, Weiss and Geller, p. 14.

14. Ibid.

15. "Cosby Threatens to Sue Tabloid over Sexual Abuse Story," March 7, 2000, Cnn.com; Mark Armstrong, "Cos Cracks 'Enquirer,'" March 8, 2000, eonline.com.

16. Ibid.

17. "Family Defends," NBC10.com.

18. William Raspberry, "Bill Cosby's Tough Love," *Washington Post*, December 13, 1989, p. A25.

19. Lawrence Christon, "The World According to Cos," *Los Angeles Times*, December 10, 1989, Calendar, p. 6.

20. Ibid.

21. Raspberry, p. A25.

22. Bill Cosby, *Fatherhood* (New York: Doubleday, 1986).

23. Frank Walker, "Cosby Daughter Fights Addiction," *Sun Herald* (*Sydney*), June 10, 1990, p. 17.

24. Ibid.

25. Ibid.

26. Ibid.

27. Ibid.

28. Ibid.

29. Elinor J. Brecher, "The Megastar's Daughter," *Miami Herald Sun*, June 15, 1992, p. 1C.

30. Ibid.

31. Ibid.

32. Ibid.

33. Ibid.

34. Jacqueline Trescott, "Erinn Cosby's Heavyweight Bouts; from the Tabs to Her Dad to Mike Tyson, the Comedian's Daughter Has Come Out Swinging," *The Washington Post*, May 18, 1992.

35. Ibid.

36. "Cosby Daughter Says Tyson Assaulted Her 3 Years Ago," *Chicago Sun-Times*, May 10, 1992, p. 41.

37. Trescott.

38. Ibid.

39. Brecher.

40. Trescott.

41. Brecher.

42. "Erinn Cosby Weds During Private Ceremony at Parents' Philadelphia Home," *Jet*, October 12, 1998, p. 32.

43. See "Erinn and Evin Cosby Discuss the Foundation Their Family Has Started for Children with Learning Differences," *The Early Show*, March 25, 2002.

44. David W. Chen, "Bill Cosby Was Target of Extortion," *The New York Times*, January 21, 1997, p. B3.

45. Ibid.

46. Ibid.

47. Ibid.

48. Benjamin Weiser, "Cosby, an Unerring Father on TV, Speaks of Affair in Extortion Trial," *New York Times*, July 16, 1997, p. B1.

49. Ibid.

50. Ibid.

51. Ibid.

52. Ibid.

53. Benjamin Weiser, "Question in Cosby Case: Scheme or Plea for Help?" *The New York Times*, July 10, 1997, p. B1.

54. Weiser, "Cosby, an Unerring Father," p. B1.

55. "Blood Test Planned over Cosby Paternity," *The New York Times*, July 29, 1997, p. B2.

56. Ibid.

57. Weiser, "Question in Cosby Case."

58. Weiser, "Cosby, an Unerring Father."

59. Ibid.

60. Benjamin Weiser, "Paternity Issue Remains Alive in Cosby Case, Despite Denial," *The New York Times*, July 17, 1997, p. B3.

61. Ibid.

62. Bill Hofmann, "Jailed Autumn Begs Cosby to Meet Two 'Grandchildren,'" *New York Post*, November 6, 1998, p. 12.

63. Benjamin Weiser, "3 Are Found Guilty of Trying to Extort Money from Cosby," *The New York Times*, July 26, 1997, Section 1, p. 1, Metropolitian Desk.

64. Benjamin Weiser, "Reporter's Notebooks; Defense Lawyer Weighs Paternity Suit in Cosby Extortion Case," *The New York Times*, July 28, 1997, p. B3.

65. Bob Herbert, "In America; No Mercy for Autumn," *The New York Times*, July 11, 1997, p. A27.

66. Ibid.

67. Ibid.

68. W.E.B. Du Bois and Augustus Dill, editors, *Morals and Manners Among Negro Americans: A Social Study Made by Atlanta University, Under the Patronage of the Trustees of the John F. Slater Fund* (Atlanta: Atlanta University Press, 1914).

69. Ibid., p. 85.

70. Ibid., p. 82.

71. Ibid., p. 83.

72. Ibid., p. 85.

73. Ibid., p. 85.

74. Ibid., p. 86.

75. Ibid., p. 87.

76. Ibid., p. 86.

77. Ibid., p. 87.

78. Ibid., p. 89.

79. Ibid., p. 86.

80. See William Julius Wilson, *The Truly Disadvantaged: The Inner City, the Underclass, and Public Policy* (Chicago: University of Chicago Press, 1987); William Julius Wilson, *When Work Disappears: The World of the New Urban Poor* (New York: Alfred A. Knopf, 1996); Michael Katz, *The Undeserving Poor: From the War on Poverty to the War on Welfare* (New York: Pantheon, 1989); Michael Katz, *In the Shadow of the Poorhouse: A Social History of Welfare in America* (New York: Basic Books, 1996); Robin D.G. Kelley, *Yo'*

Mama's Disfunktional: Fighting the Culture Wars in Urban America (Boston: Beacon Press, 1997); Elijah Anderson, *Streetwise: Race, Class and Change in an Urban Community* (Chicago: University of Chicago Press, 1992); Katherine Newman, *No Shame in My Game: The Working Poor in the Inner City* (New York: Alfred A. Knopf, 1999).

81. Ward Harkavy, "The Numbers Beyond the Bling," *Village Voice*, January 4, 2005.

82. Barbara Ehrenreich, *Nickel and Dimed: On (Not) Getting By in America* (New York: Holt, 2001); David K. Shipler, *The Working Poor: Invisible in America* (New York: Alfred A. Knopf, 2004), p. ix.

83. From Michael Males, cited in Ta-Nehisi Coates, "Mushmouth Reconsidered: You Can't Say That on TV—But Bill Cosby Can," *Village Voice*, July 13, 2004.

84. Lawrence Linderman, "Playboy Interview: Bill Cosby—a Candid Conversation with the Kinetic Comedian-Actor-Singer-Entrepreneur," *Playboy*, May 1969, pp. 170, 172, 175.

Chapter Five Shadow Boxing with a Scapegoat?
(or, Do White People Matter?)

1. Thomas B. Morgan, "I Am Two People, Man," *Life*, April 11, 1969, p. 74.

2. Sut Jhally and Justin Lewis, *Enlightened Racism: The Cosby Show, Audiences, and the Myth of the American Dream* (Boulder: Westview Press, 1992), pp. 71–72.

3. Ibid.

4. Lawrence Linderman, "Playboy Interview: Bill Cosby—a Candid Conversation with the Kinetic Comedian-Actor-Singer-Entrepreneur," *Playboy*, May 1969.

5. As for his dissertation, there was little doubt that most folk weren't going to read it; thus, his impassioned indictments of racist educational institutions could be safely made without fear of reprisal from this color-blind comedian. As for his television special, it might be

"excused" by those who disagreed with its viewpoint as an understandable exercise in ethnic cheerleading that, after all, all other groups, and their leading lights, might be accused of doing in one form or another.

6. After saying that Cosby didn't speak out on racial matters, a reporter noted that even "casual acquaintances know him simply as a good-humored cigar smoker who plays pick-up basketball, wears khakis and sweaters, takes vocal pride in his beautiful wife, Camille, and two daughters, and contends with a 25-year-old Spanish-style house in Beverly Hills which leaks a little when it rains." "Color-Blind Comic," *Newsweek*, May 20, 1968, p. 92.

7. Ibid., p. 84.

8. Morgan, p. 74.

9. For King's sermon comparing blacks and Japanese Americans forced into concentration camps, see Michael Eric Dyson, *I May Not Get There with You: The True Martin Luther King, Jr.* (New York: The Free Press, 2000), p. 39.

10. Linderman, p. 86.

11. Ibid.

12. Ibid., p. 86.

13. Ibid., p. 170.

14. Ibid., p. 175.

15. "Call to Action," *Detroit Free Press*, January 17, 2005.

16. Kevin Gaines, *Uplifting the Race: Black Leadership, Politics, and Culture in the Twentieth Century* (Chapel Hill: University of North Carolina Press, 1997), pp. 1–2.

17. Ibid, p. 2.

18. Evelyn Brooks Higginbotham, *Righteous Discontent: The Women's Movement in the Black Baptist Church, 1880–1920* (Cambridge, Mass.: Harvard University Press, 1993), pp. 14–15.

19. Ibid., p. 14.

20. See Megan Taylor Shockley, *"We, Too, Are Americans": African American Women in Detroit and Richmond, 1940-54* (Urbana: University of Illinois Press, 2004), pp. 5–6.

21. Shane White and Graham White, *Stylin': African American*

Expressive Culture from Its Beginnings to the Zoot Suit (Ithaca, N.Y.: Cornell University Press, 1998), p. 230.

22. Ibid.

23. Cited in Ibid.

24. William Ryan, *Blaming the Victim* [Revised, Updated Edition] (New York: Vintage, 1976).

25. Joe R. Feagin, *Subordinating the Poor: Welfare and American Beliefs* (Englewood Cliffs, N.J.: Prentice Hall, 1975), p. 95.

26. Ibid.; Matthew O. Hunt, "The Individual, Society or Both? A Comparison of Black, Latino, and White Beliefs About the Causes of Poverty." *Social Forces*, September 1996, p. 293.

27. Hunt.

28. Ibid.

29. Ibid., p. 8.

30. Cited in Archie Epps, ed., *The Speeches of Malcolm X at Harvard* [New York: Morrow, 1968], p. 171.

31. Robert V. Robinson and Wendell Bell, "Equality, Success, and Social Justice in England and the United States." *American Sociological Review* 43:125–143. Cited in Hunt.

32. Herbert H. Hyman and Charles R. Wright, *Education's Lasting Influence on Values* (Chicago: University of Chicago Press, 1979). Cited in Hunt.

33. Hunt, p. 7.

34. Ibid., p. 11.

35. Ibid.

36. Ibid., p. 12.

37. Ibid.

38. Ibid.

39. Bishop T. D. Jakes, part of forum, "Bill Cosby Can't Say That, Can He?" *Dallas Morning News*, June 3, 2004.

40. Robin D. G. Kelley, *Yo' Mama's Disfunktional: Fighting the Culture Wars in Urban America* (Boston: Beacon Press, 1997), p. 96.

41. Dorothy Day wanted a world where it was easier for all of us to behave decently. The quote was cited by Studs Terkel. See "An Hour with Legendary Broadcaster and Author Studs Terkel," an interview

on Pacifica Radio's *Democracy Now*, hosted by Amy Goodman, November 4, 2003.

42. Cited in Walter Higgins, "The State of Black America, Part Five: Our Empathy Deficit," BlackAmericaWeb.com, January 19, 2005. http://www.blackamericaweb.com/site.aspx/bawnews/stateof/empathy118

43. Jonah Goldberg, "The Cos Takes on Benign Neglect," *National Review Online*, July 12, 2004, www.nationalreview.com.

44. Cited in "Ranting and Raving; Personal Responsibility Talk Shouldn't End with Cosby," in *The Houston Chronicle*, May 26, 2004, p. 28.

45. *The O'Reilly Factor*, Fox News Network, January 14, 2005; *Hannity & Colmes*, Fox News Network, January 14, 2005.

46. Leonard Pitts, "Perfection Fatigue: Cosby's tired and frustrated to boot," *Milwaukee Journal Sentinel*, July 10, 2004, p. 15A.

47. Henry Louis Gates, Jr., "Breaking the Silence," *New York Times*, August 1, 2004, Section 4, p. 11.

48. Camille Cosby, "America Taught My Son's Killer to Hate Blacks," *USA Today*, July 9, 1998, p. 15A.

49. "Camille Cosby Responds Back . . . ," afrikan.net, August 26, 1998.

50. Cameron Jackson, "Cosby Encourages Black Youths," *New University Newspaper*, January 10, 2005.

51. Star Parker, "Cosby Must Not Back Off," *The Cincinnati Post*, July 12, 2004, p. A10.

52. "Declaration of Rights of the Negro Peoples of the World: Preamble," in Manning Marable and Leith Mullings, Editors, *Let Nobody Turn Us Around: Voices of Resistance, Reform, and Renewal: An African American Anthology* (Lanham, Md.: Rowman and Littlefield, 2000), p. 261.

53. "An Appeal to the Conscience of the Black Race to See Itself," Ibid., p. 265.

54. W.E.B. Du Bois, "Separation and Self-Respect," *W.E.B. Du Bois: A Reader*, edited by David Levering Lewis (New York: Henry Holt and Company, 1995), p. 560.

55. Martin Luther King, Jr., "The Rising Tide of Racial Consciousness," in James Melvin Washington, Editor, *A Testament of Hope: The Essential Writings and Speeches of Martin Luther King, Jr.* (San Francisco: Harper and Row, 1986), p. 148.

56. Ibid., p. 149.

57. Ibid., p. 150.

58. Ibid., p. 149.

59. Cited in Robert McClory, "Rev. Jesse Jackson's 'Push' to 'Excel'" *Illinois Issues*, May 1978.

60. Jesse Jackson, Speech before National Press Club Luncheon, February 17, 1994.

61. "Jesse Jackson: The Mother Jones Interview," by Douglas Foster, *Mother Jones*, March/April 2000.

62. Cited in Walter Higgins, "The State of Black America, Part Five: Our Empathy Deficit," BlackAmericaWeb.com, January 19, 2005. http://www.blackamericaweb.com/site.aspx/bawnews/stateof/empathy118.

63. Luke 12:48.

64. W.E.B. Du Bois, *The Philadelphia Negro: A Social Study* (Philadelphia: University of Pennsylvania Press, [1896] 1996), pp. 392–393.

Afterword "Niggas Come in All Colors"

1. "The Congressional Black Caucus—Ossie Davis & Bill Cosby." B455L *Black Forum*. A sound recording, 1972

Index